Advance Praise for *Verbal First Aid*™

"You can use Verbal First Aid everywhere: in the streets, in schools, at home. It is therapy of the people. It may help to prevent trauma and it could help children to heal themselves however and wherever they may be."

　　—Helena Guo, MD, chief clinical officer of PsychCN, the largest psychology institute in China, and CCO of the May 15 Soul Care Program for Earthquake Victims; winner, The Most Influential Charity Project of 2008 in China

"*Verbal First Aid* is far more than a parenting guide. It is a profound prescription drawn from current medical research toward nurturing our children and evolving civilization to the healthiest levels possible!"

　　—Bruce H. Lipton, PhD, cell biologist and bestselling author of *The Biology of Belief: Unleashing the Power of Consciousness, Matter and Miracles*

"Verbal First Aid is not merely a communication tool—it is a developmentally appropriate, child-friendly, and compassionate approach to children. It fosters supportive relationships between parents and children. When used by parents, it empowers children to master their fears around illness and injury, develop resilience to stress, and participate actively in their own healing. It is an overwhelmingly positive approach that can be invaluable to parents of children with chronic illness, but can also serve healthy children and their families."

　　—Ruby Roy, MD, chronic disease pediatrician at the University of Chicago

"As an osteopath and a parent, I find the Verbal First Aid techniques to be invaluable to teach both adults and children how to control and reduce their pain. They are a highly effective, nonpharmaceutical way of relieving discomfort and calming an often stressful situation."

　　—Karen Farrant, BSc (Hons), D.O. London

"As parents, we would like to create a perfect world for our children filled with good health, beauty, peace, and lots of fun! But life happens, and our perfect world is shattered. What then? How we cope determines if an event is perceived as a part of life or a catastrophe. This book is a must for parents and health-care workers. It helps to guide their responses to the events in life that are unavoidable. Through the proven techniques of Verbal First Aid and positive reinforcement, a seemingly tragic event can be turned into an experience that is understood and accepted . . . thus leading to healing in a real and immediate way."

　　—Deborah McCurdy, MD, associate professor of pediatrics. Mattel Children's Hospital at UCLA

continued . . .

"Who knows the possibilities for health and well-being, now and in the future, when we use these communication tools to speak to our children!"
— Susan Clark, MD, medical director of endocrinology at Children's Hospital of Orange County

"*Verbal First Aid* is a book that will change the lives of children for the better. It might even save lives. As beautifully written as it is practical, it is, in my opinion, an indispensable book for parents and for all those involved in child care."
— Charles Montagu, member of the Board of the British Council for Complementary Therapy

"In times of crisis, a child—any patient—can hang on your every word; a good doctor should know how to choose the right ones. The golden rule of 'First do no harm' applies to language, too. This book should be compulsory, not only for all parents, but as a text in all medical schools."
— Leah Kaminsky, MD, coauthor of *Your Child's Health: The Essential Companion for Every Australian Home*

Most Berkley Books are available at special quantity discounts for bulk purchases for sales promotions, premiums, fund-raising, or educational use. Special books, or book excerpts, can also be created to fit specific needs.

For details, write: Special Markets, The Berkley Publishing Group, 375 Hudson Street, New York, New York 10014.

Verbal First Aid™

Help Your Kids Heal from Fear and Pain—
and Come Out Strong

JUDITH SIMON PRAGER, PhD,
and JUDITH ACOSTA, LISW

BERKLEY BOOKS, NEW YORK

THE BERKLEY PUBLISHING GROUP
Published by the Penguin Group
Penguin Group (USA) Inc.
375 Hudson Street, New York, New York 10014, USA
Penguin Group (Canada), 90 Eglinton Avenue East, Suite 700, Toronto, Ontario M4P 2Y3, Canada
(a division of Pearson Penguin Canada Inc.)
Penguin Books Ltd., 80 Strand, London WC2R 0RL, England
Penguin Group Ireland, 25 St. Stephen's Green, Dublin 2, Ireland (a division of Penguin Books Ltd.)
Penguin Group (Australia), 250 Camberwell Road, Camberwell, Victoria 3124, Australia
(a division of Pearson Australia Group Pty. Ltd.)
Penguin Books India Pvt. Ltd., 11 Community Centre, Panchsheel Park, New Delhi—110 017, India
Penguin Group (NZ), 67 Apollo Drive, Rosedale, North Shore 0632, New Zealand
(a division of Pearson New Zealand Ltd.)
Penguin Books (South Africa) (Pty.) Ltd., 24 Sturdee Avenue, Rosebank, Johannesburg 2196,
South Africa

Penguin Books Ltd., Registered Offices: 80 Strand, London WC2R 0RL, England

This book is an original publication of The Berkley Publishing Group.

PUBLISHER'S NOTE: Every effort has been made to ensure that the information contained in this book is complete and accurate. However, neither the publisher nor the authors is engaged in rendering professional advice or services to the individual reader. The ideas, procedures, and suggestions contained in this book are not intended as a substitute for consulting with your physician. All matters regarding your health require medical supervision. Neither the authors nor the publisher shall be liable or responsible for any loss or damage allegedly arising from any information or suggestion in this book.

The events described in this book are the real experiences of real people. However, the authors have altered their identities and, in some instances, created composite characters. Any resemblance between a character in this book and a real person therefore is entirely accidental.

While the authors have made every effort to provide accurate telephone numbers and Internet addresses at the time of publication, neither the publisher nor the authors assumes any responsibility for errors, or for changes that occur after publication. Further, the publisher does not have any control over and does not assume any responsibility for author or third-party websites or their content.

Copyright © 2010 by Judith Simon Prager and Judith Acosta.
Cover design by Annette Fiore Defex.
Cover background art: Danilo Moura / Shutterstock.
Text design by Tiffany Estreicher.

All rights reserved.
No part of this book may be reproduced, scanned, or distributed in any printed or electronic form without permission. Please do not participate in or encourage piracy of copyrighted materials in violation of the authors' rights. Purchase only authorized editions.
BERKLEY® is a registered trademark of Penguin Group (USA) Inc.
The "B" design is a trademark of Penguin Group (USA) Inc.

PRINTING HISTORY
Berkley trade paperback edition / June 2010

Library of Congress Cataloging-in-Publication Data
Prager, Judith Simon.
    Verbal first aid : help your kids heal from fear and pain—and come out strong / Judith Simon Prager and Judith Acosta.
    p.   cm.
    Includes bibliographical references and index.
    ISBN 978-0-425-23427-3
    1. Children—Preparation for medical care.   2. Communication in pediatrics.   I. Acosta, Judith.
    II. Title.
    RJ61.P76   2010
    618.92—dc22
                        2009053854

PRINTED IN THE UNITED STATES OF AMERICA

10   9   8   7   6   5   4   3   2   1

I dedicate this book to Jennifer Youtt Hatzmann,
mother of my four grandchildren and a woman who deserves a
black belt in Verbal First Aid. Her example and thoughtfulness resonate
throughout the stories herein that bring the techniques to life.
—JUDITH SIMON PRAGER

To Dave, the most healing person I've ever known.
—JUDITH ACOSTA

ACKNOWLEDGMENTS

This book has been uniquely lived for me in the ongoing blessing of my work with the wonderful parents and children who have allowed me to share their childbirth and child-rearing experiences with them.

Thank you to the new mothers and fathers who attended my "Bonding with the Baby Within" workshops and whose children amazingly seemed to have bonded with each other as a result of the shared sessions while in utero. Thank you to all the mothers and fathers and children who participated in pregnancy and birthing hypnosis techniques with me, especially Lisa Hills and Kelly Klaus and their son, Owen; Cindy and Bill Coffey and sons Cole and Mason; and Mari Brusseau and Rick Sowers and sons Oliver and Owen. Thank you to Anne Hulegard and Alex Perloff for allowing us to use part of their wonderful healing story. And thank you to the mothers and fathers and children whom I've adopted as my own over the years, including Inger and John Lanese and their children Illeana and William, and Sarah and Rocky Akin and their children Adara and Oliver.

As I wrote this, I had a growing appreciation for the nurturing beginning that was given to me by my late parents, Al and Pauline Simon. And I am filled with gratitude to my own children, Danielle and Brad Prager, for the rewarding and beautiful opportunity to be their mother. To my stepchildren, Jennifer Youtt Hatzmann and Jonathan Youtt, and son-in-law George Hatzmann, thank you for your wonderful presence in my life.

And thank you to my four amazing grandchildren, Jack, Tanner, Madeleine, and Isadora, for allowing their parents and me to explore Verbal First Aid with them as our classroom.

I owe a debt of gratitude for their generous encouragement to the many mentors who awakened in me the search for who we truly are and how to best support each other in this process: Bruce Lipton, Donald Trent Jacobs, Ronald Wong Jue, Elmer Green, Larry Dossey, Candace Pert, Charles Montagu, Marilyn Simon, Timothy Trujillo, and Arnold Blume, among many others. Thanks to Corrine Jones and the European School of Osteopathy for welcoming me to share my work in Great Britain. And a note of thanks to Linda Venis of the UCLA Extension Writers' Program, who has welcomed my husband and me as instructors and made a creative home for us in her program for more than twenty years.

Thank you to all the many physicians whose support for this book and whose wisdom I so appreciated, including Susan Clark, Ruby Roy, Helena Guo in China, Deborah McCurdy, Bernardine Celoni, Todd Davis, David Springer, Chuck Dumont, Francesca de Picciotto, and Hugh Thompson. And thank you to Kathleen Archibald Simon, RN, HN-BC, for so believing in Verbal First Aid.

It's my pleasure to acknowledge and thank Babette Sparr, the best agent a writer could ever hope for. She has been wonderfully wise, generous in sharing her time and knowledge, kind, available, and supportive, and she held our hand throughout this project. Thank you, as well, to Adrienne Avila, our wonderful editor, who loved our book and whose care showed it. She was thoughtful in all ways, helping us make this book better with each suggestion. We have been blessed to have these extraordinary women on our team.

And, of course, thank you to the love of my life—this life and any others I may have lived—my husband, my best friend, my kite string, and true north star, Harry Youtt, whose love (and book of poems to me—*Love Songs to the Moon Woman*) has been as important to my life as the air I breathe. And who has made my life richer by far than any dream my poor imagination could have conjured. Thank you, thank you, thank you.

JUDITH SIMON PRAGER

The other day I was talking to a spiritual adviser and confessed an unusual amount of restlessness in my spirit, that I had an urge to travel, move, pack up tents, puppies, and ponies again. I was afraid it was a symptom of coveting—that things seemed somehow better elsewhere when I knew that was never really true.

He gave me wise advice: "You are where you are because that's where God has you to be of service. The best antidote to coveting is gratitude for what you have and what you are given to do."

And perhaps not so serendipitously, his suggestion came on the same day as the reminder to write this dedication and acknowledgment to all those who not only helped me in the writing of this book but sustained me spiritually, emotionally, and physically while I did the day-to-day work.

Thus the message was received, and I began to consider all the love and grace I am surrounded by daily. As I sat to write, my legs and heart stilled.

First, to my husband, best friend, teacher, and the love I waited so long for, thank you. My gratitude knows no bounds. Nor does your patience with me.

To my parents for their unfailing love and support. I am very, very lucky to have you both.

To the Wilson and Gelfand families for sharing their pain and struggle through the loss of Papa Bill and for allowing me to share it with you.

To Winnie Maggiore and Dave Johnson, for the blessing of friendship and their unfailing belief in the power of the spoken word. Verbal First Aid could not have better advocates in the medical profession. And an added special thank-you to you, Winnie, for sharing the stories of rescue that were made possible by words that were well chosen and well said.

To Patrick Tyrrell and Angie Wagner at NASW-NM for truly understanding the concept of Verbal First Aid and encouraging hundreds of mental health professionals to do the same.

To everyone at JEMS/Elsevier for their continued support of Verbal First Aid, with an extra thank-you to A. J. Heightman, editor-in-chief, Jennifer Berry, Lisa Bell, Lauren Coartney, and Michelle Barbeau.

To Tullie Ruderman and Dorothy Larkin, once again, for their continued inspiration in my heart and for starting that first therapeutic communication program for first responders back in 1993. My thanks for their part in all that Verbal First Aid has become.

To Jill at IRC Physical Therapy in Albuquerque, whose magic hands and expert use of magic words ("melt the butter") have begun the true healing from an intransigent and painful injury.

To all the physicians, researchers, first responders, law enforcement officers, and military personnel I have worked with, taught, and learned from. Every story you've shared has been invaluable in creating this. A special thank-you to Lieutenant Colonel Barry Howard for his unbounded enthusiasm about Verbal First Aid.

And always, to God, above all, through all and within all, for lending me His strength, faith, and hope when I need it most and feel it least.

Verbal First Aid is a language of healing. And perhaps, as I still learn how deep and high that healing can go, I should add "thank you" to the list of words that can magically change not only what we feel but what we can achieve.

AMEN.

JUDITH ACOSTA

CONTENTS

AUTHORS' PREFACE

In 2002 we wrote a book called *The Worst Is Over: What to Say When Every Moment Counts.* It detailed the protocol for what we call Verbal First Aid, specific communication techniques that can help a person to set a course for healing, for recovering physically and emotionally from a crisis or emergency. It was very well received by both first responders (law enforcement, fire departments, emergency medical service) and the medical community. That book's premise was that there are words and ways to say those words that could mean the difference between panic and calm, pain and comfort, even life and death. *The Worst Is Over* had the honor of being dubbed "the 'bible' for crisis communication" by *The International Journal of Emergency Mental Health.*

Since that time, we have been invited to teach Verbal First Aid and how to use words to set the course for recovery to doctors, nurses, first responders, and other healthcare professionals throughout the United States and in England. The Verbal First Aid protocol has steadily grown to become the standard of care for emergencies and our e-mail boxes are filled with reports of its successes out in the field.

In 2008, when China experienced devastating earthquakes and floods in which eighty thousand people died and millions were displaced, we were asked to teach crisis counselors there this protocol. Dr. Helena Guo, who had invited us, described Verbal First Aid to government officials this way: "It's therapy you can use in the streets, in the schools, wherever you are." And the government approved the program on the spot.

Then it occurred to us, if Verbal First Aid works this beautifully in such difficult circumstances, imagine the difference it can make if begun early enough in a child's life to become part of what has been called their hard wiring as they faced each of life's challenges. Children's brains are developing with every encounter they have with their environment. It is generally agreed in early childhood education circles that what is learned in the formative years affects not only the child but the adult she will become and her ability to learn and to regulate her own emotions throughout her whole life.

We decided to write this book to help parents, teachers, pediatricians, nurses, baby-sitters, anyone who takes care of a child, to help that child create a mind-set that will allow him to heal faster and more comfortably whether from larger crises or from kitchen-variety boo-boos.

We believe that the principles of Verbal First Aid should be everyone's birthright. When we know how our minds and bodies hold the power to heal, then we can teach our children how to heal themselves and help them not only turn pain into comfort but transform difficulty into demonstrations of their own wisdom, imagination, and courage. When children learn from parents and caregivers to put their scrapes and bumps and bruises into perspective, and especially when they learn that they have the ability to change their own reactions to injuries, they acquire the power to move through life in an entirely different way. They become more adaptable, more flexible; they learn internal mastery and self-confidence. This is the core gift from which many other resources spring.

FOREWORD

SUSAN CLARK, MD, MEDICAL DIRECTOR OF ENDOCRINOLOGY AT
CHILDREN'S HOSPITAL OF ORANGE COUNTY, CALIFORNIA

I am a pediatric endocrinologist and take care of children with chronic illness such as diabetes. I was initially given *The Worst Is Over* a few years ago by a friend and began reading it out of curiosity. Having been trained as a pediatrician and totally immersed in the medical model of care, I was two-thirds of the way through the book before I began to comprehend the message. As I reread the chapters, I gradually began to see the amazing possibility that I could amplify the healing process by the way I spoke to my patients and their parents.

Only as I began to try out some of the Verbal First Aid communication techniques explained in the book—began to speak to my patients using words that promote healing while medical care was given—did I begin to understand the power available to me to truly participate in the healing process. I discovered that this way of speaking in an emergency, in the intensive care unit, and when helping children and their families live with chronic illness has an impact that results in improved health and ability to cope with the illness.

Recently I went to the pediatric intensive care unit (PICU) to see a very sick but alert twelve-year-old boy with newly diagnosed diabetes who seemed very sad and withdrawn. His parents told me that when the physician in the urgent care clinic told him that he had diabetes and would have to take shots for the rest of his life, he sobbed uncontrollably. I started by telling him that his body was already better and in a few hours he would be feeling much better and we would teach him and his family how to take care of the diabetes so that he could go home. Then, his face brightened, and he asked me if he would be able to play video games! Of course! He had hope again! That evening, I did not recognize him standing in the hallway with his family until he came over to me and gave me a hug! It was remarkable for me to see how quickly the transformation occurred from being overwhelmed and helpless to empowered and confident with learning to manage his diabetes.

I became a physician for children because I desired to be a healer for children. Children are different from adults. Children show us how they are feeling by their behavior. Medical staff who work with children know that a sick, fussy, crying child is going to have a high heart rate and high blood pressure. Breathing rates increase, and the child doesn't eat well; with diabetes, being upset can even raise the blood sugar level. Nurses regularly assess the behavior of the child in addition to their vital signs (temperature, heart and breathing rates, and blood pressure) so that we know how to interpret the numbers. Changes in these behaviors tell us how well or how poorly a child is doing in the hospital.

One day I walked into the PICU to see a two-year-old who had several serious medical problems. I approached her mother and asked her if she understood the medical conditions and how her child was responding to the treatment. She said she did not understand, so I sat down to talk with her. I explained to her that the worst was over, we now knew the diagnosis and had already started treatment. I showed her the evidence that her little girl was getting better. We reviewed all the symptoms, and problems that had worried Mom now all made sense. We talked about the treatment and that improvement would be slow but steady and that her daughter would completely recover. At first the little girl was very fussy, squirming, and appeared very uncomfortable. As we talked, the child relaxed and drifted off to sleep. On the third day that this change in behavior was repeated, I joked with the mother that her daughter must be very bored with our conversation. "No," the mom said, "it is because your voice is calm when you talk to us. You take time and don't seem rushed. You sit down and answer questions."

This experience clearly taught me that it is not only what is said but the manner in which it is said that makes a difference in helping children get well and in helping parents cope with their child's illness. This experience causes me to wonder whether the use of Verbal First Aid communication tools could *decrease* the amount of medication needed for sedation or pain.

Before knowing Verbal First Aid, I would not have made a point of saying "the worst is over" to my patients and their parents, of telling them that the uncertainty, worry, and fear of the unknown are behind them. I would not have made a point of describing the positive changes (obvious to medical staff but not to patients and parents) that demonstrate that the patient is getting better, of emphasizing the small steps that show healing is occurring and that the child is improving.

Now, in addition to the medical care and because of Verbal First Aid, I ask myself, *What can I say that might make a difference?* I wonder how much these Verbal First Aid communication skills, which help us communicate with our patients and their families and which help parents help their children, might speed up the recovery of any illness or perhaps shorten a hospital stay.

Outside the hospital, in a different location, I had a completely different lesson to learn about the importance of Verbal First Aid. At a diabetes summer camp for teenagers, I introduced a program to the campers for treatment of low blood sugar that involved using a small amount of a medication (glucagon) to correct low blood sugars quickly and without side effects. As a physician I had always thought of glucagon as a friend, a useful medication for serious low blood sugars. I did not realize that to the teenagers and counselors with diabetes, it was associated with fear and very negative thoughts of emergencies, seizures, passing out, embarrassment, and sometimes vomiting, headaches, and feeling badly. As soon as I said the word *glucagon*, the teens did not hear another thing I said. They immediately hated the idea and rejected it. The counselors told me clearly that everyone was very upset! I quickly realized it would be a disaster to try to institute this program when the campers and staff felt this way.

At camp, however, we had an opportunity to use Verbal First Aid to turn this around. Some of the medical staff and I created a little skit explaining the new treatment compared to the emergency treatment the kids already knew about. We used a glass of water to represent the small dose glucagon I was introducing them to and a bucket of water to represent the emergency dose they were familiar with. We dumped the doses of water on the medical staff, who were pretending to have low blood sugar. It was funny, and the kids easily understood the difference between the two treatments; many of the campers who needed it accepted the new treatment. The following year, most of the teens who needed glucagon accepted it and some even asked for it!

This experience totally convinced me that even in nonemergency situations Verbal First Aid works. How I introduced the treatment, the words I used, made the difference in whether the campers accepted the treatment or not. The new treatment worked quickly without side effects, and very soon the teens were back having fun with their friends. *The words I used were as important as the medical treatment.* Verbal First Aid works!

Verbal First Aid is primarily a book for parents, but is also a powerful book for anyone who works with children. The communication tools described in *Verbal First Aid* teach parents how to speak to their children in a way that will make a difference in how they look at life and solve their own problems, whether they have a cut finger or a broken bone or live with diabetes. Parents often do not know how to speak to their children to help them get well and be well. When they know what to say, they can teach their children how to use their own resources for strength and well-being when they need it. When the words children hear adults say in crisis situations or times of worry or illness are positive ones, then the words they hear in their own minds during difficult times throughout their lives will also be positive, which helps them begin the healing for themselves, physically and emotionally.

These are the reasons *Verbal First Aid* is such an important book for parents, caregivers, medical personnel, physicians, and all who work with children. In my experience, speaking positively in difficult or crisis situations does not come naturally. Using the simple tools described in this book makes a difference. I have seen it work with my own children, with the children I see in the office and hospital, and with the parents of my patients.

Who knows what the possibilities for overall health and well-being are now and will be in the future when we use these communication tools to speak to our children!

INTRODUCTION

We've all heard the saying "Sticks and stones may break my bones, but names will never hurt me." While the idea may be well intentioned, science and our experience tells us it is not true: Words, the wrong words, do hurt. The power of words, the thoughts they provoke, and the images they create can and do remain long after the bruises from those sticks and stones have healed. Think back to your own childhood. Perhaps you have a memory of falling over a chair and toppling your dad's favorite lamp. Instead of hearing something soothing and helpful to your recovery, what you heard was, "I told you not to run in the house. Look at what you just did." And the sting was only partly in your knee. Most of it was in your heart. You can still feel it.

We retain much more than we realize and hold it in our bodies. Sometimes we're not even conscious of it. Why do you still feel the pain of a hurtful situation when the wound has healed? Many people—therapists, researchers, and physicians—believe that we retain and hold memories in our bodies. Candace Pert, PhD, is a former section chief at the National Institutes of Health, one of the discoverers of neuropeptides, a founder of the field of psychoneuroimmunology, the author of *Molecules of Emotion,* and an expert whose work has revolutionized the way medicine views immunity and the impact of emotions. The title of her famous CD shows her views on the subject: "Your Body is Your Subconscious Mind." Verbal First Aid works the way that it does because this response to words is a natural phenomenon; it is the way we operate all the time, not just at catastrophic events such as September 11.

Words have the power not only to influence one's emotions but to actually ignite a child's imagination and belief system. Consider the following scenario in which a little girl is playing with friends, running and laughing. She lives in the present, and the present is filled with giggling girls, teasing boys, and a ball that everybody wants. Suddenly, she trips. Her knee skids along the concrete, and blood begins to trickle from the scrape.

She holds still for a moment, stunned, her play so rudely interrupted, her belief in her limitless abilities suddenly shaken. And within seconds, before deciding what to do, she looks up to find her mother.

She might not be crying yet, partially because it takes a moment to recognize what has happened, partly because it is to her mother that she turns to learn how serious this situation is. Should she cry or is everything going to be all right? In her world, with her limited experience, she needs a few clues on how to cope with the situation.

When a child is hurt, it's not just the boo-boo that's involved.

It's not just the knee, the pain, or the bleeding.

There is also the fear, the humiliation, the confusion.

There is also the need for solace, empathy, attention.

The physical, the psychological, and the social all coalesce in that one moment.

What you say right then and there can set the course for both physical and emotional recovery. That is because the body is listening. And whatever happens, happens to every part of us.

Science is now verifying that every thought we have sends chemicals through our bodies that aid or impede the healing process. Indeed, how wounds and broken bones heal is affected by the very thoughts and pictures held in the mind based on the words we hear and tell ourselves. The little girl's physiology responds differently to fear than to calm. What she is hearing, being told, and thinking influence the blood flow, heart rate, breathing, and more through her autonomic nervous system. Saying the right thing to her at the moment she's holding on to her skinned knee can literally help the wound heal faster.

However, the physical scars of sticks and stones are only a small part of the effects that linger from an accident or incident. What the child will remember about this incident can have repercussions throughout her life, sometimes as post-traumatic stress, sometimes as lingering emotional pain.

If the mother of the fallen child cries out, "Oh, no! Look at you! You're bleeding, oh, my baby, my poor baby," she adds to the child's fear. If bleeding is upsetting to her mother, then perhaps a phobia of her own blood will develop. And if she comes to believe, as her mother's panic has indicated, that this is cause for alarm, her body will respond by creating chemicals that will impede healing.

Picture then a boy falling off a jungle gym and breaking his arm. If his father, trying to bolster his son's spirits says, "You're all right. Buck up, buddy. It's not that bad," what does the child learn at that scary moment? Perhaps he learns to keep his feelings to himself. Perhaps he begins to feel that he cannot get sympathy for his pain and begins to feel very alone. Perhaps he even begins a long path of disregard for his own feelings, all patterned on what his well-meaning father has said.

If those parents had known that what you think = what you feel = how you heal and that every word we hear influences every thought and sends chemicals through our bodies that aid or impede healing, they would have chosen different words. This is where Verbal First Aid steps in as an invaluable tool that can set the course for children's healing, physically and emotionally.

When you use the techniques and suggested responses provided in this book, you will be able to say the words that set the course for your children's physical and emotional recovery. You'll be able to short-circuit traumatic memories, sometimes just by speaking a sentence or two. You will be able to model for your children how to respond to the moment in the healthiest way, thus providing them with a technique they'll always have. You'll be able to say the words that communicate signals for healing to the child's body. This will give the child's mind a perspective for dealing with hardships and difficulties throughout life, a model for confidence.

Now let's return to the scene of the mother picking up her child and cleaning her bleeding wound. Imagine how the look on the frightened child's face would change if the mother were to say: "See what a good job your blood is doing cleaning out that cut. Now you can even use your mind to stop your bleeding. We'll wash it off and put a bandage on, and you'll be so surprised at how fast it will start to feel better." With these few words, the child experiences self-confidence instead of fear.

How different it would have been if the father had said to his son:

"You know I broke my arm when I was about your age, and you'd never guess it now. I can throw a baseball just the way I could before I broke it. Even better. Your body knows how to heal itself, and before you know it, you'll be climbing again." With these words, the boy begins to use his imagination to start the healing process. Because what you think = how you feel = how you heal.

You're probably wondering how you'll be able to stay calm and coherent when your child is in pain, bleeding, or scared. That's understandable. It's never easy for a parent when a child is hurt. But we are here to teach you ways to center yourself so that you can speak calmly to your child and be the voice that guides him to healing. The truth is that you're stronger than you realize. It might mean you'll have to let go of some of your own fears and anxieties, but the payoff will be enormous. You'll be giving your child a legacy of inner strength and confidence. Verbal First Aid can provide some of the most effective skills a parent can give his or her child because it facilitates and nurtures an awareness in the child that will last a lifetime.

This is a book that is set up to be read from beginning to end because the information herein is not just valuable but revolutionary in its approach. You might, however, want to focus on areas of greatest interest to you. Perhaps you'd like to learn about the theory behind Verbal First Aid (Chapter 1) or to fully appreciate the magical mind of a child and how children are different from the rest of us (Chapter 2).

We believe you'll benefit most from learning how to work Verbal First Aid (Chapters 3 and 4) before you go to the scripts for specific issues because the scripts are just examples. And once you understand the simple principles, you can use your imagination to color a script any way that works in the moment with your particular thoughts and with the particular child before you when he is in need of just the right words to get through something tough.

There are scripts for burns, boo-boos, and fears (Chapter 5), scripts for taking the child to the doctor or for surgery (Chapter 6), for talking to children about illness and death (Chapter 7), and for discussing some of the frightening things in our world (Chapter 8). Chapter 9 takes us into the future of Verbal First Aid, and the appendix provides you with a quick chart of magic words.

Most of the chapters have overviews at the end so that you can find important information as you go along, or any time you pick the book up when you need a quick refresher right in the moment.

Many of the stories included in this book are true, and although the names have been changed for the sake of privacy, parents and children were happy to share experiences that proved the value of Verbal First Aid.

It is our hope that you read this and then make it your own. And that as you do, you—parents, medical personnel, caregivers—discover that, with a word, the right one, you can turn a scare into a comfort, a hurt into a healing, and a pain into a memory of courage.

That would be a win for everyone.

PART ONE

The Extraordinary Science Behind Verbal First Aid™

1 What We Hold in Our Minds, We Hold in Our Bodies

Kids will be kids, and accidents will happen. From sudden nosebleeds to emergency visits to the doctor for stitches, childhood can be filled with scary moments that children and parents aren't prepared for. While parents do not have the power to prevent their children from experiencing burns, bruises, and other bumps in the road of life, parents do have the power to prevent little scrapes from becoming gaping psychic wounds and can give children the tools they can use to feel brave and confident in the world throughout their lives.

Moreover, parents have the power to help their children heal from life's hurts on every level: physical, mental, emotional, psychological, spiritual, and social. Verbal First Aid gives parents such powers, allowing them to transform an otherwise traumatic moment into a teachable one. This is because when we are in crisis, whether it's large or small, we become more finely tuned and receptive to whatever is being said around us or to us. What we hear not only affects how we respond in the moment but it becomes part of our unconscious programming for future similar events. The following two examples demonstrate this premise.

TWO ACCIDENTS, TWO APPROACHES

Meet Lily and Oliver. Each has a story, both of them true. In one story you'll find that a crisis was not handled well, and the repercussions are obvious. In the other ... well, you'll see.

Lily

Lily was three when she fell against the coffee table and cut her upper lip. It was bleeding badly, and her parents, loving her as parents will, were so upset they reacted in instantaneous horror, "Oh, no, she's going to need stitches." "Not stitches! Oh my God!" "What can we do, what can we do? We'll have to get her to the hospital!"

The drive to the hospital was filled with more awfulizing and dire predictions, and Lily's encounter with the medical establishment did nothing to improve the outlook for her. "Hold her down," the doctor commanded, and Lily felt as if there were no safe place for her, anywhere.

Many years passed, and she grew up believing she had forgotten all about that frightening incident. She became a medic in New York whose job one day took her to the scene of the September 11 terrorist attacks on the Twin Towers. Everyone there was stunned and frightened, Lily included, but she managed to work with the rescue workers and tend to the emotional suffering the disaster had caused. However, she found herself in a state of abject shock, which she couldn't release. For three days, her body shook and she felt drained, paralyzed, and helpless. In her years of helping others, she had never felt quite this way. Finally, she realized that her reaction was more profound than what she might have expected given her experience in the field, and she sought therapeutic help.

Initially confused and disturbed by how she had reacted, Lily began to understand that it was not Lily the adult, the medic, the professional, standing at the scene. It was Lily the three-year-old girl. The utter helplessness she experienced was the same feeling she'd had when she'd been held down for stitches. Because no one then knew how to give her some sense of control, some empowerment or emotional *redirection*, Lily's early childhood experience in the emergency room had become embedded in her body and unconscious mind where it lay dormant.

Up until that point, she dealt with her early incident by taking control of very difficult and frightening situations and helping others. But when she was faced with a situation she could not readily control, the embedded terror and helplessness resurfaced with the same virulent charge it had when she was three. No one at that time had said words of reassurance and comfort that would have allowed her to remember that moment as one in which she was supported and could be brave.

So, because of the way the original incident was handled, the fear lingered under the surface, waiting for another fearful situation to revive it.

Oliver

Now let's look at Oliver, four years old, kept inside the house one rainy day and so full of energy that the only way he can think to discharge it is by jumping up and down repeatedly and somewhat noisily on the sofa. Suddenly, his foot slips off a loose cushion and he skids toward the floor, hitting his head on the radiator. He shouts for his mom, Donna, who comes running.

He's bleeding fairly profusely, ready to cry, but he awaits her judgment on the seriousness of the matter.

"Oliver, what happened?" Donna says, taking him into her arms and calmly examining the wound. "Oh, you banged your head. *Owww.* Well, I'm right here, and I've got you. But, we're going to have to go to the hospital right away, because it looks like you'll need stitches. The doctors will know how to fix you right up."

He's still whimpering when she looks into his face and continues, "It's going to be all right, Oliver, because you're a good healer."

She washes the cut, makes a compress of a cloth and some ice, which she asks him to hold as she drives. On the way she tells him about the time when she was young and had to have stitches. He is so impressed that she lived to tell about it, that he makes her tell that story three times.

When they arrive at the hospital, she reminds him of the book they just read in which someone was turned into a statue. She asks him to imagine he's turned into a statue while the doctor fixes him up.

Watching the procedure, she says, "Oh, he's a wonderful doctor. That was a great stitch. You won't even have a scar."

She tells him they'll be going to Target afterward to get a Hot Wheels car, and asks him which kind would he prefer: a sports car or a classic car. He wants a classic—a red one. Then she tells him that he can tell his friends in school tomorrow what happened to him. Won't they be amazed at how brave he was!

Three days later, when Donna takes Oliver to the pediatrician's office, the doctor tells them that the cut was deep but it's healing really well and confirms that Oliver probably won't even have a scar.

Several months later, Oliver is still four, so jumping up and down on the sofa still seems entertaining. And when he falls off again and his mother hears the thump, she comes running in. She had been so calm the last time, but she's feeling like she's run out of patience with this behavior, so she yells exasperatedly as she sees the blood on his forehead again, "Oliver!"

And he looks up at her and says, "It's okay, Mommy. I'm a good healer."

And so he is. And he knows it. And that changes everything.

Donna used the Verbal First Aid techniques you're going to learn in this book to help Oliver's healing in the present and to help shape his future responses to fear and pain. Regrettably, Lily's parents didn't realize the power of their words and reactions. We'll be coming back to Oliver's story in later chapters to show you step-by-step how Verbal First Aid is done, so that you too will be the person who says the right words to make the difference that can last a lifetime.

These stories illustrate two important principles. First, our bodies are listening and responding to everything we see and hear. Literally. We know experientially for ourselves that our bodies respond to our unconscious minds every time we wake up from a nightmare and find our hearts palpitating, our palms sweaty, our throats dry. We look around, and there we are in our bedroom, safe and sound. But can we go back to sleep? No, because the image in our minds has created that biochemical array that we must process before we can again snuggle under the blankets, wrapped in calmer emotions.

We witness this principle at work on a daily basis in our own lives: We watch movies and we cry. We read books and we laugh. Someone tells a ghost story and we get goose bumps.

Why do our children almost forget to breathe as they watch, so gripped, so believing, so visibly moved by every twist and turn in the plot of a meaningful movie?

And two, these stories also illustrate how emotions are often internalized in our unconscious minds and bodies. And what we hear when we are in crisis becomes a part of the way we approach the next crisis.

Because Lily's experience was one of fear and lack of emotional support, her response to future crises became a replay of the earlier one. Because Oliver's experience was one of support, encouragement, and an expectation of ultimate success, he came prepared for the next crisis with a belief in himself and his own healing power.

FAMILIAR CONCEPT, NEW TERRITORY

Indeed, every word we hear, every thought we think, every picture in our minds, every memory revived affects us. This is not a new concept. But we've taken this idea one step further—we believe that what we think = how we feel = how we heal. Science has demonstrated that words, thoughts, images, and memories actually generate an instantaneous cascade of chemicals, causing a physiological reaction within us.

This physiological reaction is most marked when we are in crisis, panic, fear, or pain. When involved in such situations, people tend to slip into what we call an *altered state of consciousness*. What is said, heard, and imagined at such times goes directly to the autonomic nervous system, which regulates such vital bodily functions as breathing, bleeding, heart and pulse rate, and perception of pain. Whether one physically recovers easily or gets worse is directly affected by those thoughts and images because those thoughts and images directly affect the biochemistry of the body.

Furthermore, in an emergency words spoken sink deeper into the unconscious mind, where they are held and where they run us without our being aware of them. Thoughts and responses during a crisis affect not just the present moment, although that is where Verbal First Aid is highly effective. Their impact can be felt for days, years, even, over a lifetime. When children have a voice in their heads that supports and empowers them, especially in emergencies, everything is possible. What a person remembers about how an incident was handled determines whether he holds those memories in fear or whether those memories help prove his own tenacity, resilience, and courage.

GOT PROOF? SCIENCE SUPPORTS THE CONCEPT OF VERBAL FIRST AID

Reporting on a 2009 University of Kansas study covering more than 140 countries and titled "Human Emotions Hold Sway over Physical Health Worldwide," *Science Daily* explained, "Most strikingly, the association between emotion and physical health was more powerful than the connection between health and basic human physical requirements, like adequate nourishment. *Even without shelter or food, positive emotions were shown to boost health*" (emphasis added). That is, people who could find happiness in their situation, no matter how dire, benefited themselves *physically* over those who couldn't.[1]

When you change your way of thinking, you change your way of being. That includes the way you behave with other people, the way you sleep, the way you eat, and the way you heal.

When Dr. Bruce Lipton began studying epigenetics (the science of those things "beyond" genetics), he discovered that DNA could not turn itself on. Instead, what he revealed was that proteins could express themselves in almost limitless variation, no matter what the initial program, and that their expression (as physical traits, personality, or intelligence) was not predestined, as we had always believed. If our DNA is not a fixed blueprint, what, he wanted to know, determines how these genes express themselves and which genes decide to activate, and why?

He discovered that it was the environment—emotional as well as physical—that determined how a gene expressed itself. Perhaps more specific and important, it was our *perception* of the environment that was the pivotal issue. Whether a gene expresses as health or as disease is a function of what we are thinking. He realized that not only can belief make us happier or more depressed but that it profoundly affects health in this fundamental way: Belief changes genetic expression.

When we feel safe, our cells are programmed for growth and survival. When we are frightened or stressed, our cells shut down in self-protection, limiting our ability to adapt to the environment in a healthful way.

There are many studies supporting the concept that your feelings are not just influential but pivotal to your health. At Johns Hopkins, for example, over a seven-and-a-half-year period, researchers assessed six hundred adults with heart disease in their family history. The study accounted for age, gender, and race and adjusted for the usual suspects—smoking, cholesterol levels, and weight. What factor was the most influential in saving lives? The conclusion was dramatic: "A positive outlook may offer the strongest known protection against heart disease in adults at risk."[2] The strongest known protection was not giving up cigarettes, which would be a good idea, or exercising, which would be great. It was just your garden-variety positive attitude. And if it could be bottled, it would be called a miracle drug, a silver bullet. And so it really is.

As you can see, this movement into hope can make a difference between life and death. Another example of the power of words and thoughts is Masaru Emoto's work. The author of *The Hidden Messages in Water*, among many other books, tells a story about children undergoing chemotherapy at the Cancer Care Center. The children were given the option of choosing words they would like to see written on their IV pouches. It is interesting that about 50 percent of the children chose *love* whereas others chose words such as *health*, *peace*, and *humor*. What they found was that the children who saw the IV fluid as love (instead of a more conventional description of the drug as a "poison that kills cancer") not only felt better about the treatment but recovered faster and expressed a greater sense of confidence in their treatment. What the caretakers learned may have been as important as what the children experienced: How we hold an event, how we see it and receive it, and what we tell ourselves about it may be as important as the event itself.

This idea that what we feel determines how we heal has the power to change the way we approach medicine from beginning to end. Thoughts and images affect our bodies in ways we're only just beginning to understand. Many studies in the fields of guided imagery and hypnosis now demonstrate the effects of the pictures in the mind, the mental images, on the immune system and even on the panic and suffering of conditions like asthma. In one pediatric study, the results were vividly dramatic: 80 percent of children with asthma had measurable improvement, none of the children's symptoms worsened, and, best of all, some patients' symptoms resolved—were *cleared up*—after one guided imagery session.

The researcher, Ran D. Anbar, MD, professor of pediatrics at State University of New York University Hospital, reported in a paper titled "Identification of Children Who May Benefit from Self-Hypnosis at a Pediatric Pulmonary Center" that of eighty-one patients receiving instruction in self-hypnosis for anxiety, cough, chest pain, dyspnea, or respiratory difficulties, 75 percent returned for follow-up and 95 percent of those patients reported improvement or resolution of their symptoms.[3]

Researcher and author D. P. Kohen found that simply *teaching* hypnotic techniques for calming, storytelling, and positive imagery to preschool children who had asthma and their families helped the children both physically and emotionally. Not only did the children require fewer office visits, indicating fewer acute asthmatic episodes, but the parents and children both reported feeling more confident and comfortable overall.[4]

What this all means in terms of your child's well-being—in relation not simply to asthmatic episodes but to all the frights, hurts, and crises—is that you can influence the pictures in his mind, which will effect change in his physiology, his emotions, and the way he holds the memory.

The Power of the Placebo

What we're discussing may remind you of what is known in medical circles as the *placebo effect*. The word *placebo* however, is often feared by researchers and pharmaceutical companies because it is founded on something that is out of their control and beyond the scope of contemporary scientific measures—belief alone. The placebo in an experiment is nothing more than a suggestion, a state of mind, an image of healing. It is so important a variable in a clinical trial that no matter how strong the drug against which it is tested, it must be considered and statistically ruled out if the drug's efficacy can be taken seriously. Verbal First Aid does use belief in a thought as one of its attributes, but it goes further than the placebo effect because of its lasting impact.

Dr. Larry Dossey, author and one of the foremost proponents of mind–body medicine, says, "Images create bodily changes—just as if the experience were really happening. For example, if you imagine yourself lying on a beach in the sun, you become relaxed, your peripheral blood vessels dilate, and your hands become warm, *as in the real thing*" (emphasis added).[5]

The placebo effect generally works this way: Unbeknown to them, people in a control group are given an inert substance and an assurance by an authority figure that the pill they are taking will help them. In 35 percent of cases, as a rule, the bogus treatment works as well as any medication it is measured against. Herbert Benson, founder of Mind/Body Medical Institute at Harvard, says that as many as 60 to 90 percent of people diagnosed with angina pectoris, bronchial asthma, and herpes simplex (a virus) find relief with a placebo.[6]

A *New York Times Magazine* article by Margaret Talbot reported on a series of placebo studies that clearly demonstrated the mind–body connection and how thought influenced the body's reaction. In one study, doctors used an inert, brightly colored dye on patients who had warts. The patients were told that as the color faded, the warts would be removed; the warts, in fact, disappeared as predicted. In another experiment with bronchodilators filled with a simple saline solution, patients with asthma felt their airways dilating when they believed that they were using a powerful new medication.[7]

Taking it a step further, a study at the University of Michigan, published August 24, 2005, in the *Journal of Neuroscience*, showed that if we believe that a medicine will relieve pain, our brains actually react physically and release their own painkillers (called endorphins) to soothe painful sensations.[8]

If our brains can produce a similar substance to the one we believe we are taking, then you can see that the placebo effect is not only in the mind, but that the body literally contributes to the healing when belief is called on.

What contributes to our state of health is not only what we say but how we see things in the present moment. And how we see things will, in fact, determine what we say. And what we say will begin to move the listener either to fear and contraction or to detached interest and flexibility. It is why we say what you think = how you feel = how you heal.

Pain, Perception, and the Imagination

We've seen how we can influence our ability to heal. But what about something as amorphous and subjective as pain? How do we approach that? The truth is that pain is simultaneously one of the most mysterious and well-studied aspects of medicine. It is the creaking wheel of treatment and as such, it has in recent years become a subspecialty of its own.

The research demonstrates that pain does not exist separately from our perception of it. It is not like a tumor or a broken bone. Because it is what we might call a pure perception, it can change according to our immediate priorities and needs. This isn't to say that pain isn't real, only that its intensity is relative and therefore can be modified.

Therefore, what we hold in our minds and what your children hold in theirs in turn determines the grip that pain has on us. Our thoughts can help modulate the intensity, duration, and persistence of pain.

This is true for all of us: When you are involved in something you love doing, pain can take a backseat until you're finished. A friend was taking movies of his three-year-old granddaughter, Sophie, and six-year-old grandson, Josh, as they twirled about dancing. The children were delighted and delightful as they put on a show for all to see. After each song, they rushed to watch themselves on the computer monitor.

Sophie, in her exuberance, performed a wild and sophisticated turn, only to bump into a coffee table and tumble over. It was one of those falls that makes the people who are watching it wince, even though it wasn't particularly serious. With a slight red spot growing on her cheek, Sophie was clearly considering the possibility of crying, but she was looking for a confirming response. It easily could have been a reasonable cause for attention-getting theatrics. But it wasn't. The reason was the response of those around her.

Her grandpa, who had been holding the camera, calmly said, "Ooops, look at that. I'll just turn the camera off until you're sure you're okay."

If Grandpa had gasped audibly and rushed to her saying, "Oh my goodness, Sophie. Are you hurt? What a bad fall," a completely different result might have ensued. He wasn't dismissive, just offered her the alternative of paying attention to the pain or the dancing.

Because her pain was less important than her performance, Sophie, still just a little stunned by the tumble, straightened herself out and refocused on the camera, saying, "Watch my moves," to an appreciative crowd. Pain is to this extent subjective. It is a matter of where we place our attention. It is a matter of mind more than of body. Because of that and because her grandfather intuitively understood that simple fact, the evening went on as delightfully as it had begun.

Everyone knows that it's almost impossible to hold two things in our consciousness at once. As one friend has said, "Anxiety and faith are mutually exclusive. You can't be trusting and afraid at the same time." The same is true for much of what we feel, experience, or think. If our minds are filled with one thing, there isn't room for anything else. We've all had the experience of being persuaded to go out to a movie when we really wanted to stay in bed with a headache or a cold. We may have reluctantly agreed, but once we joined the activity, it wasn't until the end credits began to roll that our headache returned. It's hard to enjoy something and be miserable or in pain at the same time. A good way of explaining it is that we are like radios or televisions. By adjusting a small knob, we can tune into a station, but only one. The question becomes for us, which one would we like to tune into?

One man was in the hospital and quite ill. Nothing the doctors were trying was working. They were entering his room every fifteen minutes, trying new procedures, another scalpel, another needle, or presenting him with another form to fill out. Between all the dialysis, medications, check-ins, blood pressure readings, and help he was receiving, he was exhausted and felt his health declining. Finally, he remembered something he had learned when attending a book signing for *The Worst Is Over*—of all the millions and billions and trillions of bits of information available to us at any given moment, it is within our power to pay close attention to only two thousand. So he looked around his room, listened to the sounds coming from the heart monitors, the television screens, and the staff in the hall, and decided that he'd rather be fishing. Imaginary pole slung over his shoulder, bucket in hand, off he went. He called us to report some time later that he didn't catch anything and he didn't care. He hadn't felt as rested or as peaceful in weeks.

One study by Diane Tusek, RN, showed that guided imagery has been clinically successful in the treatment of headaches. "Patients who listened to the Guided Imager Tape, produced by Diane Tusek, decreased headache frequency and severity by 62 percent." That is an astonishing statistic: headache frequency and severity were reduced by two-thirds by an alteration in thought! In yet another study, Tusek reports, "Numerous guided imagery research studies have shown that anxiety and pain can be reduced by up to 65% within minutes."[9]

As it turns out, then, a significant component of pain is the *perception* of it. And an answer to lessening pain might involve perceiving the pain as something else. This is a cognitive device that often involves visualization.

An example of this was given by a dentist who, because she had to deliver rather large injections of Novocain into the little mouths of young children, decided to reposition the experience for them. She would say, "I'm going to make your tooth better, and, so that it's comfortable, I'm going to spray 'abracadabra drowsy sauce' on it. You know what it feels like when I do this? It feels like when you're playing with a hose with your friends in the summer and they turn the hose on you and it hits your face and stings a little and you laugh and grab it to get them back." The child nods, remembering the sensations and the feelings. "Well, I'll need you to close your eyes, so it doesn't splash into your eyes," she would continue, "and then you won't feel anything as I work on your tooth."

With closed eyes, the child doesn't see the giant hypodermic needle, but feels the sting, imagines playing with a hose, and, although there is some pain, it is the pain of horsing around, and therefore acceptable pain.

Even when the pain is a signal that something is awry, the sensation we describe as pain can also be separated out so that it is more manageable and therefore more malleable. We would want to ask a patient: What exactly does it feel like? Is it warm? Is it cold? Is it tight? How long? Does it have a color? A weight? A density? When we can visualize it in those sensory ways, we can alter it, eventually helping make *it*—the perception of the pain—disappear altogether.

Science supports this understanding. T. M. Ball showed the power of perception over pain in a pilot study reported in the journal *Clinical Pediatrics*. He and his team of researchers studied the use of recorded guided imagery in the treatment of recurrent abdominal pain in children and found it successful.[10] A 2004 study published in the journal *Pain* reported that guided imagery or visualization could reduce a child's pain after surgery.[11]

Perception is important, as is imagination. How we see the pain affects how much it hurts.

There are many ways to see pain—as a harbinger of something terrible, as information, even as something hopeful. How we see it changes how we experience it. Clinical observations of soldiers who have been wounded and are being sent home from the front talk about how much easier it is for them to manage their pain than those whose pain has no perceived purpose.

An example of a hopeful perspective is the way Colonel Barry J. Howard, USAF (Ret.), saw his pain when he came home from the hospital. After numerous, lengthy surgeries on his knee and much obvious discomfort—not to mention inconvenience—he finally returned home from a month in the hospital and rehabilitation. While a friend was fixing one of the leg supports on his wheelchair he winced.

"Are you okay?" his friend asked.

"Oh, yeah," the colonel answered. "This is great. It's a healing pain."

"What do you mean?" The friend looked at him sideways.

"You know the difference between a pain that means something is wrong and a pain that tells you something is going right. This is good. It's sharp and clear and right where it should be."

On another occasion, our friend Timothy Trujillo was at a college reunion where a little girl was bitten in the hand by a dog. Everyone surrounded her and was making a fuss as the girl screamed and cried. Because there was a doctor on the scene, Timothy (a well-respected hypnotherapist, founder of First Medicine, and researcher on hypnosis and pain) did not step forward to help. But finally the cries of the child bade him try his magic. He went over to her and asked to see her other hand. Perhaps five people were gathered around her injured hand and she was puzzled by his request. Still crying in pain, she offered her unbitten hand to Timothy. He took it and pushed his thumb hard into her palm. Her eyes widened. "Let me know when this hand feels like the other one," he said. Her attention immediately went to the place where he applied pressure. Suddenly she started to laugh. Timothy started to laugh too.

Everyone else was startled, but the child realized to her amazement that she could play with the feelings, moving in her mind back and forth between the real pain and the Timothy pressure. And that meant that she had control over *what* she experienced as well as the extent to which she experienced it. Surely a little girl did not articulate it that way, but the kinesthetic, or body, learning is the same. Perhaps deeper.

These two stories illustrate again how pain is a perception. In one case, rather than being resisted and resented, it was perceived as healing pain, a good pain that said things were getting better. And picturing that outcome sent those messages to the body. In the next, the pain was perceived as mutable: As the child moved her mind back and forth, the quality and intensity of the pain changed. And that gave her a sense of her own power rather than one of victimhood.

What this means is that you and your child are not at the mercy of forces beyond your control. Verbal First Aid gives you and your child the tools to reduce pain, manage or eliminate meltdowns, soothe fears, untie the knots of misunderstandings, and see otherwise frightening events such as visits to the doctor in a whole new light.

Beyond Positive Thinking

Verbal First Aid empowers children to think differently—about themselves and their capacities to heal as well as the effects of their words on others. It is not just about being nice, nor is it about just being optimistic. It is much, much more than that.

You may encounter, as we sometimes do, people who reject *positive thinking* and therefore do not understand how the use of guided imagery and positive suggestions can work. Clearly it does no good to try to convince yourself of something you don't *believe*. In fact, it can make you feel worse to repeat that you are as slim or rich or brilliant as media icons if it simply reminds you that it is not so.

The words used to help a child or any other person to recover from a physical or emotional injury must ring true. That is why we emphasize rapport, which consists of believability and credibility among other things. Telling a child, "I'm right here with you" or "Your body has healed itself before. That's what it wants to do" speaks to the part of us, our physiology and our minds, that can hear, believe, and use those words in the best way.

So don't be confused between wishful thinking and the wisdom to which the body is listening. Make the words positive, healing, and true and watch how they are accepted and used physiologically and socially for beneficial results in the present and in the future.

USING THE MIND TO HEAL

Stimulating the brain by providing alternative scenarios and images to a person in crisis can engender *measurable changes in our bodies* as well as alter the way we perceive ourselves and our health. In so doing we are also enhancing our sense of mastery. This is a very important idea when working with trauma, because one of the primary complaints in trauma treatment is an overwhelming sense of powerlessness. Terror and hypervigilance are compounded and embedded by a feeling of impotence. When Verbal First Aid is used right away, people are more likely to experience a sense of personal control and thus mitigate the possibility of an acute stress disorder.

Studies help us understand "how the brain becomes sensitized to a traumatic event, and how there can be a cumulative effect," said Dr. Bruce McEwen, director of the neuroendocrinology laboratory at Rockefeller University.[12] In a study at Mount Sinai School of Medicine and the Jewish Board of Family and Children's Services in New York, parents of children between one and five years old who were nearby when the World Trade Center collapsed were surveyed about their children's behavior. "Children who had been rattled by a previous experience were about 20 times as likely to show signs of depression, anxiety, or attention deficits as children who had not known a significant trauma before September 11."[13]

How children react to an incident, whether they are rattled or soothed, determines what is emotionally retained as a trauma that is echoed cumulatively. When Verbal First Aid is used well, as it was in the case of Oliver related earlier and by the fireman in the story at the end of this chapter, what is remembered is not the fear but the sense of ultimate safety. Teens who experienced the ugliness of the 1998–1999 war in Kosovo, who had lost friends, who had seen their homes destroyed, and who were surrounded by violence, were part of a study by the Institute of Mind/Body Medicine, which included guided imagery and many other mind–body techniques. The conclusion: "The data indicate that mind-body skills groups were effective in reducing posttraumatic stress symptoms in war-traumatized high school students."[14]

What about the more ordinary experiences and traumas of childhood, the ones you will most likely be dealing with? The following three stories serve as excellent illustrations of how easily and quickly Verbal First Aid can work. It's not necessary to be a therapist or to engage in a very elaborate protocol to know what to say and how to say it when you really need it. Your knowledge of Verbal First Aid can do your child a world of good in just a few moments.

The Windshield Wipers

At a typical, noisy, busy playground, a five- or six-year-old girl ran up to a man, likely her father, crying plaintively because she had gotten sand in her eyes. Her father, meaning well, picked her up and began rubbing her eyes with the sleeve of his wool sweater.

Although it was none of her business, a bystander who knew Verbal First Aid couldn't bear the thought of the child's scraped cornea and walked over to the child. "Oh, there's sand in your eyes," the woman said. "I wonder if you could imagine that your eyelids were like the windshield wipers in Daddy's car, and your eyes were like the windows that had dust on them. And if you blink a lot maybe fifteen times, I'll bet you could wash those windows off."

So the child blinked some seven times or so, considered where things stood, said, "It's better now," jumped down from her dad's arms and rushed off to play. The woman told us that she believed that the image as well as the blinking helped the situation resolve faster.

Spider-Man Takes a Dive

Andrew, five years old, had fallen out of a tree and broken his arm. A neighbor who knew Verbal First Aid saw him flourishing his cast with bravado. But under that gesture was clearly the sadness that he was confined to the front steps of his house when he'd rather be out and about making trouble again.

"Who's your favorite superhero?" she asked him.

"Spider-Man," he answered without a doubt.

"What do you think Spider-Man would do if he had a broken arm?"

"He'd probably wrap it up in spiderwebs until it was all better."

"Do you think he'd do that for you?"

"I don't know."

"I'll bet if you imagined that he was doing that every night before you went to sleep, your arm would heal faster than anything, and the doctor will be so surprised at how fast you're better."

She saw him sometime later without the cast.

"Hey, you healed really fast," she said. He looked at her conspiratorially, because his cynical mother was nearby, and just gave her that secret Spider-Man smile.

My Own Little Girl

Recently we received a phone call from a firefighter who had read *The Worst Is Over*. He always knew, he said, that there were certain first responders whose very presence seemed to change the way things resolved. They had what he called a good bedside manner and made the events, even in the face of catastrophe, seem to go better.

The day after he read our book, this firefighter was called to the scene of a car crash in which a mother and a five-year-old girl were trapped in the crushed vehicle. The mother was easily removed, but the daughter, although not seriously injured, was pinned into her seat and hysterical with fear.

Ordinarily, he said, he would have been calling out for his fellow firefighters to bring the jaws of life, shouting orders to mobilize the help that would be needed, but this time a thought, a single thought, crossed his mind and he remembered the child and what she must be thinking and feeling.

He stopped everything, just for a second, and reached into the car, touching her knee as best he could. He looked into her eyes and said to her, "I'm a daddy like your daddy, and I have a little girl just like you. And I'm going to take care of you as if you were my little girl."

Everything changed, he said. In that moment, time stood still. The quiet was dazzling. The little girl stopped crying. The air around them became charged with something unseen but felt. And the rescue happened gracefully and in such a way that, when the child thought of it later, she would think not of the fear, but of the relief, of the connectedness, of how we can be all right, even in the face of something scary.

DRAGONS, GIANTS, AND WITCHES

Maybe our lives are not about what happens to us so much as how we perceive what happens. The author E. M. Forster said that when we tell a story, there must be a mountain over which our protagonist must go in order for us to know the character of our hero or heroine. Is he brave or cowardly? Is she wise or foolish? It is only as he or she encounters the obstacle that we have the opportunity to see of what this person is made.

In the face of whatever we encounter, who are we?

What we perceive does not have to be what we actually *receive*. The research is indicating that what we think about what happens may be as important as what actually happens.

The issue, in literary parlance, is not the mountain over which we must go. It is not even whether we must slay a dragon, chop off the head of a giant, or melt a witch. Whatever our challenge may be, although it may be cancer, the loss of a loved one, or a terrible injury—all of which are tragedies and deserve their proper respect—the issue is not the mountain *but how we respond to it*. How we respond to a situation—any situation—depends less on the situation than on what we bring of ourselves to it. And this is often a function of what we are telling ourselves at such a time, of the words and images that our fear or our courage supply.

When we know that it is our thought, our attitude, that shapes the world we live in, we discover that we have within us the very answer we often seek outside.

When the firefighter stopped the world to connect with the child—when he told her that no matter how it looked, she was safe in his care—her physical, emotional, and spiritual heart shifted. And she saw the event and the world differently, then and forever.

We all are in need of rescue sometimes, but we are also sometimes the rescuer, even our own. When we and our children know the thoughts and images that can turn a car crash, a broken heart, a hurtful or frightening event around, we have gained a mastery that can help make us courageous in the face of the many dragons, giants, and witches that exist. With Verbal First Aid we are preparing our children to be and feel safer out in the world.

2 The Magical Mind of a Child

Children are special. In fact you once were one yourself.

As you look at your child, maybe you see her from the vantage point of an adult. This funny, unpredictable being may even seem a different species from you, one you sometimes don't understand. And yet, if you just take a breath and allow yourself to remember, you may find that you can connect with the awesome truth that you, that all of us, began as children, were once that mysterious, that open, that way.

You were once a child, with all the awe, innocence, wonder, helplessness, and hope that that entails.

Remember being startled by something out of your realm of the familiar?

Remember the good feeling when someone saved you or hugged your fears away or explained the mystery or turned on the light, revealing that the scary shape in the dark was your jeans draped on the back of a chair?

Maybe you can even recall a time when, as a kid, you looked out for another child, you knew what he was feeling and you protected or explained or simply held his hand through it. You knew that those feelings or fears needed to be translated, and you were there to do it. That was you, too.

Even if you had bad experiences as a child, and many people sadly have had hurts when they were most vulnerable, you still were that child. In empathizing with *yourself*, you can gain some wisdom to make a difference in future generations.

It may seem silly to you now, from the vantage point of experience, that your child is afraid of something so obviously benign to you or that your child overreacts to being hurt or to an injustice. You hear parents saying, "Oh, cut it out. You're not hurt. Stop crying."

When *they, those children*, make so much noise or when they are so silly, hit, or bite, or just plain cry that things aren't fair, or when something hurts them, it may in some ways offend us. It may seem detached from us, even beneath us as if we never, *ever* exhibited that "annoying" sort of behavior.

But if you just—for just this second—reach back, you'll find it. Those same feelings, that exquisite sensitivity, that heightened awareness, even, perhaps, that faith in magic before cynicism set in.

We grow up and we forget. That's built in. But as science is now showing us, we are also built to empathize. We have these amazing *mirror neurons* that allow us to feel what another is feeling. It's why you wince when you see someone hurt (Swedish even has a word for it—*ooofda* means "ouch for you") or smile in reaction to a smile. And part of Verbal First Aid is tuning into that ability—we call it *pacing* and will talk a lot about it—that allows you to empathize and, in understanding, know how to help.

The extraordinary capacities of childhood were in all of us once, and they are in our children now. And it is these very abilities that make Verbal First Aid so useful and so effective with them. Because children are just starting out, there are both resources and challenges involved in helping them incorporate into their imaginations and memories the words and images that can provide them with physical and emotional well-being, a trajectory of healing, and a way of thinking that offer a lifetime of the great freedom that is personal mastery.

NATURAL RESOURCES

Children Are Highly Suggestible

In professional circles it is currently a clinical given that we are all suggestible to some extent. According to one study,[1] that figure may be as high as 70 percent of the population. Imagination is a trait so rich and amazing, it allows us to know and appreciate things beyond our immediate experience in infinite ways. The ability to focus the attention inward is a fundamental and natural human experience, and if we weren't suggestible, we would never cry at a movie or suspend disbelief long enough to finish a good science fiction novel.

Research shows that all people slip in and out of these states naturally and easily, rarely even noticing it themselves.[2] Whether we're daydreaming, driving home without remembering having stopped at any stoplights, or following a thought until we can't remember where we started or what we were first thinking about, we've all been there (wherever *there* is!). Research also indicates that using the kinds of techniques we propose in Verbal First Aid, physicians and caretakers could use those states to successfully diminish patient anxiety and enhance outcome, for children as well as for adults.

As every parent who has ever tried to get a child to focus knows, children are quite often in that altered state. According to author and cellular biologist Bruce Lipton, PhD:

> Before birth and through the first five years of life, the infant is primarily in DELTA and THETA [brain wave lengths; adult consciousness is BETA], which represents a hypnogogic state (a state that is between waking and sleeping). In order to hypnotize an individual it is necessary to lower their brain function to these levels of activity. Consequently, the child is essentially in a hypnotic "trance" through the first five years of its life. During this time it is downloading biology-controlling perceptions without even the benefit, or interference, of conscious discrimination. The potential of a child is "programmed" into its subconscious mind during this phase of development.[3]

When you watch children play imaginary games you can see it in their expression as they *become* the superhero or the princess. Although we tend to want to supply them with all the fancy accouterments of costume and equipment, everyone knows that an empty paper towel roll can become a magic wand or a sword to defeat the forces of evil.

Studies show that, because children slip most easily into these altered states, these states can be used in the treatment of behavioral and physical problems in children. Lipton said "downloading biology-controlling perceptions," but for the purposes of Verbal First Aid, we call that state of consciousness in which the child is available for positive suggestion the *Healing Zone*.

The techniques used in Verbal First Aid are being incorporated more and more often into medical treatment both in the emergency room and in the doctor's office.

While we are not suggesting that you play doctor with serious illnesses, we'd like to reverse a famous phrase and say this about the things over which you do have control: Do try this at home. You probably already have—for example, when your child has fallen and has a scraped knee or elbow, you've kissed and made it better. To know that the magic, as he runs off to play again, has been love and placebo, helps you see how direct a connection there is between thought and body, belief and healing.

Remember, too, that in these altered states, words and phrases tend to become imprinted. As such, they are like tillers, setting the course down the river. Children have a greater ability to suspend their connection to the outer world and to focus in on the inner world. At times, their imaginations are even more alive than their perception of direct experience of the literal world. And it is possible to use this state to help their healing, as the rest of this book will demonstrate.

Children See Us as Natural Authorities

Babies come into the world defenseless and count on adults in their lives to tell them what to look out for ("Be careful! That's hot!") and what's safe ("You can play in the sandbox, and I'll sit on this bench and watch") and what's good for them ("Eat the broccoli, too, because it will make you grow big and strong").

My mother said or *My father told me* is almost always enough to seal the deal as far as kids are concerned. Even as adults we can identify with this dependence on or trust in authority. When we're frightened or hurt (regardless how mature or independent we believe ourselves to be), we very readily and unconsciously revert to this state and whatever our authorities say (doctor, lawyer, boss, spiritual adviser) we tend to see as ironclad law. If it happens that readily to us, consider for a moment just how open a hurting child is to that guiding hand, that kind light in the darkness, that soothing voice that tells her, "I'm right here. I'm going to take care of you."

When confused or frightened, and especially when injured, children will turn to an authority figure—parent, teacher, nurse, babysitter—for guidance. What we tell them in those moments can determine how their bodies and emotions respond and what they internalize and hold in their belief system forever.

Because we adults are such powerful authority figures to a child, we can turn a difficult incident into a moment of learning or even a lifetime belief in the world as a safe or kind place, as the firefighter in the last chapter did by telling the little girl trapped in the car that he would take care of her "as if you were my little girl." We can redefine, reposition, or reframe a difficult situation to the child's advantage. "Thank you for being so brave when you got those stitches. You were a great role model for your little sister, who was watching to see what to do when you're scared. And you showed her that when we're calm, we can heal even faster. Good job."

CHALLENGES

Honoring Trust, Especially in Crisis

Helping an incident come out better, reframing it or redefining it, of course, doesn't give us permission to lie—not even by omission—

because it inflicts serious damage to our credibility and breeds a tendency to mistrust us in the future. This damage may last for years.

One little girl living in the Midwest was told that she was going to be taken to Disneyland when actually she was headed to Los Angeles for brain surgery. The family did visit Disneyland first, but the next thing the child knew, she awakened in the hospital, head bandaged, feeling completely awful. "This," she said simply, looking up through black-and-blue eyes and noticing the feeding and monitoring tubes in what must have seemed like every vein and artery, "is the worst vacation I've ever had!"

The parents might have reframed the situation like this: "We're taking a family trip so that you can visit Dumbo at Disneyland, because we know you really like him. And you can even buy a Dumbo toy to take with you, because after that we'll be going to the hospital where they have a way to help you so you won't have so many headaches. And Dumbo can come with you to the hospital, where you can dream about all the wonderful things you saw at Disneyland as you get better and better."

We function in *relationship*—even when we disconnect or deny it. By both subtle and gross observations we make assumptions about our world, our safety, our futures. Children do the same, but they do it more quickly, more subtly, and with less intellectual interference. What we say in moments of pain or fear or confusion can either lead them deeper into the fray or into a corner of calm safety. We are the source of all the cues—to run, to sit still, to trust, or to fear. Those cues come across so quickly and so unconsciously in our expressions and our expectations. How much more important, more crucial, is it, then, to know what to say?

Fostering Rapport through Active Presence and Listening

In addition to honesty, the other challenge that goes with authority is being able to anticipate or alleviate misunderstandings, and that requires the qualities of rapport: presence and listening.

When we are teaching medical professionals and first responders how to use Verbal First Aid, we always begin by emphasizing rapport. We say that without this sense of trust, connection, understanding, and benevolent interest on the part of the rescuer, the words spoken don't have much credibility, weight, or efficacy.

In the case of children and their parents or caretakers, that rapport is often built in. But trust is the bedrock of rapport and has to be there from the start, so that everything you say, especially in times of crisis, is accepted because you have been proven honest as well as caring.

For all of us, children and adults alike, in a moment of fear or crisis, we will follow a leader. This ingrained response is part of the fight-flight-freeze mechanism that takes over our minds and bodies thanks to a flood of chemicals that allow us to fight or hide from a danger or predator. Frozen for a second while we assess the danger, we will listen and act if a leader tells us to stand, run, or duck. It is not based on a conscious thought. It is instantaneous and instinctive.

In this way, but even more viscerally, children can read when a parent's level of urgency tells them to cooperate. Whether it's a parent asserting: "I need you to do this right now!" or just the look on a parent's face that tells the child this is serious—at those times, by instinct, children respond to the nonverbal cues a parent gives in crisis.

According to a recent report, brain scans now provide evidence that emotional speech leaves distinct signatures in the brain of the listener.[4] Thomas Ethofer and a group of scientists at the University Medical Center of Geneva, Switzerland, identified emotional imprints in the area of the temporal lobes. These imprints were there even when the subjects listened to nonsense sentences. So long as the emotional message was conveyed (anger, sadness, relief, joy), it was received and processed by the brain.

Whether by emotional content or by well-chosen words, when interacting with children or anyone needing our help we are leading and they are following. But to maintain the key ingredient of rapport, we have to pace with the person, and that means listening to where she is coming from, matching her expression, and then leading her to a calmer, better state. It means following *her* lead to better connect with her.

And with children, because they are so prone to misunderstanding, this is something we always must remember.

Even for us adults, it is true that the unknown, what we don't or can't understand, can be the cause of most fear. The author Stephen King, expert at sending chills down the spines of his readers, has suggested that a partially open door, one that is slightly ajar, is more frightening than anything that might be behind it. That is because when we don't know what's about to happen, our imaginations present us with a smorgasbord of the worst possible scenarios.

From a developmental and sociological point of view there's a very good reason for that. When our ancestors in the savannah were confronted by a noise—say a crackling branch behind them—their responses were usually swift and protective. If they had ignored the signal, they might have easily become some predator's lunch. Over eons of time, we were built to respond to what is unknown with wariness and vigilance. If we don't know what's behind us or ahead of us, we instinctively, and in some cases wisely, assume the worst. To survive as a species we have had to assume the unknown was a threat. Even in modern times, although most of us have never seen a savannah or been within miles of a wild predator, the fight-or-flight response is often our first reaction to the unknown.

A child's experience with the world is so much more limited than ours; there is much they don't understand. The hard part is recognizing those times when they are upset not by what is obvious but by a mistaken notion; finding out what the mistaken notion is and helping them see the situation in a new light sets a course for healing and well-being.

What notions did you carry around as a kid that when you learned the truth made you shake your head and realize you'd lived that part of your life based on a mistaken idea? Children can have mistaken ideas about everything from illness and death to their part in their parents' divorce.

Someone in the community may have died from an acute illness that included a fever, so when the child comes down with a fever of his own he may be terrified that his fate will be the same. He may not be able to articulate that in so many words, but his panic may surprise you. Why is he so upset? He's had fevers before and so have the rest of us. In many cases—particularly with very young children who don't yet have fully developed intellectual or verbal skills—we have to do a little detective work and some good listening instead of dismissing the worry. "Tell me why you're crying," you say as you sit on the bed and take his hand, and if he says, "Mrs. Morgan . . . ," it begins to come clear.

Here, the Verbal First Aid tool of using a role model to counter the earlier one may help. "Oh, Mrs. Morgan had a different sickness than you. And she was very old. You just have a fever. Everybody gets fevers. Daddy had a fever in the winter, remember, and he's just fine now. You want to go over and hug Daddy and see how fine he is."

One mistaken notion lasted too long to allow a woman to have the career she'd dreamed of. As a child she was in the hospital with diabetes and a nurse entered her room and began admonishing her that unless she "behaved herself," she could "go blind, just like that," snapping her fingers and then disappearing like the Wicked Witch of the West, leaving behind a medical hex. The child had no idea how to behave in such a way as to avoid such a dire fate and was too frightened to ask the doctors if this was true (it is not). So she decided not to become the artist she wanted to be, in case blindness overtook her and she would lose her livelihood. Only in her twenties, when she finally got up the courage to ask a doctor if she could go blind "just like that," did she learn that the nurse had been wrong. Once relieved of her fear, she became a therapist to help others release themselves from such toxic thoughts.

Helping a child with Verbal First Aid always starts with listening and watching. Even a preverbal child is speaking to us. To know what to say and how to say it, we need to understand him and determine as best we can what is frightening or hurting him. A child who is behaving badly might simply be a child who doesn't understand what is going on and resists it out of fear. What your child may have in mind may surprise you completely.

One nine-year-old boy whose eyebrow was slashed open by a fall in the playground was rushed to the hospital, where a plastic surgeon was called in to help suture the wound so that the scar didn't disfigure the boy. But when the child heard the word *surgeon,* he went into a panic. Luckily, the mother knew Verbal First Aid. Instead of making assumptions that he was just afraid to have stitches (an unknown and something she'd already helped him understand), she asked what he was concerned about. He said he didn't want a surgeon to come near him, that he was fine, that he wanted to go home.

"Why don't you want a surgeon to help you?" the mother asked. "Surgeons cut things open or off," he said with great finality. That much he knew for sure, and he already was cut open and didn't want anything cut off. What could have been a scene, a source of fear and perhaps even trauma, became an opportunity to learn something new about what cosmetic surgeons do and how lucky he was to have one nearby just when he needed one.

Again, the most direct route to calm and a better outcome was through understanding the pictures in the child's mind and substituting other pictures and ideas that were more helpful, allowing him to heal.

ADMINISTERING AGE-APPROPRIATE VERBAL FIRST AID

When we talk about children, we are in fact talking about a large and diverse group of beings who differ in stages by the year, if not the hour, from the child they just were. As a result, their needs change frequently.

Of course, using Verbal First Aid with an infant is a different exercise from helping a preteen overcome a fear or hurt. The techniques, the thoughts behind them, and the choice of words and images are necessarily different depending on the verbal and cognitive abilities of each specific child.

A Child's Unique Theory of Mind

A little girl was walking through a museum one day when she came upon a display that incorporated a long string of bright lights. "Look how funny the lights look when I blink my eyes fast," she said.

Forgetting as we do that we were once children, we may forget how it feels to be so egocentric that we can't even conceive that others do not think the same thoughts, see the same things, experience the world exactly as we do and, moreover, that they have separate and other feelings.

The theory of mind is the study of when and how children begin to realize that perceptions and thoughts exist beyond their own. Young children who are perfectly aware of how painful it is to get hit or kicked may be blithely unaware that those very same kicks hurt someone else.[5]

Somewhere around the age of two, children can begin to identify emotions: "I'm sad." "I'm happy." By two years, they are able to express their own emotions verbally and begin to assign emotions to others through pretend play.

By about four, they begin to understand that other people have desires, emotions, intentions. By six, they realize they can question their own and others' beliefs.

Younger children and preadolescents may think literally and can misinterpret what we say. A playful "I'm not going to bite you," can scare a child more than reassure her. Maybe even the game of Boo! would not be appropriate in a medical setting or in a new place because everything in that environment may be out of context and come as a (usually unpleasant) surprise.

On the other hand, sometimes the literal can lead to healing. Our friend hypnotherapist Timothy Trujillo tells the story of being in a restaurant at dinner where an eight-year-old boy complained of a headache. Timothy said, "I'll buy that headache from you." Surprised, the boy said, "You don't want my headache," but Timothy said, "Not now, but I may want it sometime. I'll give you five dollars for it." The child decided that was a good bargain, and shortly thereafter announced to the table that his headache had gone away. Timothy explained that we say in English that we *have* a headache, and we can't have it if we've sold it (or given it away) to someone else!

Some children think in graphics, others think in numbers, some think in words. When shown a pain chart, for example, the faces are meaningful to some, not to others.

Joseph Chilton Pearce explains that there are two types of learning, but only one of them is true learning. The other is conditioning. When we feel threatened or are in a state of fear, the blood reflexively goes to our survival-maintaining hindbrain (also called our reptilian brain), which embeds fear, anger, and anxiety.

True learning, Pearce has said, involves the higher frontal lobes, the part of the brain that creates, that is logical, that is intellectual. For actual learning, children need a positive, supportive environment because when anxiety creeps in, the brain defaults to its old defenses. And it remembers the fear more than the intended learning itself.[6]

In essence, parents are brain architects. This is metaphorically and literally true. They have an opportunity to help shape a brain physically as well as emotionally in those frightening times when children learn or become conditioned to fear.

So, before we introduce to you the protocol, let's take the time here to understand the child so that we may better apply the Verbal

First Aid techniques in ways that are most effective with each age group and that do the most good.

Every age also has its own vocabulary of solace.

Prenatal Babies

Although the kind of studies that can prove consciousness in the womb are not being done in large numbers, partly because of a belief system that rules it out and partly because no one wants to or can put electrodes on the head of a fetus, there *has* been research that tell us the fetus is listening.

A study carried out by Dr. Alexandra Lamont at the University of Leicester's School of Psychology in England provides evidence not only that babies remember and recognize music that they heard in the womb but that they retain the memory of that music for at least a year. This is much longer than was originally thought possible. This was not an intelligence test but a memory test.

The test involved babies who heard the music up to three months before they were born but then not again until they were a year old. They were shown flashing disco lights and heard music from a nearby loudspeaker. When they lost interest and looked away, the music stopped, teaching them that they had to look at the lights to hear the music.

That the infants preferred music they had heard in the womb showed long-term memory. And, just a note here, they preferred to recall more fast-paced music.[7]

In a study by Anthony DeCasper and W. P. Fifer, at the University of North Carolina, pregnant women read aloud the popular Dr. Seuss book *The Cat in the Hat* twice a day to their unborn child. A few days after birth, the newborns were outfitted with a special nipple that let them signal their approval of what they were hearing. A host of studies on infants rests on the observation that when babies are offered a nonnutritive nipple and a choice of listening materials, their enthusiasm in sucking is a fairly direct measure of their interest.[8]

These newborns were given the opportunity to hear a different Dr. Seuss story than the one they'd heard in utero. They quickly learned they could change the story read by altering the speed of their sucking. "As demonstrated by their sucking speed, the newborns remembered *The Cat in the Hat*, liked it better than the new story, and adjusted their sucking speed to hear the familiar one. They preferred the story read by their mother over another female reader. Furthermore, they preferred it read forward instead of backward."[9]

These studies show that fetuses were able to hear songs and stories, remember them, recognize them, and prefer them. There are thus strong indications of consciousness in the womb.

Other studies on language recognition, the recognition of a father's voice, and on prenatal responses to violence and smoking have been reported in Dr. Fredrick Wirth's book *Prenatal Parenting*.[10]

So Verbal First Aid begins in utero. Babies hear the voices but also the thoughts of their mother, which are translated, according to Bruce Lipton, into chemicals that are shared via the placenta with the fetus, so that the fetus experiences what the mother is feeling. This influences, Lipton explains, the selection of which strands of DNA are turned on, thereby shaping the future child's physiology and psychology.

Studies have shown that a mother's stress can manifest in an increased chance of premature birth, reduced birth weight of their baby, sleep disorders in toddlers, reduced motor maturity in infancy, unconscious coping and survival skills like hypervigilance and hyperreactivity, deficits in regulatory control of behavior during childhood, and psychiatric disorders in adulthood.

In fact, recent understanding in human pathology clearly reveals that issues that affect us as adults, such as cardiovascular disease, cancer, and obesity, actually have their roots in the peri-conceptual, fetal, and neonatal phases of life. The conditions under which a child is developing in utero profoundly shape her for the rest of her life in regard to behavior and physiology.

In terms of Verbal First Aid, then, when we send chemical messages of being wanted, of love, of peace, and of calm across the placenta, we can afford our fetus a healthy start. Thoughts of love and gratitude can help create a template for emotional and physical development that, according to Wirth, "builds the brain architecture that will determine [the baby's] behavior after birth and probably for the rest of his life. . . . Everything you think, feel and do while pregnant has a profound impact on your child both before and after birth. You are a brain shaper, a life shaper. Your role as a loving, powerful parent begins long before your baby's first cry or smile."[11] Programs like Bonding with the Baby Within, which provide guided imagery for supporting babies, offer Verbal First Aid techniques for accomplishing just that.

Premature Babies and Other Infants

Premature babies are defined as children delivered before nine months of gestation. They are often in need of special care both emotionally and physically until their development catches up with their calendar age. However, according to Dr. Ashley Montagu, every newborn is a premature baby. Montagu's theory is that, unlike other mammals— elephants and giraffes, horses, dogs, cats, and others who can step up and walk away from their mother from the minute they're born—we humans may be unfinished when we are delivered into the maternity ward. That may be, as he suggests, because our heads would be too big to pass through the vaginal canal if we waited to be born until we could stand on our own two feet. Therefore, we are *all* born prematurely, and we require another nine months or so in our mothers' arms before we're ready to meet the world.

Premature babies require nurturing that can be similar to a kangaroo-like repouching immediately after birth: frequent touch, constant exposure to the sound of the heartbeat that accompanied them in utero, and a physical sense of security.

A McGill University study, reported in the journal *BMC Pediatrics* in 2008, noted that regular cuddling helped reduce the stress in babies born as early as twenty-eight weeks of gestation when they had to undergo painful medical procedures. The study indicated that skin-to-skin contact with the mother reduced the pain response.[12]

As with the premature infants, holding and cuddling is invaluable for newborns through the first year. Hugging, massage, music, rocking, stroking, and patting communicate volumes. Touch is extremely important for development, as was shown by the desperate emotional state and susceptibility to illness in the tragically untouched infants found in institutions in Ceaușescu's Romania.

Joseph Chilton Pearce, child development expert and author of *Magical Child* and *Evolution's End*, discusses touch-starved American children who have never received enough emotional or physical nurturing. Pearce notes that the emotional and physical are essentially the same and when we deprive children of love and touch in the earliest stages of life we see the results of that deprivation in their rage later on. The absence of touch has been linked to numerous psychiatric problems, one of which is attachment disorders.

In *The Biology of Love*, psychologist Dr. Arthur Janov, who was on the staff of the psychiatric department at Los Angeles Children's Hospital, said that you can "kiss a brain into maturity." What he meant by that was that an unloved brain has different chemicals and ultimately a different structure from the brain of a loved being—and touch and kisses are a big part of the difference. Research now concurs that this process of becoming is not just emotional but physical and biochemical.

You don't have to be a skilled orator to use Verbal First Aid with a baby.

Verbal First Aid offers many tools for this age group. Words, even when not cognitively understood by the baby, can be used to heal and soothe. An example of this is singing and rhyming. Distraction with music, soft toys, human interaction, cooing, rattles, driving in a car, gentle movement, or anything that takes the child's mind away from whatever is disturbing him or her often works to change the focus and relieve the pain. How we do this is as important as doing it. One pediatrician we know advises that *thrusting* a distraction at a child only increases the anxiety and agitation, although she believes that distraction is a valuable tool when used properly. She tells the story of one woman who shakes a toy in front of her baby daughter's face every time the doctor approaches her, which has so far made the baby more anxious.

The way to distract successfully is gently. Talk to the child calmly. Use words of love, of safety, of blessing—whether you believe that the baby can understand the precise meaning or not. "I am here," "You've got your favorite toy to make you feel better and protect you," and "Can you feel my hand? I've got you," are words of love and safety. The words and, most important, the manner in which they are conveyed communicate your own state of mind. If you are calm, the child receives comfort. If you are anxious, he receives a reason to fear.

You are your child's emotional and environmental barometer. He can absorb your meaning on some level because it is the *connection* that matters as well as the quality of that connection. Infants are extremely intuitive and mirror the emotions of those around them. When you soothe your child from the bottom of your heart, you will both feel more calm.

Children Aged One to Four

One of the characteristics of toddlers is that they are both highly concrete and highly imaginative. Both these tendencies have to be taken into account when we use Verbal First Aid.

If a toddler is frightened, reassure her, acknowledge that something scary has happened, but spare her the details that she cannot yet understand. Toddlers don't have to know the specifics, how their bodies work, or why the house caught fire, only that they and their family are safe and loved. Too much information often serves to take the focus away from that important message, the only one that they are really looking for.

A sentence as simple as: "I see you have an owie and Mommy [Daddy, Sally, Dr. York] knows just how to fix it up so you'll be all better, good as new, and be able to go out and play again soon" says just the right amount for this age. Or you can say: "I know that was scary when that dog started barking. I think he was scared, too, when that big truck went by and that's why he started to bark. Lucky he was behind the fence. And lucky we have each other to hug. Maybe the dog will find some other dog to hug so he can feel better, too."

By two years of age, your child's imagination has kicked in. If he's not initiating his own stories, he is responding to yours. You can use toys, puppets, dolls, drawings, bubbles, or storytelling for distraction and to explain a difficult situation or, as psychologists do, to allow the child to express what he can't talk about by himself through the dolls in play.

A technique that has a proven track record with toddlers is known as Pretend Time. By using play, you and the child can imagine successful outcomes. You can rehearse situations that might be unpleasant (like a visit to the doctor), before and after, with dolls getting the injection instead of the child, and with the child in control, administering it and telling the doll it will be "okay real soon."

It is also possible to engage the imagination by using metaphors of experiences with which a two- to five-year-old is familiar to explain a more complicated concept. For example, you could say, "See, this could disappear, just the way a bubble pops and disappears!"

For the older toddler, using his interests and favorite characters goes a long way in picturing the healing—look to television, movies, books, games, and activities for appropriate characters. For children this young, you can use favorite characters as a point of reference and involve them in creative solutions to a problem or situation. For example, a little girl complains of a tummy ache that you know to be a nervous stomach about a fear (like leaving you to go to nursery school), but she is not ready to talk about it. You might try using a third party:

> **You:** What would SpongeBob do about that stomachache?
>
> **Jayden:** I don't know.
>
> **You:** Could you pretend to ask him?
>
> **Jayden:** (Pondering.) He says he would blow a few bubbles and then do a few karate moves.
>
> **You:** And that would help?
>
> **Jayden:** The bubbles would.
>
> **You:** We could blow some bubbles. Would you like to?

Jayden: Maybe.

You: How would that make your stomach feel?

Jayden: Good.

And then while you're blowing bubbles, you might take it further and have a conversation that more specifically addresses the pressure on the belly.

Sometimes a simple "What would SpongeBob do about that stomachache?" provides the child with an opportunity to come up with her own answers. This is a very important part of the process.

We don't want to prescribe too quickly. In this case, we might ask for the child's participation and let his imagination begin to wander and wonder about what it takes to feel better. As he calls all those possibilities into his mind, we can assist rather than immediately take over. When it seems that the child needs help or if you think that stomach needs physical tending, you might offer a suggestion such as, "You know what I think? I think SpongeBob would eat the toast and drink the ginger ale that his friend dropped off at his house. So how about we get you some toast and ginger ale."

Children Aged Five to Twelve

Children from about age five understand causality, so the word *because* can be both an explanation and a positive outcome or suggestion. For example, a five-year-old child with an upset stomach due to anxiety about a performance at school or fear about trying something new can be distracted with a game and an encouraging sentence like: "Your belly can feel better now because of the fun we're having playing hide and seek." You can also ask if it helps to rub the tummy, put something warm on it (blanket, towel), or have a favorite stuffed animal nearby to protect the child. Let the child guide you (and ultimately herself) in this process because it is *she* who is drawing on the information about herself and her own healing resources that will make the difference. When she has let you know that she's found some relief, you can add, "Because it feels good now, you can continue that feeling all day long."

The children in this age group are generally very suggestible and have a great ability to fantasize. Use their area of interest for metaphors. To the more mature child, you might suggest, "You know the way you can delete something from the computer screen? Just imagine that you can delete . . ."

Stories and games with successful outcomes can be used with this age group to great benefit, especially ones that incorporate their favorite characters. Stories like *The Little Engine That Could* illustrate the power of positive thinking quite beautifully. As always with Verbal First Aid, speak in the child's vocabulary and use references to his or her world. For instance, you might ask: "What would Batman or Dora the Explorer do to feel better?"

It is helpful to use guided imagery with these age groups, carefully tailoring it to your child's needs per his age. "The use of imagery by children is really a no brainer," says guided imagery expert Diane Tusek, RN. "Kids are naturals at using their imaginations. Guided imagery is just an active form of daydreaming. They think it is a neat way to help themselves calm down, manage anxiety, build confidence, and sleep better."[13]

If a child is clearly upset about something but acting out instead of addressing it, it's most likely because he doesn't even realize in concrete terms what is bothering him. To help your child heal emotionally, consider asking open-ended questions to get him to sort through his feelings. For example, imagine how your child could feel upon learning that his grandma has died. To get him to open up, you could ask open-ended questions like "What are you thinking about?" and "What do you wish would be different?" and then really listen without judging. If it's something you can do nothing about, like "I wish Grandma was still here. I miss her a lot," you can at least support the child in his feelings. "I do too. Let's draw a picture of her to remember her by. You want to?"

Children from five to seven years old are generally concrete and have a fairly rigid concept of morality. They see it as a form of economy. You do this, I'll do that. Things have to be exchanged fairly. In Verbal First Aid we seek most to strike a balance with children in this age group. This does not necessarily mean negotiating but means presenting options to them so that they feel they have a choice and input. "Would you rather take the medicine and then brush your teeth, or brush your teeth and then take the medicine?" Either way, they have agreed to taking their medicine because they had a choice and the matter seems fairly handled.

The use of role models becomes more important as the child matures. Somewhat older children like to know how you, the adult or parent, dealt with difficult situations. "You see this tiny scar? Can't even really see it, can you? Well, when I was just about your age, I was ice skating, and I fell, and Marsha Olson couldn't stop in time and she just tripped right over me. And her skate cut me right here. And we had to go to the emergency room, just like we're doing for you now . . ."

These children are moving from childhood to adulthood in the sense that their prefrontal cortex is rapidly developing. The prefrontal cortex is the last part of the brain to develop and become fully functional. It controls decision making, personality, and complex cognitive behaviors. Even though this part of the brain will not be fully functional until the children are approximately twenty-two years old, children of this age group are already beginning to use more sophisticated modes of interaction. As you will see in the chapters ahead, Verbal First Aid can help you move your children toward wisdom.

IN SUMMARY

- Children automatically see adults as authority figures.
- As an adult dealing with a child, what you say has great weight.
- Children are often more willing than adults to seek help and learn new things or change their view of the unexpected as reframed by an adult.
- Children slip easily into the altered state that can accept healing suggestions for the mind, body, and spirit.
- Children's spirits have a healthy curiosity as well as a tremendous capacity for imagination and self-awareness.

All of these qualities can be engaged, especially in moments of fear and uncertainty.

PART TWO

How It Works

The Verbal First Aid Manual

Somewhere right now a child is climbing up onto something a bit too high or a bit unsteady. A child is touching something too hot and pulling her hand back just a second too late. And somewhere a child is waking up from a nightmare and crying for his mommy or daddy. The scenarios are a part of growing up. Bumps, bruises, tears, and fears will happen to them just as they happened to you.

When scary things happen to our children, though, we want to offer more than "You're okay" or "It's just what happens." We want to offer support and perhaps even more. We want to offer them a vision of life that may be quite different from the one we received as children. We want them to know that they have the resources to help them recover, pick themselves up, and even grow from the experience. We want them to see for themselves the power they have over their own thoughts and their own bodies. And we want to show them how to use it.

In Part II, we will present you with specific examples of how you can facilitate the process of giving your child self-power. We'll teach you the Verbal First Aid protocol that will accomplish it. We've separated the process into easy to remember, manageable steps that can be put to work in your life—and your children's lives—right away. Know that the more you take these steps, however faltering you may begin, the smoother and more natural you'll feel as you go on. The positive feedback you will receive when you see the results of Verbal First Aid in real life will keep you moving forward.

3 Three Steps to the Goal

Watch your thoughts, for they become words.
Watch your words, for they become actions.
Watch your actions, for they become habits.
Watch your habits, for they become character.
Watch your character, for it becomes your destiny.

UNKNOWN

So, you're probably thinking right about now, What's the magic formula? Well, much as we'd like to march you right over to the words that heal and show you how to use them, there are three basic steps we have to take you through first that will make all the difference in using the right words effectively. They are:

Step One: Centering yourself
Step Two: Using rapport
Step Three: The ground rules

Once you've mastered these steps, the techniques for giving healing suggestions can fall into place and you can use them with easy grace and make them your own.

OLIVER REVISITED

You may remember the story of Oliver from Chapter 1. When Oliver fell and injured himself, his mom, Donna, used a variety of Verbal First Aid techniques, and Oliver emerged from the experience without a scar or a scare, taking with him a greater confidence in his own healing powers.

How did she accomplish it?

Let's put the process in slow motion and focus on each step that you can use, and you'll see that while it might take some practice, you can begin to speak Verbal First Aid. You'll see its good effects in the faces of parents and children as the words set the course for recovery. You may want to read through this chapter to understand the process; later you can refer to the recap on p. 78.

So, here's Oliver, doing the job of a typical four-year-old, jumping up and down on the sofa. Donna is in the other room when she hears a sharp thud followed by Oliver's cry. She runs into the living room to find Oliver on the floor, with a large gash in his forehead bleeding profusely from having been slammed against the radiator on the way down from a bounce.

Put yourself in her place. Whether you're a parent, teacher, professional, or medical caregiver, this is a difficult moment. Maybe your heart begins pumping loudly in your chest. Maybe you feel faint or even feel like crying yourself. We know that wouldn't be useful to the child because, as we've seen, he is basing his response on yours. In a conversation, Dr. Bernardine Celoni, former chief of pediatrics at Methodist Hospital in Arcadia, California, put it this way: "There is power in the use of the voice, itself. We learn it in mothers taking care of infants. Unless the child is bursting into flames or has his neck stuck through something, take a deep breath, walk slowly towards him or her, and start talking. Talk slowly, calmly, purposefully. Your anxiety aggravates the situation."

How do you accomplish this?

Step One: Centering Yourself

As a loving parent, you probably don't even want to think about the possibility of your children harming themselves. As parents we say with a mixture of concern and pride, "I don't know. He's fearless. He just runs off and . . ."

But for those times when *we* must be brave, when *we* must be wise and steady and calm, it's good to know that we can use tools at everyone's disposal—words and images—to set a healing course.

If we're imbalanced, terrified, or overwhelmed ourselves, we will further upset the child; moreover, we will not be able to get to step two, establishing a healing rapport, which is really the heart of Verbal First Aid.

We're all familiar with the instructions we get before every plane trip: "If the oxygen masks descend and you are traveling with small children, please place one on yourself first." Every mother in the plane thinks to herself, "No! I'd put it on my child first." But of course, you're no good to your child or anyone else if you can't breathe, so we're recommending that before you attend to anyone else you consider the following: No matter what the crisis or how urgently you wish to rescue the child, when you take a quick moment to find your center, you can be most effective, starting from a place of wisdom and calm.

1. *Take a Breath*

Please take a moment right now to inhale. Good. Now let it all go. Breathe in again, slowly, deeply, and hold it for a second, then let it go, even more slowly and carefully. Let your shoulders sink gently from the position in which they were probably hunched. Feel the difference in your body, in your muscles, in your heart rate.

There are many reasons why taking a breath is emphasized in times of crisis.

When we're frightened, it is natural to fall into a pattern of shallow breathing. As a result, the brain—the organ that needs the most oxygen to function—gets a bit less oxygen than normal, which in turn renders us less aware, less resourceful, and less effective. In short order, the body senses the oxygen depletion on a cellular level and begins to panic. Because the body's panicked, we breathe even more quickly and shallowly. It's easy to see how quickly a vicious cycle is activated. Luckily, it is just as quickly deactivated if you deliberately pause to take a slow, deep breath. It is an instant stabilizer.

Breathing consciously this way has a dual function in that it also brings us into present time. If you find yourself in a frightening or worrisome situation, your unconscious mind may be automatically playing reruns from your past, as we learned from Lily's story in Chapter 1. The past encroaches on us, uninvited when we are at our most vulnerable. It takes but the smallest of triggers—a similar sound, a familiar smell, a recognizable expression. Although our past experience is useful because it is warning us that we might not be safe, it also can cloud our perceptions, confusing what *has* happened with what *is* actually happening, mixing up what we once did and what we need to do now. Flooded by the stream of our own histories and fears, we project needlessly into the future, worrying about things that have not yet happened. *The simple act of taking a breath helps us orient properly in time and space.* When we become aware of our breathing, we become aware of where we are and what needs to be done.

Breathing also works to help the child center herself. There is a lovely technique taught to us by a mother of four that you can use with your children right away. Not only does it calm the adult, it calms the children. When a child comes running up to you in a frenzied state, you can stop the panicky hyperventilating by putting out a finger and saying, "Blow this out as if it were a birthday candle. Good. Now take a nice deep breath." Exhaling first makes lots of room for a good refreshing breath, and maybe the birthday suggestion brings with it a fleeting good feeling as well. Within moments, the off-balanced child is back to herself again.

So, whether you are being asked to help in a serious emergency or in a kitchen variety incident, when you're called on to help remember to breathe in and breathe out. Simple to do and all too often forgotten. Nothing will happen that you can't handle in the space of a good, deep, mind-clearing breath. When you are in calm control, it is far more likely that children around you will be calmer as well. And when they're calm, their natural endorphins—those healing hormones—can be properly released.

Consider the Sufi story about a young man who was walking down a dusty road lined with gnarled old olive trees. Sitting down against the base of one tree was a man quietly meditating. Suddenly the young man heard a peace-shattering howl and glimpsed the swirling dust and whirling skirts of an ecstatic dervish. The seated man continued meditating without batting an eyelash. The young man, confounded by the older man's outer calm, went up to him and asked, "How can you sit there so quietly when that dervish is making such a racket?" The older man never opened his eyes but answered, "I let him spin." So even if your child is upset and cannot slow down his breathing, do not allow yourself to lose your center. As a parent, your sense of calm and control is vital to your children. Let them spin if they must. You are the eye of the storm.

2. Do a Self-Check

Once you've taken a deep breath, do a *mental self-check*. How are you inside? How are you outside? How are you presenting yourself? Are you frantic? Calm?

Then remember that the emergency is not about you, although it's true that you are a critical piece of how it's handled. It's about the child in front of you who needs you. Know that if you are the adult on scene, you are the one who is there to help, and as such, you are equipped to do it solely by virtue of your being present. And in a short while, you will see that your presence alone may be one of the most powerful factors in facilitating a calm, healing state in another person.

If you are concerned about your capacity to be of help, remember all the people who at one time or another effectively helped you. See them clearly. What did they do? Maybe it was your tough, sweet old grandmother who used to cross herself three times and then roll up her sleeves, or a teacher perhaps who was cool in a crisis and whose shoes you can now step into. If you are spiritual or religious, you may feel the presence of angels or divinity when you need it. If you are not, you may feel your own competence kicking in as if the right program were instantaneously accessed.

Next, do a *physical self-check*. If you are somehow involved in the accident or incident (for example, a car crash), make sure you're okay. If you are capable of helping someone else without doing further harm to yourself, get centered in your body. One of the first reactions in an emergency is to dissociate, a natural reaction to extreme stress. We've called it *leaving the scene.* To be helpful, however, you have to be present in your body. Find something physical that grounds you. Feel your feet on the floor. Take hold of something that gives you comfort or meaning (a charm, a religious symbol) or something that steadies you. Know that whatever has been presented to you at the moment, you will be capable of handling it.

3. Cultivate a Loving Presence and Intention

No matter how many techniques we learn, no matter how many tools and ointments and gauzes we keep in our medicine cabinet, if we are truly wise, we know that healing occurs by the grace of an Agency far greater and more ineffable than mere routine. The more experienced the practitioner, the more he or she knows that a sense of love and safety are the greatest of medicines. Words are the vehicles. And you can take great comfort in learning how to give therapeutic suggestions. But we want to remind you that the words are just that and no more—they are *vehicles.* Words convey intention, presence, compassion, love, and hope. They give direction, to the mind, body, and soul. The engine that moves them is your love and your empathy.

For example, the simple words *come here* can convey a multitude of meanings, depending on our intentions. Just here, on the page, the words *come here* are neither loving nor threatening. They are simply two words. If said in a semi-harsh tone, however, *come here* can mean, "Get over here, young man. You're in *big* trouble." If said in a pleasant tone, *come here* can mean, "I've got so much love and a safe place in my arms for you." It's a hug. Intention is everything, and tone is crucial to the atmosphere we create. How we say something is as important as what we say. "I love you," said without conviction doesn't work any better than "I need you to be calm," when said to someone who is upset by someone who doesn't care. Expression, both verbal and physical, is also a vital part of Verbal First Aid.

No one loves your child more than you do. If you can't immediately recall or imagine what to say, allow your calm compassion to speak through your eyes, your tenderness through touch, your gentleness through your patience. Your love is a far more important part of healing than mere technique alone. The rest will come with practice.

Here's What Donna Did

When Donna found Oliver on the floor bleeding, she quickly took a breath or two, checked herself so that she walked calmly but lovingly toward him, and knelt down beside him to see what needed to be done. He watched her and waited, wondering whether to panic. But her body language and her loving examination of his forehead said the equivalent of "I'm here, I'm right here with you," and they gave him confidence that things were already under control.

Step Two: Using Rapport

Verbal First Aid is more than simply the delivery of healing suggestions. It is the way of delivering them that makes the person to whom you're speaking more likely to receive them and use them to recover.

And having rapport is that doorway. Rapport is the result of establishing authority and a meaningful connection. Having rapport means letting someone know you understand how she feels and can help her through whatever crisis she is in. When we are in rapport with someone, we both have that luxurious feeling of being understood, a rarity in today's busy society. In a time of hurt or crisis, it is that moment of "I'm here to help you. I hear you. I see you. You can count on me" that helps the body relax into a mode in which healing can happen. One nurse once put it into these words for us: "You can't always cure, but you can always care."

When we teach Verbal First Aid to medics, police officers, and firefighters, rapport is the pivot point. More than anything else, their ability to gain the trust and confidence of the people they encounter in the field is the single greatest skill they have. Once gained, it is that rapport that will enable the victims to accept their therapeutic suggestions for healing.

When we talk about building rapport in a situation in which someone needs help or attention, we always emphasize that it is more than a technique; it is a way of *being*. It is the building of bridges between people that lets them know that you hear them and care, so their parasympathetic nervous system—the part of the nervous system that turns on the chemicals that help us rest and digest—can kick in and allow them to begin their own healing. Rapport is heartfelt and empathetic. It is not the same as charm or being nice, and for it to be truly healing it cannot be manipulative or insincere. The difference between genuine rapport and salesmanship is enormous and very readily intuited by others. High pressure salesmanship or manipulation almost always puts someone on guard, even if he or she couldn't say why. It just *feels* wrong. Real rapport is experienced as safe and supportive. It always feels right.

And, although it is most necessary when we talk to children, rapport is the absolute center of all Verbal First Aid and the most important ingredient of the entire protocol, partly because people who are hurt, frightened, or in fear or crisis may regress to childlike feelings and needs themselves. But mostly it is vitally important because, without rapport, you can say and do it all so correctly, and it can still fail to accomplish your goal. With rapport, however, mistakes are forgiven, ambivalences are interpreted in the best possible manner, and healing is moved forward even when we stumble over ourselves.

Little children may intuitively recognize and practice rapport. Studies have reported that infants show facial distress signals when they hear a recording of another child crying much more frequently than when they hear a recording of their own troubled sobs.

When one child in a school yard has been wounded, either physically or emotionally, it is such a moving sight to notice the caring reaction of another child standing nearby, watching hesitantly. Slowly, the heart-centered little one comes over and sits next to the injured child in silence. They will sit together for as long as it takes until the injured one feels better. And often that's all it takes.

Sometimes it takes a little more. When two-year-old Cole saw a sad little girl curled up, head buried in arms wrapped around her knees, sitting in a concrete play tunnel, he walked over and sat beside her quietly, waiting for her recovery. She continued to mope, seeming to ignore his loving presence. Finally, he stood up, walked over to an abandoned tricycle, dragged it with every ounce of his energy, and delivered it to her hiding place. She looked up, paused, accepted the gesture if not the gift, made eye contact, sighed, perhaps felt better at being understood, got up, and walked away—as did Cole, without saying a word.

As a parent or caregiver, it's likely you already have a good basis for rapport with your child. When a child feels heard and understood, you have created a sense of safety that allows the child's own body and spirit to kick in and help do the work of healing. Albert Schweitzer, the great physician famous for his reverence for life, put it this way: "Each patient carries his own doctor inside him.

They come to us not knowing that truth. We are at our best when we give the doctor who resides within each patient a chance to go to work."[1]

To simplify, we've broken down the process of gaining rapport into three steps, which we call the *ABCs of rapport*.

1. Authority

There is a natural state of affairs in parent-child, caregiver-child, teacher-student, and doctor-patient relationships. Plainly stated, by virtue of your experience and position, you lead the way. By both your example and your words, you tell your children how the world works. They look to you for information, protection, direction, and understanding. They will either duck and cover or open their shades based on your perception of reality and how you communicate it to them. If you tell them the situation is serious, that makes it so. If you tell them you can see the injury and that you have it handled, the sense of safety is built in.

Depending on their age, children are in one way or another gauging the severity of a situation based on your response to it and to them. Keep your response even, temperate, and kind. They're watching your every move and following you where you lead.

2. Believability

While we often advise first responders not to say, "You're going to be all right" if they don't know that to be the truth, parents have some more latitude. They can soothe in reassuring ways just because they are Mommy and Daddy or the authority figure, the first and last refuge in a scary situation no matter how brave their children have been up until then. But believability is an important credential to reestablish with your children and to maintain over time. If you were believable before, you will be believable in the future. On the other hand, if you say something won't hurt and then it does, how can they trust you the next time?

One nurse at a rehabilitation center raised her hand with great animation when we discussed pain and how to avoid using words like *hurt* or *painful.*

"But you can't lie to them," she stated strongly. Agreed. We can't.

The nurse worked with young children who had been injured severely, many of them long-term patients with whom she'd developed very caring relationships. She knew their families, their friends, she'd read them letters from their schoolmates. She sincerely cared about them.

"So you want to tell them it hurts?" we asked.

"Well, if I'm putting in an IV, sure. I have to be honest."

"How do you know for sure precisely *what* it is that they're going to feel? Or how they're going to feel it? What if instead of saying it's going to hurt, what if you said, for instance, that they were going to feel some kind of pressure as you gave them this medicine to make them *feel better* but you don't know exactly what kind of pressure it will be—warm or cool—or whether it'll feel like it has a color, like a blue feeling or a pink feeling ..."

The nurse nodded, understanding our strategy. She saw that she could give her young patients choices about how they would react and possibilities about what they would feel. The truth is we don't know what anyone will feel. By offering options, however, we are showing empathy and can therefore gain rapport and provide children with opportunities to choose their own response.

What was important for us to understand was her passionate commitment and her strong need to maintain the integrity of her relationship with the children under her care. When she understood that she could honor them *and* guide them to more comfort and a quicker recovery, she was more than satisfied.

One dentist has a particularly intriguing way of handling the discomfort and fear that young patients often experience when given their first shot of anesthetic into the gum. He pinches the cheek near the injection site and wiggles it as he inserts the needle into the gum. He makes no references to pain, to needles, or to hurt. He simply says, "I'm going to put this cool, pink gel on the back of your mouth, right there. Feel that? Good. And you're going to count with me to, oh, I don't know, we'll see how long it takes you, maybe five or ten—one boy I know only made it to six, he was really fast—until it starts to tingle and it's really numb like you get from playing in snow without gloves . . . okay? You'll let me know by saying 'all numb.' Ready? One . . ."

Then when the child says "all numb" the dentist responds: "I'm going to pinch your cheek now and it's going to feel really funny as I give you this medicine to make your mouth even more numb, like a whole day in the snow."

And that's it.

No drama. No lies. Just a clear, guided redirection of attention and thought. The integrity of the relationship is honored and believability maintained.

3. Calm

Being calm applies to both you and the child. In an adrenal or fight-or-flight state, the blood rushes from the prefrontal cortex, where we think logically, to the limbic or emotional brain, where we are at the mercy of more primal feelings instead of rational thoughts. Our job is to call that blood back, to balance the chemicals flooding us from our sympathetic nervous system, which is on the lookout for danger, with the chemicals of our parasympathetic nervous system, which keep us calm. We can do this. We can place ourselves in the eye of the hurricane and protect our children's psyches from the storm.

Remember to take deep breaths and slow down before you approach your child. Bring yourself back to where your feet are. You don't have to be in the past, where earlier traumas can haunt, or in the future imagining the worst. Breathe to be in present time, and center yourself in your own authority. You know what to do.

Here's What Donna Did

When Donna came over to Oliver, after she centered herself with her breath and body check, she examined him and reassured him that she knew what to do. She said, "Oliver, what happened?" She unobtrusively examined his wound as she held him in her arms. He really couldn't explain it, and she easily translated it into language and action that allowed him to turn his concern over to her. "Oh, you banged your head. Owwww," she said, building rapport by showing that she saw, felt, and understood what he was going through. "Well, I'm right here and I've got you," she said, calmly.

"But we're going to have to go to the hospital right away, because it looks like you'll need stitches, and the doctors know how to fix you right up," she then said. She evidenced authority—have to go to the hospital—and believability but began giving him suggestions even as she diagnosed the problem. When she said, "the doctors know how to fix you right up," she was using a technique you'll learn next called future pacing.

Oliver was still in some fear and shock when, again using rapport,

Donna read his concerns and said, "It's going to be all right, Oliver, because you're a good healer." With that little incantation, she calmed his present and blessed his future, as you will see.

Step Three: The Ground Rules

We're almost there. Just one more thing first. What *not* to say.

As with any new skill or program, there are certain ground rules that help you learn the technique and use it automatically, and some include avoiding the old ways of warning or admonishing your child "for his or her own good." It's essential to eliminate the negative.

The Verbal First Aid ground rules are simple and once you understand them they will seem as natural and obvious as if you had been using them all your life.

1. Keep It Positive: Say What You Want to See Happen Because What We Say Tends to Become Real

We recently watched as a mother warned her adventurous son, "Don't play on the fence. You're going to crack your head open." We didn't stick around to see what transpired, and of course, accidents do happen and children are always risking danger, but we must make every effort to avoid suggesting or prescribing them.

People are so accustomed to speaking in negatives that for most of us it is wholly unconscious. Spend a day noticing how many times you use words like *not* or *don't*. It can be enlightening and informative on more than a few levels. We are a fearful culture, and when people are afraid, it's natural, though not healthy or helpful, to see things in negative terms. When we are afraid and see things in a negative way, when we imagine the worst, it's like putting a hex on life, using our imaginations to conjure up what we don't want to happen. Everything we are surrounded with—the Internet, radio, television, security alerts—everything tells us to be afraid and to prepare for the most unimaginable catastrophes. Those are our states of mind on ordinary days. When we are faced with a crisis, particularly when it involves someone we love and want to protect with our very lives, it is even easier to fall into that habit of fear and negativity.

The good news is that our thinking makes a very real difference—not only for us but for the people we so want to help. Remember, what we think determines what we say and how we say it. What we say and how we say it determines to a great degree how we facilitate healing in ourselves and others. For instance, it's common practice in sports to focus exclusively on the positive, imaging the performance we *want* to give. No coach spends his whole session telling his students or players *not* to drop the ball or *not* to fall. The reason is simple: When we're anxious, we bypass the *not* and go straight for the image we don't want, which in this case would be dropping and falling. What we *want* to see is the ball going *swoosh* through the basket without ever touching the rim. We want to feel our chests breaking through the ribbon first and our bodies flying effortlessly through the air as we tuck tight then open like a pocket knife into a perfect, water-slicing dive. When Milton Erickson, MD, was asked to help train the U.S. Olympic rifle team, he trained them in the art of imagery and taught them to see the perfect shot. And he had them see it over and over and over until they saw themselves to victory.

Here's a way to really see for yourself how this visualizing of language works. Close your eyes and picture and imagine any animal but elephants. Don't picture African elephants with their big tusks and their big ears. Don't picture mother elephants and baby elephants. Don't picture circus elephants balancing on their trunks. . . .

What are you picturing? Elephants, of course, because there is nothing in the sentence *Don't think about elephants* to picture *except* elephants!

So the *don't* is not heard. When we tell our children don't fight, they hear the word *fight*. If your child says, "My stomach hurts," in Verbal First Aid you wouldn't say "Don't vomit." It would be more effective (and often less messy) to offer an empathic rub or elicit some information. "Tell me where, sweetheart. Here?" "What does it feel like?" "When did you start feeling that way?" "What makes it feel better? Does it feel better if I do this [rubbing] or just hold your hand?"

If the lower lip of your tiny tot is quivering, the very words *Don't cry* may be all she needs to hear from you to start the wailing in earnest. Instead, you could kneel down to eye level or hold her up to you so that you face her and gently, subtly mirror her pout as you say, "Tell me what's going on. What are you feeling?" In a very young child that may elicit a flow of blubbering words, but that's an improvement over the helplessness she would otherwise feel. Even the attempt at communication on her part is a form of self-empowerment and ultimately a learned source of self-control.

Because children are more visual and less analytical than we are, what we say to them is soaked up without the intellectual interference we expect to find in adults. When we use Verbal First Aid, this can be an enormous benefit for children. A study published in the *Journal of Neuroscience* in 2008 measured the effects of positive and negative feedback on learning in children. What was found was that eight- and nine-year-olds learned primarily from *positive* feedback when they received "Well done!" signals for getting an answer right on a computer. Negative feedback was hardly registered in the brain. As one of the researchers, Eveline A. Crone, explained, "The information that you have not done something well is more complicated than the information that you have done something well. Learning from mistakes is more complex than carrying on in the same way as before."[2]

This research supports the tenet in Verbal First Aid that we help children best by telling them what we *want* to have happen, not what we don't. And telling them what they do or did well. One mother, upon seeing her child fall off his bike, rushed to him and said, "That was a really good fall. You protected your head and face with your hands. Good job!" The child, starting to cry, stopped mid-wail and thought about it. He *had* fallen well. No humiliation, just a positive learning experience. That and a kiss and a little bandage set a helpful course for recovery, with a picture in his mind he could use in the present and in the future.

In fact, everyone, children and adults, have the same area in the brain that responds to positive feedback. It's the basal ganglia, just outside the cerebral cortex. So even though older children and adults can learn from the negative, we all respond very strongly to direct and clear feedback about what we're doing right.

The simple idea: No one can do a *don't*.

The simple rule: Tell your child what you want to see or have happen, not what you don't.

In the case of a child playing on a fence or a kid running in the hall with a pencil in her hand, all an authority figure has to say is,

"Let's play on the jungle gym that's meant for climbing, when we get to the playground." Or "You can slow that pace down, now."

2. At the Moment of Pain, Crisis, and Hurt, Offer Support and Forgiveness Instead of Criticism

You might say that the more dramatic the response by someone in authority, the more traumatic the memory.

One patient had a pain in his right shoulder that was intractable. It had built up over the years and would not relent despite physical therapy, massage, and pain medication. He was examined by MRI and X-rays and in many doctors' offices until he wanted to bang his head against a wall just so he could stop thinking about his arm. After numerous psychotherapy sessions, it was finally revealed that when he was a very small child, he had disobeyed his father's warning to stay off a particular stool in the kitchen. As he was standing on it, his father came into the room and saw him, immediately scowled, and yelled, "Tommy!" The patient remembered his father's voice as he fell toward the floor, his right arm hyperextended: "Damn it! What did I tell you about standing on that?" The boy's arm was broken and though the doctors told him the bones had healed, the wound had not. Words can stick in the mind and feel like they're stuck in the body. It was twenty some years later and it still hurt.

That case is a lasting reminder of one of the most profound healing truths: Love is still the greatest medicine. Reminding your child that you *told* him he would hurt himself or asking her what she was thinking serves little purpose. Honestly, she has no good answer, and inspiring guilt and shame only sends chemicals through the body that impede healing and increase pain. There's always time later to deal with the lesson in the catastrophe, when everyone is cool and calm and can hear and understand that there was a better way to reach that high shelf than climbing on the cabinet drawer. Even if your child is naturally inclined to blame himself and openly calls himself bad or stupid, it's important to deflect that thought, so that the interpretation is not embedded and the event locked in as traumatic.

A simple way to avoid focusing on what went wrong and thereby creating a negative atmosphere is to say, "We can talk about that later. Right now, it's more important that you feel and get better. Here, take my hand. The worst is over. I've got you."

Here's What Donna Did

Donna's approach to Oliver was not to shame him, but to encourage him to be part of the healing. She knew that they would be having a discussion about being careful as well as jumping on furniture sometime in the future, but not while he was hurting and feeling helpless and perhaps foolish.

3. Expect Compliance; Expect Healing

Too often we rely on the word *try* because we are afraid to expect too much. But in Verbal First Aid we are telling you that you can *expect* amazing things, extraordinary things. You can expect them because they are not only possible, they are true and readily available to you right now.

From a Verbal First Aid perspective the real problem with half-hearted communication is that when we use the word *try,* we are implying that we expect failure. At the very least, the mind interprets the image of trying as a struggle, a hope against hope. You can almost hear the grunt of effort behind it. "Try . . ."

"Try to eat something" automatically means you probably haven't been eating and more than likely don't feel like eating, but you can try. Listen to the difference when you say with confidence: "Here, you can eat the peas and a little of the potatoes." Saying, "Try to blow your nose," may elicit a flaccid attempt at best. "Here, blow your nose into this and you'll feel better" is an instruction any child can follow. Who doesn't want to feel better?

There is a simple demonstration of this principle that you can do with yourself right now to illustrate the downside of using the word *try*:

- Select someone you know who is the kind of person who, if you asked her, "Please move that chair for me," she obviously would.

- Then, pointing to a chair, say to that person, "Try to move that chair." With that puzzling instruction the person might respond, "Why, is it nailed down?" Trying implies the probability of failure.

Moreover, when we want to help someone get well, we want *our* belief in his ability to accomplish a task to engage *his* belief. When we say to a child, "Try to sit up," it could sound to him as if we were not certain that he can. When we say, "Let's sit up and see how you feel," we are affirming our belief that he is ready to do so, and in that way, he and his body may agree.

Also be aware of using the words *pain* and *hurt*. If the child uses that word, you can mirror it, but a more general "Tell me what you're feeling" or "Is it feeling better now?" can direct the mind to a better outcome than asking, "Does it still hurt?"

IN SUMMARY

- Center yourself through your breathing. Remember a model of calm and become one yourself.
- Use rapport.
- Model the ABCs of Verbal First Aid: authority, believability, and calm.
- Pace so you can lead. When he is calm and he hears you, you can direct the healing.
- Keep it positive.
- Don't criticize or give in to anger at the moment of crisis. This generates chemicals that prohibit healing.
- Expect success. Children (and all people) live up to or down to what we expect of them.
- Remember, whatever the question, love is the answer.

4 What to Say

Words are, of course, the most powerful drug used by mankind.

—Rudyard Kipling

Now that you see how important it is to center yourself, develop rapport, and eliminate the negative, you are ready for the protocol. This is the what-to-say portion you've been waiting for. But please remember that what you say is only part of Verbal First Aid. For it to work its wonders, everything that comes next must be applied in the context of what has come before.

GIVING HEALING SUGGESTIONS: REALLY TALKING TO THE HAND

Every conversation is filled with suggestion, whether we are conscious of it or not. Ordinary comments and questions such as, "Do you smell something?" "Isn't it hot in here?" and "Being out here in the country watching a soft cloud drift across the sky makes me feel so lazy" are all suggestions in that they conjure images in our minds and make us feel a certain way. Communicating an experience brings it to mind in another person, sometimes quite literally and directly, sometimes more tangentially or indirectly. And the more vividly it is expressed, the more the person who hears the comment can see, taste, feel, understand what we have experienced or want them to experience.

Healing suggestion works in much the same way, but its purpose is more specific. Its technique is more targeted because when people need healing suggestions, they are frequently in some kind of crisis. And when they're in crisis (mild, moderate, or extreme), they are more suggestible. Everything you say matters. As we've shown, this is especially true of children. And, as the parent or caring adult, you are the authority figure. You're the one who—with a touch, a glance, or a word—can turn something horrifying into something challenging or at least manageable. Therefore, whatever you say becomes a suggestion to the mind, the body, and the spirit. As with Oliver, who took the suggestion "I'm a good healer!" a positive suggestion can make all the difference during a crisis. And once that suggestion is accepted and used for healing, the body will remember it whenever it needs it again.

Just as there are different sorts of people—oppositional, passive, defiant, competent—there are different sorts of suggestions. Some may be better than others for your child. If your child is normally resistant to instructions, you might stay away from more direct suggestions and use more indirect methods. If your child is looking for very clear guidance, make your suggestions very direct and positive.

In this chapter, we'll take you through the various types of suggestions you can use with different kids and when dealing with an injury or emergency, many of which Donna used with Oliver. But first we'll reveal to you the underpinning of all suggestions—a technique therapists call *pacing and leading*. Essentially it is an extension of rapport. When we pace, we read the other person's signals and move along with her for a bit to build rapport and gain her cooperation. Leading is the verbal version of taking someone by the hand and guiding her from where she is to a position of safety.

Pacing

Pacing is very simply what it implies: keeping pace with. Psychologist Carl Rogers was a genius with this process. His patients came out of his sessions feeling that they were supremely understood. Pacing is vital in healthy, loving parent–child relationships. In that context, particularly in infancy, it is used a great deal in what Heinz Kohut, MD, called *mirroring* in his book *The Search for the Self*. Parents do it all the time—they smile as their baby smiles, they frown as their child frowns. It is so lovely to watch as a person feeding a child sympathetically opens his or her own mouth with each spoonful. When sincere and loving, it automatically validates the experience of the other person. Even without language or sophisticated cognitive skills, babies respond to this. It lets them know they are part of a social world.

It continues throughout life: Everyone's had the experience of walking in step with someone down the street, realizing that both of you are keeping the same rhythm. Perhaps you were sitting with someone and your faces took on the same expression. It is the most natural of phenomena. We all do it, and it is a preeminent rapport builder.

Studies of mirror neurons help us understand how we naturally have compassion. These neurons cause us to react similarly in our brains whether we're doing an activity or feeling an emotion or watching another person doing or feeling something. They are why we smile when being smiled at and why we wince as if being hurt when we witness someone else fall. It's as if we had experienced the emotion ourselves. New research suggests that mirror neuron activity is fully developed by age seven.

There are many ways to pace.

When Donna said to Oliver, "Oh, you banged your head. *Owww*," she was building rapport and letting him know she could feel what he was feeling.

Repetition can also be a form of pacing. If your child says, "I got scared and forgot to be careful," you can say, "Oh, you got scared."

Now you might be saying, I thought the ground rules included not saying the negative. And that's generally true. But when building rapport, before giving the positive suggestions, it can be helpful to acknowledge and reflect back to the person what he is feeling. This is a valuable technique, although there are two concerns to be conscious of:

1. Too much repetition can sound forced and unnatural, breaking the rapport.

2. Your tone of voice is important because repetition can also be perceived as sarcastic and dismissive or mimicking or mocking. It must be done with great care and thoughtfully, as though you were chewing on the thought itself or requesting some additional information.

Leading

We're now in the giving suggestions part of the Verbal First Aid protocol, and that means that we go from rapport and acknowledging the problem to moving a child in the direction of healing. That's the leading part of pacing and leading.

It is best exemplified by pacing and leading with a child who has asthma. This technique is especially effective if the child is hyperventilating. By breathing with her, you can join in. You might say (all the while pacing the rhythm of the breath), "I know ... how difficult ... it is ... for you ... to breathe ... easily ... right now." At this point, your breathing rate is in sync with hers; you can gradually begin to *slow down the rate* and watch how she starts to follow your lead. (You can find a full script of this scenario and scripts for many others in Chapter 5.)

The following are types of suggestions that you can use with your child.

HEALING SUGGESTIONS AND TECHNIQUES

Direct Positive Suggestion

It has been demonstrated that it is possible to say to a person who is bleeding even from a minor vein or artery, "I'd like you to stop your bleeding and save your blood," and he will be able to do so.[1] Not all bleeding in every situation can be abated in this way, but it happens far more than you might think.

Even people with hemophilia have benefited directly. When such individuals, who are frequently in life-threatening danger of bleeding, are given this suggestion in hypnosis, they are able to live with greater confidence and even undergo dental work without losing excessive blood.[2] A self-hypnosis program for hemophilia patients at the University of Colorado has decreased frequency and severity of bleeding episodes while increasing feelings of control and self-confidence.[3]

Direct suggestions are just that—direct commands to the person, to the body, or to emotions telling them in so many words how to effect the healing or set its course for the better. One of our favorite direct suggestions is this:

> Your body is already working on making it better. Right as soon as it happened, your body called a "red alert," and your white blood cells were sent down to fight the bugs. One kind of white blood cell is attacking them; others are making a scab, which is like your body's own bandage, and making new skin. If you're very quiet, you can hear it happening, if you listen very hard.

Other favorite suggestions include the following:

- "Take a nice, easy breath."
- "Hold my hand, look into my eyes, and sing the alphabet song as I call 9-1-1."
- "Notice your stomach becoming calmer and more comfortable."
- "Pretend you are blowing out a birthday candle, and then let yourself inhale softly with a smile."

Notice is one of those magic words that send the mind on an errand to pay attention to what is working or may soon be better. "Notice how your breathing has become easier," is a direct suggestion to someone having a panic or asthma attack.

Allow yourself is also a gentle command that gives permission to do something therapeutic. "Allow yourself to let your shoulders settle softly as you exhale."

Indirect Suggestion

Although the more serious the crisis, the more direct you must and can be, with some smaller crises, you can use an indirect approach.

Indirect suggestion is not reverse psychology, but rather a tangential way into a subject that may cause the child to come up with his own conclusions and not feel coerced. If the child is defiant or contrary or even just prefers to "do it myself," you can suggest pain relief/numbness or relaxation in a variety of indirect ways:

- Everyone knows how to feel tingling and numbness in his arm when it falls asleep.

- I wonder what you will think of that will allow you to comfortably close your eyes now.

- Isn't it nice to be able to sit easily and let your breathing do all the work?

- Some of us remember very well what it's like to be in a snowball fight and have so much fun we didn't even know we weren't wearing gloves and that our fingers were already numb.

Changing the Focus

One woman at a talk we gave told us that when she would complain of a stomachache to her sweet old grandmother, the elderly woman used to say, "And how's your head?"

The surprised child would say, "Oh, that's okay." And the grandmother would say, "Good. Go and lie down for a while and soon your stomach will feel like your head."

Next time you hear your child express concern or upset about what seems like a minor discomfort or injury that requires more emotional attention than medical, you can also suggest, "You bumped into the chair? Well, I'm going to have to have a private word with that chair. But first you have to tell me what makes it feel better. Can you walk around the table and see if that helps? And then let's see if moving your hands up over your head helps. How about . . ."

Changing the focus not only distracts the child but allows him or her to see beyond the discomfort. Seamus has a very long and impressive splinter in his ankle from climbing an old wooden fence. You remove it, clean and bandage the wound, but he insists it still hurts. "Hey," you suggest, "it's certainly a giant splinter, a mongo splinter, maybe the world's largest splinter." Seamus feels proud of himself for having been speared and lived to tell about it. "Let's put it into an envelope and mail it to Uncle Joe," you say. "Won't he be impressed that you managed to survive that! You want to write a letter to go with it?"

While most medical interviews focus on what makes it hurt or what makes it worse, what we want to know in Verbal First Aid is what makes it better. And sometimes what makes it better is just seeing how we've overcome something and putting that experience in a new light.

Guided Imagery

Guided imagery is truly a most important tool for you to use in all kinds of circumstances.

Guided imagery can be used to give pain relief, to send chemicals through the body that can literally change the way physical healing occurs or even change a mood or a ragged emotion. You'll want to choose imagery and suggestions that are appropriate to the situation and to the child's age and imagination. Other examples and uses of guided imagery will appear throughout the book.

Always use as lush and vivid details as you can muster. Help the child see an alternative reality, to put her mind somewhere where feeling safe and happy manufactures the neuropeptides that communicate well-being. It's possible for your child to imagine recovery and feeling better in the present and the future.

Be as imaginative as possible. "Here, take my magic ring and when you put it on, you'll feel a wave of good feeling come over you. Maybe you'll feel just like you did when we were at Grandpa's farm last summer and you saw the new baby lamb, and it was so soft and it licked your hand, and you laughed. And then you'll know that you're okay and safe. Here, try it! Yes! See?"

Here's What Donna Did

Let's return to Donna and Oliver.

Donna reminded Oliver about the Harry Potter book they had been reading in which Harry was turned into a statue. Donna asked Oliver, "Can you lie that still and be a statue, while the doctor fixes you up?" Donna encouraged Oliver to picture what it would feel like to be a statue, and Oliver had to use his imagination to find out.

Donna combined future pacing with guided imagery when she told Oliver that when they were done at the hospital, they would be going to his favorite toy store to get a toy car. Which would he prefer, she asked, the sports car or the classic car, making him use his imagination to leave the scene and be in a toy store in his mind while the procedure was happening.

Role Models

We have had really interesting healing interactions with children when asking them a question like, "What would Spider-Man do in this situation?" Children's imaginations are wonderful and they love hanging out with their heroes and superheroes. "What would Dora the Explorer do?" Answers pop up, the imagination begins to soar, and the child feels a part of an adventure.

Depending on their age, children also like to learn what other children in this situation did, or what you, the adult, the parents, did when this happened to you. Go ahead and use a role model the next time your child bumps his head, has a bad fall, or needs to know that he will come out strong from the situation.

On the way to the hospital to get these unknown things called stitches, Donna told Oliver about the time when she was a girl when she had to have stitches. He was amazed. She'd lived to tell about it, and here she was, perfectly content as if nothing had happened. But it hasn't happened to him yet, so he needed her to describe it to him in detail. How did it happen that she needed stitches, what was it like, how quickly did she recover? He made her repeat the story three times on the way to the hospital. But it reassured him. She was his role model in this. And all turned out well.

Be My Partner

When we involve anyone, but most especially a child, in the act of helping herself, then she can become part of the solution and feel her own competence rather than play the role of a victim.

Victimhood is powerlessness, whereas rescue is empowering. When a child learns that there are things he can do, ways he can affect the outcome, he has a sense of mastery that he can carry with him throughout life. You can't always be there for him, but if he is helping himself, realizing that he can help himself, you have provided him with a coping skill that allows him to overcome obstacles and appreciate his own fortitude and resilience throughout his life.

This is perhaps the most important resource we can give the next generation—the profound understanding that the solutions to what they encounter are available to them, that they can consciously participate in their own experience of life, and that they have the capacities within to change how they receive whatever comes their way.

One of the most surprising stories along these lines involved an incident in Big Sur, the part of the northern California coast where cliff side meets ocean. Some of the cliffs are hundreds of feet above the shore, and a young teenager had been walking along the edge of one of them when she slipped and began to slide; she now found herself clinging by her fingernails to a ledge three hundred feet above the beach. James Barrow, an EMT firefighter in the area, told us the story.

He had gone to rescue her, had been lowered by a rope beside her, and found her screaming uncontrollably in fear. Of course he did *not* say, "Don't look down, you'll fall," or even "Don't fall," because he wanted to give her suggestions that would give her a picture in her mind of safety while he worked to secure and save her. So he said, "You know those superheroes Batman and Robin? Well, I'll be Batman and you be Robin, and we'll get you out of here."

Suddenly her crying ceased and she unexpectedly and forcefully said, "No!"

"No?" What could this mean?

"I—" she said, her sobs abating and her eyes flashing, "*I* want to be Batman!"

It's amusing in retrospect, now that the danger's passed, and she did become Barrow's partner in the rescue, which is what he was going for in the first place.

So, change the dynamic from victim to hero by making the child your partner. Ask her to hold the bandage while you clean the cut, ask her to let you know when it's three o'clock or to keep a chart of the times when the medicine must be applied or taken. Use the child's own desire to help to allow her to help herself.

Here's What Donna Did

After Donna washed Oliver's injury, she made a compress of a cloth packed with ice and asked him to hold it against his forehead as she drove to the hospital. He had a job to do. He was part of the recovery, rather than being just a victim, lying there in fear and pain. And that job both distracted and supported him and that moment.

Expect the Best Outcome

Your expectations are also suggestions. You're the authority. If you know that children can participate in their own healing and recovery and expect the best from them, they will believe they can. Teachers see the evidence of this all the time in their classrooms. When they expect success from their students they get it. When you speak about your child's recovery with conviction, it gives her a picture and a road map.

Here's What Donna Did

When Donna told Oliver, "You're a good healer!" he believed her, because she had been a truthful authority figure in his life before, and it proved true. Beyond that, and this shows another level of the power of Verbal

First Aid, it became a future belief, part of his own self-description and expectation, that helped him gather his strength the next time he was injured.

In the 1990s Robert Rosenthal and Lenore Jacobson reported on their schoolroom studies, the results of which are often called the Pygmalion effect. In the studies, teachers were told that certain seven-year-old students were about to blossom and that they were potentially very smart. Those students did blossom in part because of the belief that they would. Those very same students who performed well when the teachers believed they were exceptionally bright, performed poorly for teachers who were told they were slow.[4]

In Greek mythology, a king of Cyprus named Pygmalion carved a beautiful sculpture and did such an amazing job, he fell in love with her. Taking pity on him, Aphrodite brought the sculpture to life as Galatea. Picking up on that myth, in 1916 George Bernard Shaw wrote a play titled *Pygmalion* about a linguistics professor who made a bet that he could turn a flower girl into a lady, which he did, and then he fell in love with her. (The play was the basis for the Rex Harrison/Audrey Hepburn musical *My Fair Lady*.) The key to all of these stories is that someone who is believed in comes to life as they are seen. The Galatea effect is even more a self-fulfilling prophecy in which the person/statue herself believes in herself and becomes what she believes.

In each of these stories we see the Verbal First Aid model of what you think = how you feel and how that goes on to affect your life. And we can all be Henry Higgins to our children, encouraging them to become the elegant blossom that is inherent in their very being.

The Yes Set

The Yes Set is another variation of suggestion. It focuses on generating a rhythm of agreements so one can lead the person to a beneficial conclusion or outcome. It has been found that when people say yes more than twice, they tend to continue saying it. For a child who is in need of Verbal First Aid, observe and comment on three indisputable truths.

For example, in the case of a child who typically protests taking a dose of medicine or an antibiotic, you could put him at ease by offering these truths, "Sometimes medicine can make things all better. You see this medicine I have right here? Nice color, that pink, right? It's going to make that cut all better."

Or if a child is hurt, you can practice the Yes Set by acknowledging a couple truths, and then suggesting that he feels more comfortable because you are there. More specifically, you could say, "I can tell that your leg needs attention. I'm right here with you, and I've got you. I've called nine one one, and the ambulance is on its way so you can focus on my hand holding yours and be a little more comfortable right now as I start to check the rest of you." A child agreeing to these truths may also, then, agree to feel more comfortable or to breathe easier.

For children who suffer from nightmares, you can offer some truths and a suggestion that might help them to better understand their unconscious mind. Begin by saying, "At night, while you sleep, your mind can dream. You know, though, you dream all the time. And in those dreams you can hear, you can see, you can move. You can have any number of experiences, just as you can now. You could even find some answers your daytime mind doesn't know yet."

A pediatric nurse found that, instead of jumping in with the "it-will-just-hurt-for-a-minute-but-let's-do-the-IV," right away, a Yes Set eased the child into the situation.

"You're Jared, right?"

Jared nods.

"And you're here with your mommy?"

Jared looks at Mommy, nods.

"And you're wearing those running shoes with the lights in them?"

Nodding.

"You like to run?"

Jared nods and smiles.

"Running is fun. And now we're going to do the IV, and it's going to be all right."

Jared nods.

Here's What Donna Did

Donna used a Yes Set with Oliver.

When Donna was watching the procedure, she said, "Oh, he's a wonderful doctor. That was a great stitch. You won't even have a scar." As it happens, although the cut was deep and significant, Oliver did not have a scar. Whether or not it was great technique on the part of the doctor, it was a great technique on Donna's part, and she helped Oliver use his own healing and belief systems to make that so.

The Because Clause

A special form of pacing and leading particularly useful with children is the Because Clause. *Because* is a word that has an almost magical effect on many people. Why? Because. Because it's rife with explanation and possibilities. Because we begin answers to many questions, profound and simple, with it. Because it so often can be satisfactory. "Put on your coat before you go outside." "Why?" "Because it's cold out there, and your coat will help you stay warm and toasty in the wind."

Therapeutically, it seems to be helpful because it puts the motivation right up front. "Because you really want to get better quickly, you can rest your leg in bed today and by tomorrow, you'll be up and playing with your friends." There's a double blessing here, an embedded suggestion hanging on the *because*. It's the reason why you're stuck in bed (so you'll get better quickly), and because you do, you'll have the reward of playing with your friends.

For children with sleep issues, the contingency of a *because* can offer the suggestion and gift of anticipating an easier slipping off into dreamland: "Because you've been having so much fun with your cousins, you'll have lots of great things to dream about."

Here's What Donna Did

Donna used the Because Clause with Oliver.

Donna didn't just spring a trip to the hospital on Oliver with a sense that he'd done something awful or it was dire and they would now—oh no!—have to have surgery. Instead, she used a Because Clause to get to the desired picture in his mind. She said to Oliver, "We'll have to go to the hospital right away, because it looks like you'll need stitches, and the doctors know how to fix you right up." That was a suggestion he could use.

Contingency or Implied Suggestions

One technique is called a *contingency suggestion* since the first part is an indirect suggestion to do something, and the second part implies a healing response to the suggestion. This involves using a template that says, "As I do this, you can feel this." For example, "As I put this medicine on your knee, you can begin to notice that it first feels cool, and then it feels a little tickly, and then it feels much better." And another example is, "When you put this heating pad on your tummy, it'll start to feel nice and warm, and more relaxed with every breath you take."

Illusion of Choice

We use the illusion of choice technique often with children. "Do you want to brush your teeth first and then read a book before going to bed or read the book first and then brush your teeth before going to bed?" They're going to bed. But at least they feel like they have some say in the matter. It's the outcome that we're focusing on.

So, with a sick or injured child, the desired outcome is comfort. "Are you more comfortable lying down or sitting up?" Sitting up. "Okay, then, let me help you sit up so that you can be more comfortable." Which is what she agreed to.

Medicine taking can be a chore, but this technique may make it go down a little more smoothly: "Would you rather take your medicine before you eat or after you eat?" Whichever he agrees to, he has agreed to taking his medicine.

Future Pacing

Similar to regular pacing, future pacing allows you to project what you want to see—out into the future. I am with you, not only here but in your future, where you are better, more comfortable, and happy.

You might say to a child who is wondering when she can go out and play or take a cast off a broken arm, "Imagine how surprised the doctor will be when your arm gets better so much faster than she thought it would."

At the doctor's office, after he has finished the procedure and is telling the child that he expects the child to heal just fine, you might add, "When you get home, we'll be careful you don't overdo it, even though you'll be feeling better faster than you thought." The real suggestion, as you can see, is the last part.

When we use future pacing, the child has both the wonderful relief from pain because we took her mind off the immediate problem and a revised picture of what happened and how well it will turn out.

Here's What Donna Did

Donna told Oliver that the next day he'd be able to tell his friends in school what happened to him. She assured him that they'd be amazed at how brave he was! Suddenly, he was not a victim but the star of his own movie about this adventure. He began to wonder what his friends would think about his story. He almost couldn't wait to tell them.

As you can see, there are many ways to phrase suggestions. In Chapter 5, you'll find actual scripts for some of the most common scenarios a parent or caretaker might encounter. Once you understand the principles of Verbal First Aid—the value of centering and rapport and saying only what you want to have happen, not what you don't—you can begin to speak to your child's body and spirit to help her heal and to help her internalize the ideas so that they are available to her, naturally and automatically, when she can use them best.

IN SUMMARY

- Literally or imaginatively, *say what you want to have happen,* not what you don't. The frightened mind doesn't hear the *don't*. So avoid suggestions with words like *pain, vomit,* and *cry,* unless that's the outcome you want.

- Give therapeutic suggestions. People in pain, fear, or panic are in an altered state of consciousness, and everything you say can be a suggestion to the body for good or ill.

- Practice pacing and leading—join your child in his breathing or emotion and then slowly lead him back to well-being.

- Use direct suggestion, such as "Stop your bleeding and save your blood."

- Use indirect suggestion, including the following techniques:

  1. Changing the focus

  2. Guided imagery—picturing a better or different place or outcome

  3. Role models

  4. Be My Partner

  5. Yes Sets—you gain agreement on small things and work up to the desired outcome

  6. The Because Clause

  7. Expect the Best Outcome

- Use contingency or implied suggestions in the form of Illusion of Choice or Future Pacing.

5 Where Does It Hurt?

Scripts for Burns; Asthma; Nosebleeds; Cuts and Boo-boos; Falls, Bumps, and Bruises; and Fears, Nightmares, and Bedwetting

Words can sometimes, in moments of grace, attain the quality of deeds.

—ELIE WIESEL, AUTHOR, ACTIVIST, AND NOBEL LAUREATE

In this section we will provide you with scripts for most common childhood emergencies: burns, asthma attacks, nosebleeds, cuts and boo-boos, falls, bumps, bruises, fears, nightmares, and bedwetting. These issues will be covered in detail so that you will feel prepared and capable of handling anything that comes up. All the scripts in this chapter are written so they can easily be adapted to your own situation.

VERBAL FIRST AID FOR BURNS

If your child has been burned with fire or hot water, or in any other situation, immediately place the body part under running tap water or cover the area with a clean, cool, wet towel. *Do not* apply ice, butter, or ointments and do not break any blisters. You may cover the burn with a sterile dressing and immediately call your doctor for further instructions.

The simple rule of thumb in burns is to follow standard first aid protocol, use gauze or towels that are as clean as possible (if not sterile), keep the wound protected until proper medical care is secured, and give repeated suggestions for "cool and comfortable" while you attend to it.

Always remember to call 911 if a situation appears to be more than you can handle or gives you cause for more serious concern. If a burn is both red and moist or turning white or larger than the palm of the child's hand, call 911. While you are waiting for help to arrive, you can speak to your child to help him stay calm and facilitate healing right away. Verbal First Aid can help set the course in the right direction.

Remember: First center yourself; then exhale and take a breath.

Use your authority. What you say and how you say it set the course for recovery. Stay calm, in loving presence.

Scenario 1

In this scenario we will provide you a script that employs pacing and leading, guided imagery, and indirect positive suggestion to handle a common kitchen crisis: a burn.

It's dinnertime. The water boils in the pot of pasta sitting on the stove, the handle tilted slightly forward. The meal is almost ready. Sara is at the sink, washing vegetables for dinner when five-year-old Matthew, naturally curious, in search of an adventure, saunters into the kitchen, looking to help.

She senses his presence, but before she can turn around and say,

"Matthew, don't touch tha—" he has reached for the pot handle and, nearly in slow motion as she watches in horror, the water and pasta cascade toward the floor, splattering her child.

Matthew is stunned. This is so unexpected, so scary. Mom has rushed over. He doesn't know what he's done wrong—just wanted to see what was up there and to help.

He follows her gaze to his arm, which is wet and becoming red, and he begins to feel the sting of it.

Sara follows the instructions for burns, calling 911 or the doctor if necessary.

She takes a deep breath, so she can be centered and calm.

Sara: Well, Matthew, looks like it went *kaboom*.

Matthew: (Lips quivering, not sure what to say or do.)

Sara: Oh, sweetheart, I know you just wanted to help.

Matthew: Yeah. (Nodding, tears forming in the corners of his eyes.)

Sara: Show me your arm, darling.

Matthew: Owie.

Sara: Yes, it's an owie. I see. I'm going to turn it around so I can see it, and we can start to make it better right away. Okay?

Matthew: (Nods agreement.)

Sara: (Examining the burn and seeing it needs minor medical attention.) Well, it looks like some of the water fell on your arm. Can you see it, Matthew?

Matthew: Uh-huh.

Sara: What color does it look like to you?

Matthew: Red.

Sara: Does to me, too. So, you know what we're going to do? We're going to get some cool, clean towels for it, and you're going to help me with that, okay? (Sara quickly takes a clean, white towel and wets it with cool tap water. She is physically reacting quickly to this situation, even though it is not a serious emergency, but she is also staying calm so that Matthew can pace that sense of safety with her.) As I put that on there, like that, you can hold it there for me while I get the phone and make a quick call. And while I talk on the phone, you can think about how that cool, cool towel is making your arm nice and cool, all the way down deep, just really cool like the time you played with the snow without your mittens and your hand got so cold, really cool until the red is less red and starts to look a little pink, and then not even so pink anymore, but kind of like your other arm, just nice and cool and comfortable. So, you can do that now—right—while I get the phone.

Matthew: (Takes the towel and holds it to his arm.) Uh-huh.

Sara: Good job. Cool and comfortable.

Even if Matthew were sobbing uncontrollably, Sara would say the same thing right through Matthew's tears. If more urgent medical attention were needed, she would either call 911 or take him to urgent care immediately, all the while giving the same suggestions for "cool and comfortable down deep."

There's a story told by a medical doctor with a knowledge of hypnosis. His son had gone skiing and had forgotten to put on sunblock. When he came home his face, neck, and ears were beet red and painful. The doctor gave his son suggestions for "cool and comfortable" but only mentioned his face. In the morning when his son came downstairs for breakfast, his face was a normal color, but his ears and neck were still flaming.

Scenario 2

In this script, we will show you how to use slightly more directive, but more detailed, suggestion. This may be useful with older or more sophisticated children. For this scenario, let's assume that instead of Matthew, Sara's ten-year-old daughter, Emily, dropped the pot and that the burn covers a larger area, including her hands, chest, and stomach. She is in much more pain and sobbing.

Sara: I'm right here and I'm going to help you make it get better. To help you, I need you to stay with my voice and help me by doing what I say. Can you do that? Good. Now, take off your clothes. I'll get a towel. (They each do what they have to do.)

Emily: It hurts!

Sara: I know, Emily. To help it go away, I'm going to put this towel on you like this, sweetheart, so you can feel it getting cooler and more comfortable right away. You hold it there now while I make a phone call. That's right. Hold it so it's comfortable for you.

Emily: Ow! Mom. Make it stop.

Sara: (Gets off the phone after calling 911.) I'm going to help you make it stop, Emily. The medics are on their way. But until they get here you can stay with my voice and do what I say. You can do that, can't you?

Emily: (Nods affirmatively.)

Sara: Good. First thing you can do is tell me exactly what color the hurt is.

Emily: Red. Really red.

Sara: It's red. Okay. Hold my hand. Good. Now, close your eyes. Make that area cooler, real cool, like you're putting all that hurt in a big cool lake or the way it feels when you're really hot in the summer and you get a glass of ice water, the way it feels as it cools you down deep inside. What color is it now?

Emily: Lighter. But it still hurts.

Sara: It still hurts, but it's a little lighter.

Emily: A little.

Sara: Good. And you can keep making it lighter and lighter, letting it get cooler and cooler as I get another really cool towel and you give me the one you've been holding. You're doing a good job, Emily. Your body knows how to heal itself, sweetheart. Remember that time you got that awful paper cut and you cried and cried and you thought it would be open forever, but by the morning it was all closed and by the day after you couldn't even remember exactly where it was. And you can be surprised the same way when this injury goes away and you can try to remember where it was, but it'll be so far gone and away you probably won't be able to. You'll just be pleasantly surprised that it's all gone.

Verbal First Aid Shortcuts for Burns

- "Mommy's right here, and I've got you."

- "The worst is over. It's going to get fixed up right away."

- "Picture that arm packed in ice and snow, cool and comfortable. Remember the time you played with snow without your mittens and your hands felt sooo cold? Cold like that."

- "What color does it look like to you? Red? To me, too. Picture the red turning lighter and lighter, more and more like the color of your other arm."

- ■ "Feel how the cool water is washing over it, like the ocean over the sand, washing away footprints and making it calm and comfortable."

- ■ "Your body knows how to heal itself. Remember the time you (fill in her experience) and your body healed it and it went away all by itself?"

VERBAL FIRST AID FOR ASTHMA

Asthma has become a major concern for children and their parents in communities across the country. It has affected more children in more diverse settings than ever before. For this reason, we are including the following scripts and want to remind you to always make sure you contact your doctor or call an ambulance if you feel your child is having an asthma attack. If you already have a prescribed regimen, such as an inhaler for acute attacks, give the medicine first. As you do, Verbal First Aid can help you keep both yourself and your child calm and composed, which are essential for resolving the situation. Anxiety exacerbates respiratory complaints and sometimes initiates them.

When the pediatric residents at Cedars-Sinai Medical Center in Los Angeles were trained in Verbal First Aid, they learned the pacing and leading protocol for helping asthma patients when Albuterol or other prescription medicines are not available. Breathing is so essential to life, and the panicky feeling that arises in a person whose bronchial tubes are constricted creates even greater physical tension. As is illustrated in the following scenarios, when the caregiver begins breathing in rhythm with the patient, begins talking the patient into calm, and is able to model steady, easy breathing, the patient can follow.

After the demonstration of this pacing and leading breathing at the medical center, the first patient that the physician in charge of the residents saw after the training was an eight-year-old girl who was having an asthma attack. The doctor breathed with her, reflecting back the constricted, frightened breathing at first and gradually slowing down while talking of imagining the lungs relaxing. The doctor called to say that she was astonished to report that the treatment worked. The girl began breathing normally, and the doctor extended an invitation for further training in this surprising way to help children. While this protocol can be very helpful, we reiterate that it is simply meant as an adjunct to your standard practices for treating a child with asthma.

Keep in mind that Verbal First Aid for asthma should always be soothing, reassuring, and steady. The suggestions should generally be focused on opening (e.g., the airways), comfort, and ease. In the following scripts you will learn how not only to help your child be more at ease until help arrives but to begin a genuine healing process.

Scenario 1

Mark is in his office watching his seven-year-old son, Tyler, race around the yard with a neighborhood friend. Mark is working on a report he needs to have on his boss's desk by the next morning, but something about Tyler's movements make him stop and take a closer look. Tyler has slowed down and is resting his hands on his thighs. He is bent over and looks like he can't get a deep breath. Mark drops what he's doing, runs into the kitchen, opens a drawer, and pulls out an inhaler. He stops for one second, takes a deep breath, centers himself, and walks outside. He approaches his son calmly, puts his hand on Tyler's shoulder.

Mark: Tyler, it looks like you're having some trouble breathing.

Tyler: (Nods, but can't speak.)

Mark: I have your medicine. Here, I'm lifting it to your mouth. Take hold of it, that's right, press, and let the spray move into your bronchial tubes. Y'know I had to take an inhaler once (If this is not true, say, "I had a friend who used an inhaler, and he told me . . ."), and I remember it feeling a little cool and that it opened me up pretty quick . . . and I remember feeling it working . . . a little cooler, a little more open and a little more open . . . until I was able to take a really good, deep, satisfying breath . . . just like that.

Tyler: (Breathes a bit more regularly, sighs.)

Mark: That's good, Tyler. (Sighs with his son.) And it's working a little already, and you can take another comfortable breath right now, real easy, real comfortable, feeling how the medicine opens and smoothes and makes it easier to breathe comfortably . . . That's right. (Breathes again with his son.) And you've been through this before, and you already know that your body knows what to do to help you so you can breathe deeply and comfortably . . . You remember, and your body remembers, doesn't it?

Tyler: Uh-huh. (Takes a deeper breath.)

Mark: (Takes a deeper breath along with his son.) If you did it once, you can do it again.

Tyler: I think it's better. (Sighs.)

Mark: Looks and sounds better. (Sighs.)

Scenario 2

In some cases, medicine is not immediately available. People forget to take inhalers on trips or they forget to replenish their supply, or they reach for one and find out it's empty. It is important in these situations to call 911 or start driving to the emergency room before you do anything else. Once proper action is initiated, you can begin using Verbal First Aid.

It's one of those beautiful days they just don't want to miss, so Marcy and her daughter, Elizabeth, head out with friends on a spur-of-the-moment picnic. Packing a lunch, some extra clothes, and towels, they take off for the mountains. They spend the afternoon hiking around the hills and have their lunch near a beautiful lake. Elizabeth, who loves the water, insists on going in although it is cold. When she comes out, she is wheezing. With a history of asthma, her mother always keeps an inhaler in her purse or makes sure Elizabeth has one in her backpack. Somehow, in their rush, they both forgot to take one with them. Marcy asks her friend to inform the park rangers and to call 911. Then she sits with her daughter on a picnic bench.

Marcy: Here, Elizabeth, I'm right with you and we've both been through this before and know what we need to do to make it better. You know how to bend forward a little and lean your elbows on your thighs, just like that so your airways open, open a little more, good, just like that.

Elizabeth: (Wheezing, leans forward, but her breathing is still strained and shallow. Her face reveals her anxiety.)

Marcy: (Leans forward too, gently pacing her breathing with her daughter's, then gradually, almost imperceptibly at first, slowing her breath down, leading her daughter back to a more regular respiratory rate.) Now . . . I'm going . . . to talk to you . . . as you sit with me . . . and remind you . . . that's right . . . of how you get better . . . and how you . . . already know how to do in your body . . . your body knows how to open . . . that's right . . . and as I put this towel around your shoulders . . . you can begin to feel that opening just a little more . . . that's right . . . and already you can feel the worst is over . . . and that it's getting a little better . . . a little more open . . . and I'm going to count from ten to one and when . . . I get to one . . . you can feel how open and comfortable . . . it is to breathe . . . ten, nine, eight . . . that's right . . . more open, more comfortable . . . right with me . . . seven, six, five, four . . . a little more . . . three, two . . . and all the way now . . . one.

Elizabeth: (Takes a bigger breath, but still wheezing.)

Marcy: Much better . . . so we can do it again . . . in a moment . . . opening your airways more and more each time.

Marcy has been matching her breath to Elizabeth's and then leading it back to a normal, easy rhythm, which Elizabeth slowly begins to match. Marcy can repeat this pacing and leading (see Chapter 3 to refresh your memory) as long as she needs to while she and her daughter wait for the medics to arrive.

Verbal First Aid Shortcuts for Asthma

WITH AN INHALER

- "Here's the inhaler. It will help you to breathe much easier. Just the way it did last time, remember?"

- "That's right, press, and let the spray move into your bronchial tubes. You can start to feel that cool feeling of opening and becoming more and more comfortable with every breath."

- Use a role model. For example, "I had to take an inhaler once and I remember it feeling a little cool and that it opened me up pretty quick . . . and I remember feeling it working . . . a little cooler, a little more open and a little more open . . . until I was able to take a really good, deep, satisfying breath . . . just like that." Or you could say, "My friend John had to use an inhaler and he told me it was cool," et cetera.

WITHOUT AN INHALER

- Breathe with the child, matching his breath and then leading him to easier breathing.

- "I can see . . . how hard it is . . . for you to breathe . . . but if you breathe along . . . with me, follow me . . . it will be . . . easier and easier to breathe . . . Like that . . . your body knows how to open . . . Yes, just like that."

- "I'm going to count from ten down to one, and with every number you will feel your lungs opening more and more, as you lean forward and count in your mind with me. Ten, that's right, getting a little better . . . nine, good, like that, more open, more comfortable . . . eight, easier and easier to breathe, good . . ."

VERBAL FIRST AID FOR NOSEBLEEDS

Nosebleeds are a relatively common occurrence both in children aged two to ten and in the elderly. Despite their high incidence, they can be scary and upsetting, especially for children who do not understand what's happening. Verbal First Aid can be truly helpful in not only calming the frightened child but facilitating a quick, easy recovery.

Typically, nosebleeds that do not require medical attention are generally caused by excessive nose picking and, in the winter, dryness of the mucous membranes. Of course, other normal causes for nosebleeds in children include a surprise encounter with another child's fist, toy, or head against the nose.

Generally, bleeding occurs in one nostril, and many episodes seem to occur in the morning hours. Unless the child is bleeding for more than ten minutes, has repeated occurrences, is short of breath, is vomiting up blood, or is very dizzy and running a fever, it's likely you can handle the run-of-the-mill nosebleed without a physician's assistance.

In Verbal First Aid, the way we deal with a nosebleed begins with the basics, just as it does with any other crisis—major or minor. Centering comes first. After you calm yourself you can begin to calm the child. Seeing your child with blood dripping across his lips and onto his shirt may seem like a scene from a horror movie, but as soon as you remember that nosebleeds are quite common in childhood, you can take a centering breath, knowing you have what it takes to handle the situation.

After you let your child know you see what's going on ("Oh, sweetheart, you've got a nosebleed. We'll take care of that"), you can get a clean, slightly damp cloth, walk over to him calmly, and wash the blood off his face (hands, et cetera) as you say, "Nosebleeds happen to a lot of children. Even some grown-ups. And as I help clean you up, you can start to stop the bleeding from the inside. And I'm going to show you how like magic."

As soon as you can, have him sit up on your lap or on a chair with his head slightly forward so that blood doesn't slide down his throat. Have him spit out any blood in his mouth because swallowing it could cause him to vomit and frighten him and you further.

As you pinch his nose gently at the soft end and hold your hand there consistently for ten minutes (or solicit his help by having him hold it if he's old enough or able) you can say, "In your mind, you can even think of it as a faucet that you can turn off or a hose that you can pinch just like you're doing right now. There. Just like that."

And you can help your child recognize that even though these things sometimes happen, our bodies are wonderful and seem to know exactly what to do to repair themselves, sometimes even without our knowing how. "It's like having expert mechanics with you whenever you need them."

Scenario 1

Five-year-old Melissa wakes up and shouts for her parents. They come running. She is dripping blood from her nose. The blood has run down her face and onto her pajamas. When she sees it, she is frightened and starts screaming.

Mom: Ohhh, honey, you've got a nosebleed! Well, we're right here. Dad, would you grab a nice wet towel, while I hug Melissa and let her know that everything's all right?

Melissa: Mommy! I'm bleeding all over.

Mom: Well, just from your nose, darling, even though it feels like all over. That's what happens in nosebleeds. Lots of people get them. We're going to clean you up and help it go away.

Melissa: Am I going to die?

Mom: No, my love, it's just a nosebleed. I used to get them all the time, and I'm still here, hugging you, as a matter of fact.

Melissa: I feel funny.

Dad: (Comes in with a wet towel.) Mom's going to pinch your nose while I clean you up a bit.

Mom: (Taking a clean paper towel or tissue and applying it to her nostril gently.) Or would you like to hold it shut yourself while it heals?

Melissa: You hold it.

Mom: Okay. So, here's the trick. While I pinch your nose, like this, you're going to breathe out of your mouth, like this. Let's see you do it.

Melissa: (Breathes through her mouth.)

Mom: Good. That's all you have to do and this will be taken care of. Can you imagine a little faucet in your nose like the faucet we use to turn on the hose water?

Melissa: (Nods.)

Mom: Imagine a little faucet in there and imagine that you can turn it off, just the way we turn off the water. And you can stop the bleeding. Can you do that?

Melissa: I think so.

Mom: Good. And we can read your favorite book while we wait for it to stop, and before you know it, you'll be fine again. Because your body wants to heal itself, and we're going to help it.

Melissa: I'll hold it with you.

Mom: Okay.

Scenario 2

Eight-year-old Finn is in a fight with another boy over a toy truck. There are about thirty seconds of "It's mine," "No it's mine. I saw it first," while they pull and tussle, until the other boy lets go and the truck slaps Finn right in the nose. It starts to bleed.

His mother runs over.

Mom: Uh-oh, bumped your nose. Okay, we'll clean it up and stop that bleeding pretty quick.

Finn: He hit me.

Mom: Actually, the truck hit you. And you'll be just fine as soon as I pinch your nose enough to stop the bleeding and let your body begin to heal up right away. I'll hold it for ten minutes, and then it will be done. You can look at my watch and tell me exactly when we're done. See, when this hand gets to the five, you can say "Let go! I'm fine now!"

Finn: (Sounding funny, because Mom's holding his nose) And the truck . . .

Mom: Yes, that was what bumped you. Well, we'll talk about the truck later, but for now, as soon as we can let go of your nose, we're going to have a little quiet time so it can heal for sure. I think you guys—and the truck—have had enough bumping and jumping today. Just take it easy, and it's going to heal so well you won't even know it happened by dinner tonight . . . but you'll have a great story for tomorrow. Then we can talk about trucks and see if we can find that one with the concrete mixer on the back that's been missing for a few weeks.

Finn: Okay.

Mom: So for now, while you sit here with me and watch my watch, I'll tell you a funny story about when Grandpa had a nosebleed.

Verbal First Aid Shortcuts for Nosebleeds

▨ Nosebleeds are common but can be scary. Center yourself and then let the child know that "It's what we call a nosebleed, and everyone gets them from time to time."

▨ Clean his face and hands of blood, tip him slightly forward, and gently pinch the nose at the end for ten minutes.

▨ Say, "In your mind, you can picture your nose like a faucet or a hose, turning it off until it's just a drip, drip, then a slow, slow drip and then it's off."

▨ And let him know, "Your body knows how to heal itself." And so it will.

VERBAL FIRST AID FOR CUTS, BOO-BOOS, AND GETTING STITCHES

There is an archetypal component to cuts. They open us, literally. Even when they don't hurt very much, for many people both young and old, they are frightening. When we get cut we are vulnerable. Even in the very young for whom that concept is completely unarticulated, the experience is visceral. When we see our own blood, when it seems to be flowing from us without our knowing how to stop it, that, too, adds to the fear.

Understanding our fears and anxieties actually tells us what we need to do to help our children deal with a cut or abrasion. Verbal

First Aid in these circumstances should focus generally on empowerment by using resources children already have, through role modeling or partnering, direct suggestions delivered with confidence, and future pacing.

Physicians David Cheek and Dabney Ewen reported that, in both emergency and operating rooms, ordinary (nonarterial) bleeding can be lessened and/or halted entirely with a command from an authority figure. Therefore this protocol may be used for accidents as well as for simple nosebleeds.

The following scripts will demonstrate this for you. If the cut is more serious than a household bandage can appropriately handle, either call 911 or bring your child in to the doctor or emergency room immediately. While you're waiting for the ambulance or heading to the hospital, use Verbal First Aid to set the course straight.

SCENARIO I

Janet's seven-year old daughter, Olivia, wants to help make dinner. Janet has always stressed kitchen safety and has taught Olivia how to properly handle a knife. She has been told never to use one without a grown-up present. However, one day while Janet is out in the garden, Olivia wants to surprise her mother by preparing a salad. She takes the supplies out of the refrigerator, sets them on a counter, takes a serrated knife out of the utility drawer, and gets on a small stool so she can reach everything easily.

In her excitement to help, she takes the knife in her hand before she properly steadies herself and slips off the stool. The knife slides through her hand, making a half-inch incision across the side of her palm. As soon as Olivia wails "Ma!" Janet runs into the kitchen, sees the blood, and remembers: First steps first. She takes a deep breath, banishes all other thoughts from her mind, and centers herself for the task at hand. She makes sure she is as calm as possible before speaking.

Janet: Olivia, what happened, honey?

Olivia: I slipped. Mom, it's bleeding.

Janet: I see. And that's a good thing for a cut, sweetheart, because it cleans it out so it can heal right. So, I'm going to get a good look at that cut and see what we need to do. While I look at it you can make sure it bleeds just enough to cleanse the wound . . . okay? And then you can *stop the bleeding* . . . just the way you always do when you get a boo-boo. Okay?

Olivia: (Nods with tears in her eyes.) Ow.

Janet: I know, love. It's an ow. And it looks like it's the kind of boo-boo we can make better right here, right now with a bandage from the bathroom. Want to come with me and pick one out that you want?

Olivia: Yeah.

Janet: (In the bathroom.) Here are three really good bandages, each one is made to help you stop the bleeding and make the boo-boo go away. Which one do you think is the most special and will make it go away fastest?

Olivia: (Considers all three, then points to one.) That one.

Janet: Interesting. That looked like a magical bandage to me, too. So we're going to put it on like this right here, and you can *stop the bleeding* . . . that's right, right away.

Olivia: Like this?

Janet: Just like that. You remember! Very good. And won't you be delighted and just so amazed when your skin knits itself all together and smooth again? It's a special magic you have, Olivia. So when we put a new bandage on tomorrow, it's going to look better. And even better the next day after that.

Olivia: Gone?

Janet: Very soon all gone. You're such a good healer, Olivia, that it might be gone before I even check on it.

Olivia: Really?

Janet: Remember last time how quickly your boo-boo went away? It was all black and blue, but then the next day it was just a little yellow and by the day after that it was as good as new and you forgot you ever had a bruise there. You did that all by yourself.

Olivia: I did?

Janet: Yes, you did.

Scenario 2

Sometimes a prior history with a cut or medical condition can complicate a child's response both to the current crisis and to us. It is easy for a child to misunderstand a situation, and that in and of itself can be a source of great fear. What is particularly helpful at those times is to refrain from judging or dismissing his fears but to help him reach a new and better perspective on himself and the world in which he lives.

A nurse was caring for a child she'd seen in her office a while back. The girl had originally come in for a deep cut that needed stitches. The nurse recalled that the child had been very brave when the doctor stitched her, but this time the girl's anxiety was palpable. When the doctor approached her to remove the stitches, she became hysterical. She kicked, screamed, clutched at anything that promised to take her away from the man with the scissors. There was no consoling, cajoling, or comforting her. The nurse recalled her frustration. It was a mystery to everyone present how someone who had been so brave had suddenly become so terrified. A mystery, that is, until the child's mother remembered something important. The following is a dramatic demonstration of what that conversation might have been like.

Mother: Honey, does this have anything to do with your doll?

Daughter: (Crying, nods *yes*.)

Mother: The one whose arm I sewed on a while back?

Daughter: Uh-huh. (Still crying, but now engaged in a meaningful conversation that addresses the real problem and the real fear.)

Mother: Well, I can see what's upsetting you so much, sweetheart, because the stitches I put in the doll's arm came out a few times and when they did ...

Daughter: The arm fell off!!! (She cries again, but not as loud or as fearfully.)

Mother: It did. You're right. And you know why?

Daughter: Uh-uh.

Mother: Because that was a doll's arm, not a person's arm, and they're made out of very different things. You remember that cut you got a while back when you fell on the swings? Remember? (After her daughter nods *yes*, the mother continues.) Well, you also remember then how it healed itself, even without stitches. The skin just magically knitted itself back together. All we did was wash it, kiss it, and put on a bandage and—*poof*—it came together and it *stayed together*. Wasn't that boo-boo right here? (She points to a spot on her daughter's arm.) Can you see it anymore?

Daughter: No.

Mother: You know why?

Daughter: Magic arm.

Mother: Yes. Exactly. Your arm has a magic the doll's doesn't. And when the doctor takes out the stitches, your skin will be perfect, all together.

Daughter: Promise?

Mother: Absolutely. We'll do one at a time, and you'll tell the doctor how you think it's going. Okay?

Daughter: Okay.

In the actual situation, it took a single realization and a short, loving conversation to turn everything around. When we take the time to find out what is really happening, it can lead to a discussion that will enlighten and relieve everyone.

Verbal First Aid for Getting Stitches

As several of the stories and scenarios in this book have shown, going to the doctor or hospital can be a source of quite a bit of anxiety, especially if a child's previous experience at such places resulted in great discomfort.

Stitches are particularly scary for a child because they involve the direct manipulation of a part of them that is already wounded. For that reason, Verbal First Aid encourages emotional preparation before the procedure (scenario 1) and gentle distraction (scenario 2) during the procedure to make it all go much more smoothly. For more information on this topic, see Verbal First Aid for Doctor Visits and Surgery (p. 154).

Scenario 1

Three-year-old Natalie slips on a throw rug near the kitchen door and falls against the cabinet, cutting her arm on its edge. Tracy hears the thud but doesn't hear a cry until Natalie gets up and sees the blood on her shirt. Tracy sees the laceration and realizes it is fairly serious. She takes a deep breath and assesses what she needs to do to help her child.

Tracy: I'm right here. I see what happened. That was quite a fall. Let's wash off your arm so that it starts to feel better right away. (Picks up her daughter, carries her to the sink, sets her on the counter in front of her, and gently takes her arm.)

Natalie: (Still crying.) It's bleeding.

Tracy: Okay, Natalie. As I wash this off, you can stop the bleeding then. Want to know how?

Natalie: (Nods *yes*.)

Tracy: Well, it's like a faucet. I'm going to run the water and the special medicine over the boo-boo for a count of three. And then, I'm going to turn the faucet off and put a perfectly clean white towel on your arm. When the faucet shuts off, you can turn off the bleeding. Just like that.

Natalie: Really?

Tracy: Oh, yeah. Watch and see. (Turns on the water and washes the wound.)

Natalie: (Stops crying to count.) One . . . two . . . three. Okay, Mommy, turn it off. Turn it off.

Tracy: It's off. Here's the towel. I'm going to hold it on your arm, and you can help me. Now, you stop the bleeding. Turn it off.

They go to the hospital and on the way, Tracy knows she has to prepare Natalie for the stitches she will probably need.

Tracy: Remember when you threw the pillow and it tore open? And with just a few stitches, Mommy put it back together so that you didn't even see it was ripped?

Natalie: (Nods.)

Tracy: Well, the doctors are even better at sewing than I am, and they're going to make it so that that boo-boo disappears and you're as good as new.

Natalie: Is it going to hurt?

Tracy: If they decide to do it, they have a special way to make your arm feel the way it does when you've been playing in the ice or snow without your mittens too long or the way your arm feels when it falls asleep all numb and tingly.

SCENARIO 2

Playing at his friend Damien's house, ten-year-old Micah tripped over a beanbag chair and hit his forehead on the back of a wooden chair behind it. The result was a gash across his eyebrow.

It would ultimately require twelve stitches.

Damien took one look at the blood and cried out, "It looks bad!"

As a result, until his mother appeared to take him to the emergency room, Micah experienced a lot of fear in not knowing what was happening and what was going to happen. He was even thinking they might not be able to put his head back together again.

As soon as she arrived, his mother realized he would feel much less out of control if she described the steps involved in the procedure so that he could practice it in his mind and be ready for it.

Micah was disconcerted by all the blood that poured from the wound.

Mother: What do you do when something's dirty?

Micah: Wash it.

Mother: Exactly. And that's what your blood is there for, to wash the germs away. It's already starting to take care of the problem.

She told him that they would go to the hospital and that a doctor would stitch the cut for him. Micah knew you sewed clothes, but he couldn't imagine sewing up a person!

It's a good idea to use analogies that interest the child and are appropriate for his age level when describing what will happen. If he likes dinosaurs, tell him a story about a dinosaur who injured himself in a similar way and a pterodactyl who flew back and forth over the cut with a string, sewing it up and how they became good friends.

Micah loves drawing cities and building them. So his mother described the procedure this way:

Mother: There was a breakdown on Eyebrow Street. The construction crews were called in, first, to clean up the mess. They used the blood to hose down the street. Then the engineers were called to lay down new tracks. That's the part your skin is going to do, growing back together the way it was before. An architect was hired to design an attractive new station. Right at the time the breakdown happened, everything was already in motion. But the architect has to be added, to make sure it fits together and stays together perfectly. The body knows how to do the rest of it all by itself. The stitches just help your eyebrow stay exactly in place until your body knits itself back together again.

Verbal First Aid Shortcuts for Cuts, Boo-boos, and Getting Stitches

- "Now that the nice red blood has cleaned the cut, you can stop your bleeding and save your blood."

- "Once the boo-boo is clean, you'll be surprised at how the bleeding stops all by itself."

- "When I count to three, I need you to stop the bleeding. One . . . two . . . three . . . good girl."

- "Be my partner: I need your help. Will you hold the bandage while I clean your boo-boo? As soon as I say I need it, I want you to be ready with it, right on the spot, can you do that?"

- "Your body knows how to heal itself. Remember when you cut yourself and before you knew it . . .'"

- "I'm right here. Hey, that was a great fall. You protected your face. Good job. Dust off your hands and see how you're feeling."

- Describe new procedures, such as stitches, fully, using an age- and interest-appropriate story so the child can internalize what's going to happen and feel prepared.

VERBAL FIRST AID FOR MINOR FALLS, BUMPS, AND BRUISES

Many times, especially with little ones, there are falling-down occasions that aren't critical and don't even require a bandage. They're more "Yikes!" moments, but if parents, either to prove their love and concern or to try to make it better in a hurry, make a fuss about these bumps, the child can misconstrue the seriousness of the occasion and later remember it as more upsetting than it was.

Here are three scenarios using distraction techniques after a minor injury that may help both the emotions and the body recover more completely and quickly.

Scenario 1

Some falls can be relatively harmless. A tricycle tipped over on the lawn, a shoelace malfunction, or a push (accidental or otherwise) by a slightly larger kid generally ends with the child catching himself with his hands. As the hands catch him, the impact sends pain signals to the brain.

If it is apparent that the largest part of the injury is the indignity of it all, and the major physical component is the stinging of the hands, this practical distraction technique can save the moment.

Five-year-old Eleanor was executing a turn on her new three-wheeler when she hit a small pothole and fell off.

Her mother came running up and, checking her out, said, "Oh, you fell off your bike. I'm right here. Let's look at you. Why don't you dust off your hands while I check your knees, ah, like that, and dust off the front of your shirt. Good."

Telling the child to "dust off your hands" changes the feeling in the hands as well as distracts her so that the fear and anger at having fallen translates into a useful busyness. Little pieces of concrete dust, tar, and dirt are moved around and discarded. If you get a small child to do a little clapping and then join in with her to help dust off knees, shirt, and hair, the fall becomes less of a focus. Suddenly, you are partners in returning everything to normal.

Medically, we refer to the *gate theory of pain*, a well-accepted idea that suggests the gate at the posterior horn of the spinal column can block pain when it is overridden by certain low-intensity stimulation (which is why rubbing a wound seems to offer relief). So the focus is on the dusting of the hands, not the stinging.

Of course, saying immediately, "I'm right here," makes the whole exercise seem safer.

And if you help the child see that her reaction was a good one, she can walk away from the scene with some pride:

Mother: "Boy, you did a great job of falling; you caught yourself with your hands and protected your face. Good job. This really worked out fine, don't you think?"

Scenario 2

If a child has bumped into a chair, the wall, or some other inanimate object and has come over to you in tears, it is often amusing as well as distracting to take their side against the offending source of pain.

Mia: Ow!

Mom: What happened?

Mia: The chair . . .

Mom: Which chair?

Mia: (Surprised, she points at the offending piece of furniture.)

Mom: (Going over to the chair and pointing seriously.) Don't you hurt my little girl.

If Mia is the kind of child whose sense of humor resonates to this kind of playacting, she will be thrilled at your coming to her defense, even as she realizes that it might not have been the chair's fault and that the chair might not learn its lesson.

And what this says to children is that, as protector and caring adult, you will do what is necessary to ensure their safety. Mostly, it makes them laugh and rather than a cry or whine, you'll hear something like this:

Mia: And tell it not to do that again!

Scenario 3

It was Liam's eleventh birthday and his four-year-old sister, Daphne, was so thrilled to watch as the candles were blown out and the cake was being cut that she leaned too far forward in her seat and lost her balance. First there was the crash to the floor, which surprised everybody, and then the shriek. Her mother rushed to her, checked her out quickly, picked her up in her arms and said, "I'm right here. It's all right. You got so excited, you fell off the chair and surprised and scared yourself!"

Daphne was momentarily inconsolable as she tried to figure out what had just happened, when her mother added, "You know, the person who falls off the chair gets the second piece, after the birthday boy." While Daphne considered the prospect, seven-year-old Todd deliberately slipped off his perch, claiming the third piece. Everyone laughed, Daphne pointed out what decoration she wanted on her slice of cake, and perspective and humor trumped a slight bruise and embarrassment.

And because the mother helped her daughter recognize the difference in feeling between surprise and shock and real danger, the flow of adrenaline Daphne experienced was dissipated through laughter.

Verbal First Aid Shortcuts for Minor Falls, Bumps, and Bruises

- Acknowledge that the child is safe and that you're there for her. "Oh, you fell off your bike. I'm right here. Let's look at you. Why don't you dust off your hands while I check your knees."

- Distraction can be instantly effective, if you are certain that the child is more frightened or surprised than hurt. Congratulating what a child did *right* in the situation distracts as well as helps her to find her strength. "Great job of falling; you caught yourself with your hands and protected your face."

- If appropriate, use humor or laughter to reframe the situation. You can admonish the offending couch that "hurt" your child, or help him see how funny the fall was, if you can do it without embarrassing or humiliating him.

VERBAL FIRST AID FOR COMMON FEARS, NIGHTMARES, AND BEDWETTING

Fear is generally about the unknown. It is a reflection of a state of mind as much as it is a statement about any given reality. In most ordinary circumstances, children are made fearful by things that are fermented in their imaginations—whether in daytime fantasies or in their nightmares. Therefore the task for us as caretakers and parents is to make the unknown less unknowable and more interesting, thereby giving the child more control and a greater sense of detachment.

In modern culture, our children are surrounded by fearful stimuli—

video games, television shows, radio, and the Internet—some of which we as children never had to learn to manage. National security, safety seats, air bags, helmet laws, Amber Alerts—all the things designed to protect our children are often the very same things that make them more vigilant and frightened. This goes back to the notion of a *not*. When we tell someone not to be afraid, we have already implied that there is something of which they ought to be frightened.

It is very important when we approach a child who is fearful, whether we deem that fear reasonable or not, to remember again certain philosophical basics: Take a deep breath, exhale, center, and find a calm spot in yourself. Let your presence in and of itself be a source of comfort and reassurance.

Approach the child supportively. It never helps to judge a fear. To the person in its grips (whether young or old), fear can be overpowering. It is also, at that moment, the child's reality. So whether it is real isn't the issue as much as your willingness to see the fear through her eyes. From a chemical point of view, when the fear is strong enough, it can literally bypass the executive functions of the brain, making our thinking cloudy and irrational.

Be patient. It takes a while for the physiology of fear to pass. The chemicals initiated by the adrenal glands need a chance to recede and be replaced by more cortical functions in the brain. You know this yourself, as you have to wait a full twenty minutes before you can return to sleep after a nightmare. A good part of Verbal First Aid with children who are afraid is the patient reassurance of your presence and your love.

For us to help our children we have to start with ourselves. We can help them see things differently only when we do. If we are fearful and feel victimized, it might be more of a challenge to convince our children that they have control or can achieve mastery over themselves or the circumstances of their lives. When we approach the moment without expectation or judgment, we communicate this adaptability, this fearlessness, to our children without even having to say anything. The more adaptable we are, the more possibilities we see. The more judgmental and rigid we are, the less we feel we can do in and about the world.

If the emotion is beyond words, if it is a frightening or confusing picture in the child's mind, grab a piece of paper and a crayon and let him draw it. And as he draws it, have him see that thoughts are mutable, that maybe it was a monster but if you put a smile on that monster's face then it might just be seen as a friend, like Shrek. In the Harry Potter books, using the word "Ridiculous!" helps to diffuse the power of a frightening vision. Children are born with limitless creativity and imagination. In fact, it is commonly believed that all infants are born with the capacity to learn any language and make any sound. Our capacities get restricted only over time, when we limit our exposure and our willingness to step out of our comfort zone. Encourage the child's imagination. Having the child draw the dream helps when words fail to convey the pictures in the mind. And through the drawing, the fear can be altered in positive ways. One gains mastery over it. Creativity is almost always the way out of fear.

Verbal First Aid for Fears

Children are new to the world. There is so much they don't understand. They are also by their very natures more imaginative (both in good and bad ways) as well as highly suggestible. Watching television or a scary movie, hearing things they don't understand from older children, learning to get along in complex social situations like school are all things that can produce anxiety in young ones. It is not unreasonable for them to sometimes be afraid.

Beyond the newness of the world, there are many things that do require extra caution when you are small. Nature protects us by equipping us from the start with an early warning system, a set of body signals that alert us to danger when we approach the edge of a cliff or balcony, an autonomic startle response to loud noises, a sense of dislocation or discomfort in the dark, and an aversion to the smell of smoke. Children may be afraid of specific objects (spiders, dogs, elevators) or even intangibles (like the dark). These are normal and natural up to a point.

In fact, the Child Anxiety Network reports that, between the ages of two and fourteen, 90 percent of children will have at least one specific fear.[1] Whether the fear is a phobia (or part of an ongoing panic disorder) or simply a reaction to the beliefs, environment, and experience of the child depends on how intense and out of proportion to the potential danger the reaction is.

The Child Anxiety Network breaks down specific fears by age:

- **Ages 0–2:** Loud noises, strangers, separation from parents, large objects.

- **Ages 3–6:** Imaginary things (ghosts, monsters), the dark, sleeping alone, strange noises.

- **Ages 7–16:** More realistic fears (injury, illness), school performance, death, natural disasters.

If the fear is interfering with the child's ability to focus or to feel safe in general or if you are concerned about the intensity of it, be sure to consult a professional who specializes in this area.

Fear is felt, as we've shown many times in this book, in the body. Children's stomachs, their heart rate, and their breathing rate may change in ways that frighten them further.

The following scenarios are ones that parents commonly face and ones in which Verbal First Aid can be enormously helpful.

Addressing General Fears

Fears can be irrational. If spiders push your buttons, then even though you know that you're a whole lot bigger than a spider and that most spiders are completely harmless, that knowledge may not prevent that awful feeling from arising when you see one. It's really important (if you can manage it) to avoid sharing your fears with your child, because you are the one who explains the world to him, and if you're afraid, your reaction clearly tells him that there's something to be afraid of.

Although Verbal First Aid is useful primarily for the moment of fear, so that it is handled there and then and doesn't become a greater trauma, it can also afford a teaching moment after the initial fear is over.

In the moment of fear, the best approach is to try to remove the fearful object or the child from the scene and tell him, "I'm right here, and you're safe."

Never ridicule a fear. It is as real to him as any of yours, we assure you. In the terrible moment of exposure to something frightening, when the rational part of the mind is hijacked by the emotional part, we are at the mercy of the emotion and simply want rescue. And that is what you want to be able to offer. "I'm right here. You're safe."

Later, when the fearful situation has been defused, you can use the other tools we'll discuss to help shift the child's view of the terrifying object or experience.

Addressing Fears of Creepy-Crawly Things

Remember that kids like to know how you or a grown-up they trust overcame something that they're going through because you are their role models. So a recollected family story has power to influence children. Perhaps you have one like this.

"When Uncle Tony was little, he was afraid of bees, just like you. He didn't like the buzzing. Not at all. It made him feel very scared. Then one Christmas he got a toy airplane and it really flew across the room on a battery, and it was very fancy and special. And it made the very same buzzing sound as those bees he was afraid of! And when he first heard the plane's sound, he really got scared. And then he started to laugh. He really loved that plane. And he realized that the buzzing was only a *sound*. And ever after, whenever he heard a bee, it made him think of the toy plane and remember that great Christmas."

The other main tools for helping children through fears are desensitization and engaging them as part of the solution. *Desensitization* uses repeated, gentle exposures to the feared object so that the child gradually gets used to it, and therefore, the shock and fear decrease. Reading the book or seeing the movie *Charlotte's Web* is one way to endear a spider to a child. Cute spider toys, a funny Halloween spider ring, all make the creatures more approachable in the long run. For slightly older children, *Bee Movie* might do the same for a fear of bees.

You could use desensitization to have your child draw a spider, then look at pictures of friendly spiders in books. You could have her watch videos, see the bug from a safe distance (perhaps in a glass case), and finally, when she's ready, up close.

Making children your partner in finding a solution not only involves them in rational thinking in the present but ultimately shows them how they can feel less powerless in the face of this threat.

You: You know, when I was your age, I was afraid of spiders, too. And then one day Grandma asked me, "What would you say to the spider if you could talk to him?"

Quinn: What did you say?

You: (Pausing) What would *you* say?

Quinn: Go away, don't bother me. I hate you.

You: What do you think the spider would say?

Quinn: I hate you, too.

You: Why would he hate you?

Quinn: Because I want to step on him.

You: Why do you want to step on him?

Quinn: So he won't bite me.

You: Why would he bite you?

Quinn: Because I want to step on him.

You: Oh, so if you didn't want to step on him, he wouldn't bite you?

Quinn: I don't know.

You: Maybe not?

Quinn: Maybe not.

You: So, if you could say to him, "I'm not going to hurt you," what do you think he'd say to you?

Children have wonderful imaginations. When they *anthropomorphize* (give human characteristics to) an animal or object or imagine what it would be to live life from the point of view of another creature, they increase their capacity for empathy while they decrease fear of that which is different from them.

In his book *The Spiritual Life of Children*, Pulitzer Prize–winning child psychiatrist and Harvard professor Robert Coles reports these thoughts of a ten-year-old boy: "My kid brother was throwing rocks the other day, and I told him, 'Look at it from the rocks' view—they don't like being thrown around and around for no reason!'...When we take a walk, my little sister asks if the trees notice us, like we do them."[2]

These kinds of acts of imagination generally cease as we become less fanciful and more practical, but with Verbal First Aid we can use them with children to promote healing.

Remember that your attitude is important. If you're afraid, have someone who has a more calming attitude take the child through this process. But if your heart goes out to other creatures, you can share that reverence and teach your child compassion and connectedness.

This isn't to say that you shouldn't weave in admonitions and cautions about animals that can bite or be poisonous. Let the children know that they are very big to the bug and that the bug is afraid of them, as if they were a giant. And if they get too close, the bug will try to protect itself by biting. So they should keep a safe distance, and respect the bug's fears as well as their own.

You could also point out some of the beautiful things about spiders—the webs, for example, sparkling with dew in the sunlight and catching flies for us. Tell your children about bees, about the honey and the honeycombs. And let them know that without bees, we wouldn't have fruits or vegetables! As for snakes, check out their beautiful patterns.

Appreciation and empathy might also become gifts of a lifetime. What would it feel like to move across the floor using only your body wiggling back and forth? What would it feel like to kiss a flower and have it turn into an apple or a plum? Mmm, it makes you wonder.

Addressing Fears When a Parent Goes on a Business Trip or is Temporarily Away

It's not unusual these days for one parent or the other to have to leave on business trips or even to move out of the house. This can be a fear-filled time for the child, who feels unable to control what goes on around her. She may experience the fear of abandonment and miss the support of the absent parent, and she likely feels sad and angry that things aren't the way they always were.

If the child cries when Daddy or Mommy leaves but is not exhibiting other serious behavior issues, such as biting or sleep disorders, then her crying is a reasonable response to this disruption of her routine and security. It is really important that, while she can't control her life at all because she is at the mercy of whatever the grown-ups decide in every moment, she at least knows what to expect. Thus before the parent (statistically most often the father, so that's what we'll use in these examples) leaves on the trip or moves to a separate home, you can use future pacing to offer predictability when everything seems chaotic.

You can remind the child of other times that Daddy went away and came back. When he returns or visits, you can tell the child that he's coming, that she'll go to the playground with him, that they'll have dinner—as fully as you can, describe the process. If he has to leave again, that's part of the scenario. If you tell that story over and over, the child will feel like that's the script, and she can make it work for her. Then she can practice that in her mind. Daddy's going away, then he's coming home, we're going to the park . . . and he has to go back to work. In this way, you help her to know what happens next and what to expect. And before the father leaves, remind the child of the story. *And then he has to go, and he'll be back another time.*

It's mental rehearsal for emotional issues and works in the same way as mental rehearsal for unexpected emergencies, which we will discuss throughout and more fully in Chapter 8.

What the parent is doing when he's not with the child is also a mystery. So together with the child you might create a book about Daddy's week without her. For example, how he gets up in the morning, travels far away, works, calls her at a specified time in the day or week, and how all the week he misses her and thinks about his little girl. And then comes back to see her. She can understand it if it's a routine. Having a picture of him in the book or beside her bed might make her happier. And she can read her book to herself over and over and internalize that he goes and is coming back. Make the routine as predictable as possible.

One newly divorced mother of several children noticed that they were upset about the back and forth between two homes and were feeling afraid or worried about where they were going to end up and when. She sat down with them and had them make a book that showed what Daddy was doing when he was away, and what Mommy was doing while they were visiting Daddy. They made pictures of what they liked to do at each of the houses, and pictures of what they like to take from one house to another, giving them a sense of control. The more ritualized the schedules, and the more they see the pattern, the safer and more in control children will feel.

Of course, you'd never use the child as a negotiating pawn or inflict negative feelings about these circumstances on her. You'll want to let her know that the absent parent is not leaving *her*, only that he has to go. That his leaving is not her fault might seem obvious to you, but often it needs to be said.

Pacing with children is a good first step, but sometimes they just aren't able to say what they feel. Putting their thoughts into words can in those instances really help. "I think you're so sad that Daddy has to leave." Give him time to react or think about it. "It is sad," you confirm. "Daddy's sad, too." Or even, "Maybe you're feeling angry at Mommy, or angry at Daddy that he has to leave."

Recognize the boy's feelings and let him know that it's all right to feel the way he does. "I'm sad, too, that Daddy can't stay. But he can't. But he'll be back again, because he wants to be with you." "It's okay to be scared that he's leaving and that you can't go with him. It's okay to feel angry or sad."

Give your child a lot of reassurance that he is heard and understood, even though he can't have his way. "Daddy doesn't want to have to leave you. And I'll be right here with you." Make him feel safe in your love and understanding at this trying time.

It's hard to explain to younger children that their father will be back in a week, of course. But if there's a pattern, they can begin to understand that. When you add a three-dimensional example, it can sometimes make the concept of time easier to grasp, as in the following scenario.

Scenario 1

Four-year-old Alana wakes up and, instead of having Daddy get her juice, Mommy brings it. This is not part of the routine.

Alana: Where's Daddy?

Mom: Remember, he told you last night and you read the book. He had to go on a trip, but he'll come back.

Alana: I miss Daddy.

Mom: (Pacing with her.) I know. He usually brings you the juice and tickles you. Do you want me to tickle you?

Alana: No. I want Daddy to tickle me.

Mom: Daddy will be back in three days. Can you show me three with your fingers?

Alana: This is three. (Holds up fingers.) I want Daddy here.

Mom: Me, too.

Alana: Where is he? It makes me feel scared that he's not here.

Mom: I'm right here with you. He wanted to be here too, but he had to go on a trip, and he'll be back soon.

Alana: (Snuffles.)

Mom: Remember when we went to Grandma Bea's and we had to take a long trip?

Alana: In the car. And I threw up.

Mom: Yes! It was a long trip. Well, Daddy has to go on a long trip like that. But he'll be fine. He won't throw up.

Alana: (Smiles at the thought of her grown-up dad acting like her.)

Mom: And do you remember that we came back from that trip? And here we are?

Alana: Yes.

Mom: Well, Daddy will be back in three days. I have an idea. Let's draw three pictures of Daddy and put them on the wall. And when you wake up in the morning, you can take one picture down and hug it. And when you wake up the next morning, you can take the next picture down and hug it. And when you wake up the next morning, you can take the last picture down and hug it ... and that day you can hug the real Daddy when it's dinnertime.

Addressing Fears of Elevators, Heights, or Falling

Unfortunately, many of us have a built-in fear of unnatural heights and the incredible machines that take us there, such as trams, planes, and elevators. Many of those stimuli can be avoided, but elevators (or escalators) are so much a part of modern life, that a child who is scared of them will be spending a great deal of time in fear and making his parents' or caretakers' lives quite difficult.

Much of what makes us afraid of heights (or falling) is the fear of loss of control. We are afraid of what we don't know, what we can't predict or understand, and what we can't control. Therefore, what helps children (or adults) become more comfortable and less anxiety ridden is giving them a sense of mastery and self-assurance by redirecting them to resources and information they already have but might have forgotten about. Milton Erickson used to call these *prior learnings*, and a great deal of the beautiful work he did with his patients involved reminding them of the valuable skills they had all along. With children, totems or transferential objects (objects that remind them of the skills they need or have) can be particularly helpful, as you'll see in the following scenario.

Scenario 1

Six-year-old Jackie and her mother are getting ready to go to her grandmother's home, which is in an urban high-rise. Here, Jackie's mother reminds her daughter of prior learnings as she simultaneously helps the girl better understand what she's afraid of.

Mom: Jackie, it's time to go. Put on your shoes.

Jackie: I don't want to go. (Sits on bed and kicks her shoes across the floor, hugging her teddy bear.)

Mom: What is it, honey? You love Grandma. (Sits beside her.)

Jackie: (Nods; tears start to flow.) Elevator.

Mom: The elevator? What about the elevator?

Jackie: It goes high up.

Mom: It does.

Jackie: And last time it bumped.

Mom: (Sits back, remembering how it had started and stopped with jerks that had scared Jackie and made her feel as if she were falling.) I remember, it was a little scary.

Jackie: (Nods and clings to her teddy bear more tightly.)

Mom: Well, it looks like your teddy bear helps you feel better. As you hold it, I can tell you a story about a time when you were scared—and it was a while back so I don't know if you remember.

Jackie: (Gives mom full attention.)

Mom: You were very little and you had a nightmare. It must've been a really bad one because you screamed so loud that Daddy and I thought we were having a nightmare, too, and we bumped just like the elevator.

Jackie: I did that?

Mom: Yes, you did. And after we bumped, we jumped and ran into your room. And there you were in the middle of the floor. And you were so scared because in your dream you bumped, too. And, you know, you were very little then and your bed seemed a lot higher and bigger than it does now. So when you fell out of it, it was a long way down.

Jackie: I fell out of bed?

Mom: Uh-huh . . .

Jackie: (Starts to giggle a little.)

Mom: But things change, especially the way we see things, Jackie. Like your bed and being bumped. It doesn't feel very high or very scary now. It's your bed. And you love your bed. But then . . . you were very little. Boy, did you cry. And I don't know if you remember it with your mind or just with your body, but I got your teddy bear and gave it to you and you held it just like that while Daddy and I sat on the floor with you until you felt better, and we picked you up and put you and your teddy bear in bed. And you told your teddy bear that it was going to be all right because you were there. When we went in to check on you in the morning, you were still holding your teddy bear, just like you are now. It made you feel so much better, holding that teddy bear. Even with bumps.

Jackie: (Considers her teddy bear.)

Mom: And every night we tucked you in with your teddy bear and it made you feel very safe. Remember?

Jackie: I remember!!!

Mom: Would you like to bring your teddy bear with you?

Jackie: Yeah.

Mom: I think your teddy bear would like that. I have a feeling he's going to be very excited about taking a ride to see Grandma. And it may be exciting for you to get out of the elevator on Grandma's floor and show her your teddy bear and give her a hug.

The totem made Jackie feel safer, as you can see, but it also allowed her to be brave for her teddy bear, and when she shared the experience with him and reassured him, she was really reassuring herself.

Verbal First Aid for Monsters and Nightmares

Addressing Monsters

Imagination can be a wonderful thing and is the perfect tool for Verbal First Aid, but there isn't a person alive today in the real world who hasn't been frightened by some figment of his or her imagination. Although as adults we know the difference between figments and facts, being scared is a fact shared by all. And so we don't deny the feeling, but pace with the child and lead her to a sense of safety.

Scenario 1

Jim and Gina are sleeping when they are startled out of bed by a wail from their son, Jacob. It is a bloodcurdling shriek, and they both fling the covers off and hurl themselves down the hall and into their son's room.

Jacob: Mommy!!!!!!

Jim and Gina: (Both frightened but, remembering to take a breath before they fly through their son's door, they open the door on high alert but less frantic.)

Gina: Sweetheart. Mommy's right here. (Sits down on the bed with her son.)

Jim: We're both here, Jacob. What happened?

Jacob: (Lips trembling, tears rolling down his cheeks, curls himself into a ball on his mother's lap.)

Gina: Something scared you.

Jacob: In there! (Points to the closet.)

Jim: In the closet. Something from the closet scared you. It must have been something very unusual. Tell us what you think it was.

Jacob: It was big. I don't know.

Gina: How curious. It was big. And it fit into that small closet with all your stuff in there?

Jim: How curious. What could it be?

Jacob: I dunno.

Gina: Maybe a coat?

Jacob: Uh-uh. (Shakes head no.)

Gina: What do you think, Jim?

Jim: Can't say I can imagine what it might be. Jacob, you think you can show me? We can take a special flashlight and turn on all the lights in the room and even bring your blanket with you to protect you. Would you help me get rid of that big ol' thing that scared you?

Jacob: Okay. (Pulls on the blanket and Gina wraps it around his head and shoulders like a cloak.)

Gina: You look like a superhero or King Arthur, Jake. You're gonna scare that big ol' thing right outta here so fast we might not even get to see him go.

Jim: Ready, Spider-Man?

Jacob: I want the flashlight.

Jim: (Picks up the flashlight.) Here ya go. You're gonna help me find it, right?

Jacob: Uh-huh. (Starting to feel a little braver.)

Jim: (Holds the knob of the closet door.) Okay, big ol' thing in there, we got our flashlight and Jacob's got his cape on. You better watch out.

Jacob: Yeah. Watch out.

Jim: (Opens door wide and turns on all the lights. As expected, nothing is there but clothes and shoes.) Oh, wow! Gina, it's gone. You did it, Jake!

Jacob: He's gone! (Turns around to his mother, now proud rather than afraid.)

Scenario 2

At the breakfast table, four-year-old Max is eating his cereal.

Max: Mommy. Something happened in my room last night.

Mommy: Really? What happened?

Max: There was a monster.

Mommy: Ooooh. Was it a scary monster or a funny monster?

Max: Scary.

Mommy: Mmmm. What can you say to a monster that would make it go away?

Max: I don't know.

Mommy: Can you say, "Go away, Monster!"

Max: (Quietly.) Go away, Monster.

Mommy: Can you say it louder?

Max: Go away, Monster.

Mommy: Even louder?

Max: GO AWAY, MONSTER.

Mommy: Whew, if I were a monster, I'd leave when I heard that! Say it again.

Max: (Feeling braver.) GO AWAY, MONSTER!

Mommy: Yeah. Point your finger out of the room and say it again.

Max: (Pointing.) GO AWAY, MONSTER!

Mommy: I think that'll do it.

Practicing really helps give the child a sense of his own power, and a tool he can use. And he may experience less anxiety if the dream ever returns.

Addressing Nightmares

Little children often fluctuate between a form of consciousness and dream states in their everyday life. So it becomes a challenge to explain to them what a dream is. To them it can seem very like the rest of their experience.

It's been estimated that one out of every four children has nightmares more than once a week. When we examine the fear behind a nightmare, we see that it provides us very graphic clues about what disturbs or preoccupies our children's minds, even when they can't express it in words. And when we help them overcome their fears of the imaginary, we help them prepare for overcoming fears and finding solutions in their everyday life.

The following scenario really happened to a three-and-a-half-year-old boy, who lived in New York City. His mother helped him problem solve, so that deep in the middle of the night, if he felt helpless, he could imagine how he could deal with such a situation in his waking life.

SCENARIO 1

Evan wakes up having had a nightmare, crying to his mother that he was lost.

Joann: Oh, you had a nightmare. Come and sit with me. So, you were lost. Did you know where you were?

Evan: No.

Joann: Did you know where I was?

Evan: No.

Joann: Ooooh, scary huh?

Evan: (Lip quivering, sobs, nods.)

Joann: Evan, do you know your address, where you live?

Evan: (Automatically.) 123 Central Park West.

Joann: And where you were, were there taxis?

Evan: (Puzzled. He hadn't thought about that. Shrugs.) Sure.

Joann: Okay, so whenever you're lost, you can just get into a taxi and tell him your address, and he'll take you right back home to me.

Evan: (Thinks about it for a minute. It seems to resolve it but not really.). But the Grinch!

Joann: Oh, the Grinch. Was he chasing you?

Evan: (Nods.)

Joann: Well, that's a good reason to take a taxi. Grinches don't take taxis. Did you ever see a Grinch in a taxi?

Evan: (Thinks about it and starts to laugh at the image; cuddles in his mother's lap.)

Although this may not solve the problem in the real world, it gives Evan solace and a sense of having been taken seriously. And, in that moment, he sees that there are ways in which he can feel safe, even in an uncertain world of ugly green cartoon monsters.

Scenario 2

Kayla stands at the side of her parents' bed, sobbing quietly and waiting for them to wake up and notice her.

Mommy: Kayla? What's wrong, honey? Can't you sleep?

Kayla: Too many people.

Mommy: Oh, you had a dream.

Kayla: Where's Mommy?

Mommy: You dreamed that you were lost and couldn't find me?

Kayla: (Nods.)

Mommy: (Opens the covers and signals for Kayla to come in and cuddle.) Well, I'm right here. That was a dream.

Kayla: Mommy.

Mommy: Hmmm. Yes. That was scary to be without Mommy, wasn't it.

Kayla: (Nods.)

Mommy: But when you opened your eyes, you were in your

bedroom, right next door to mine, and I was right here. Isn't that interesting?

Kayla: (Nods slowly.)

Mommy: Dreams are funny things. Sometimes in the daytime we use our imagination to pretend we're somewhere else. Like when we pretend you're a princess, and you're dancing in the forest. Right? And sometimes at night, our imagination takes us somewhere else all by itself.

Kayla: I don't like it.

Mommy: Yeah. But you know what we can do? We can take that worry about getting lost and put it away for the night. Just like you put your dolls away for the night. We can put that worry away in a backpack and let it sit outside by the old tree and spend the night out there.

Kayla: Yeah. Out there.

Mommy: We can take all the worries and put them in the knapsack, and then, when it's morning and you can see that I'm right here, you can open the bag . . . and the worry won't be a worry anymore.

Kayla: But at night . . .

Mommy: Right. We put the worries away for the night. And we read a nice book we like, so our imagination has something we like to think about and play with overnight. Would you like to do that?

Kayla: Okay.

Mommy: So, would you like to imagine what your worry sack looks like?

Kayla: Okay.

Mommy: What color is it?

Kayla: Pink.

Mommy: What decorations does it have on it?

Kayla: Ballerina.

Mommy: Like on your birthday cake?

Kayla: Yes.

Mommy: Beautiful. It looks like it will really do the job. Now, use your imagination to think about what worries you want to put in there.

Kayla: Lost.

Mommy: Yes, of course. Because I'm right here. So, into the sack, *Lost*, outside for you tonight!

Kayla: Yeah. (Snuggling down and feeling a little mastery over some of her fears.)

Mommy: And imagine it out by the tree, waiting for you until morning when it won't be a worry anymore.

Kayla: (Touches Mommy's arm to be sure she's there.) Mommy.

Mommy: Yes. (Kisses Kayla's forehead as she snuggles down to sleep.)

SCENARIO 3

Six-year-old Ryan is afraid to go to sleep because he expects bad dreams. His mother, Lisa, gets into bed with him as he's winding down from the day.

Lisa: Ryan, do you remember a good dream you had that you really liked? Like the one about when you and Poppie baked all those chocolate-chip cookies.

Ryan: Yeah. That was a funny dream. We ate most of them!

Lisa: It would be fun to have another dream like that.

Ryan: Yeah.

Lisa: What else would you like to dream about?

Ryan: I don't know.

Lisa: How about our summer vacation by the lake.

Ryan: I loved that time.

Lisa: I'm thinking I'd like to dream about that, too, so let's see what we remember about it. Do you remember the campfires and cooking the s'mores?

Ryan: And jumping off Daddy's back into the water.

Lisa: And making tunnels in the sand.

Ryan: Yeah, remember the one I made that was about ten miles long?

Lisa: Yeah, I do. Who else is there?

Ryan: Zeke and Amina and . . .

Lisa: Yeah. Let's try to dream about that.

As they add the details, Ryan becomes more and more relaxed. When Lisa says she'd like to dream about the same thing, she's giving her son a sense of how we direct our own thoughts.

Verbal First Aid for Bedwetting

Bedwetting is a difficult issue because it happens when the child has the least conscious control over his behavior and body and therefore feels the most powerless. It is embarrassing among peers, it is trying for the parents, and it makes the child feel like a failure. Anticipation of awakening in a pool again can also undermine a most important activity, sleep, when we should be regaining our strength, recentering ourselves after a busy day, and restoring ourselves for a new day.

According to the American Academy of Child and Adolescent Psychiatry:

- Approximately 15 percent of children wet the bed after the age of three.

- Many more boys than girls wet their beds.

- Bedwetting runs in families.

- Usually bedwetting stops by puberty.

- Most bedwetters do not have emotional problems.[3]

The academy reports that smaller, later-developing bladders are often the problem. Bedwetting may also be the result of childhood stresses, such as parents' divorce, a death in the family, the arrival of a new baby, a move, stressful toilet training, and perhaps emotions or fears that require attention.

The obvious steps a parent can take to help the child include having the child empty the bladder before bed, limiting liquids after dinner, taking the child to the bathroom during the night, disturbing sleep as little as possible, avoiding embarrassing or criticizing the child, and praising successful attempts to stay dry overnight.

While recognizing that this problem is unique to each individual child and being aware that a general approach cannot take into consideration what unconscious forces may be at play, we offer this Verbal First Aid guided imagery script because it has proven effective for some children. Remember that a child paces his parents and your belief in this approach may greatly influence its success.

SCENARIO 1

Chris: I'm going to try not to wet my bed tonight.

Dad: Did you know that Dora the Explorer's friend Diego had that problem when he was just a little younger than you? [Use whatever character the child will relate to.]

Chris: Diego?

Dad: Yes. Diego needed to learn how to wake himself up at night when he had to go to the bathroom, just like you.

Chris: I like Diego.

Dad: Me too. Close your eyes now [younger children do not need to close their eyes] and let yourself watch Diego coming toward you, smiling. He sits next to you on the bed and tells you how he solved the problem for himself. Can you see him on a TV in your mind? Watch him as he wakes up in the middle of the night to go to the bathroom. Do you see that?

Chris: Yes!

Dad: Watch yourself on TV now with Diego. In the next program, Diego is tapping you on the shoulder so you can go to the bathroom, too. Just like Diego. Can you see that? Can you feel how it feels to have Diego tap you on the shoulder and go with you to the bathroom?

Chris: Just like Diego.

Dad: Ask Diego to come to you in your sleep and tap you on the shoulder to go with him to the bathroom. Will he do that?

Chris: Yes . . .

Dad: Can you feel how happy you will feel in the morning waking up dry?

Chris: Yes.

Dad: So as you go to sleep, invite Diego to visit you overnight and tap you on the shoulder to wake up and go to the bathroom. And in the morning you can be so happy that your friend helped you stay dry.

Chris: Okay.

Allow the child to feel a positive feeling about this, not a worry or a feeling of needing to accomplish anything. Allow him simply to experience how pleasant it is to have his friend, Diego, or any other character he chooses, wake him up when needed. Let him relax into it, in a way that may relieve the stress that causes some of the problem.

Repeat this visualization as often as necessary and let his unconscious mind get the message and do the rest.

Verbal First Aid Shortcuts for Fears

- Reassure: "I'm right here with you."

- When the fear goes beyond words, have the child draw it. Drawing can offer mastery over fear.

- Simple fears (e.g., elevators): Give children a sense of control, help them remember prior learnings, and use totems to transfer a sense of safety.

- Fears of objects or animals: Desensitize by gentle exposures to friendly representatives of the species, and allow children to use the gift of their empathy by identifying with or understanding the feelings of the feared object.

- When Mommy or Daddy have to be away: Future pace, draw pictures, and make stories about what they're doing and what will happen when they come back. Use mental rehearsal to give the child a sense of continuity, security, and predictability.

Verbal First Aid Shortcuts for Monsters and Nightmares

- Problem solve: Come up with ways to send the monster away.

- Teach children to direct their thoughts: "Sometimes we use our imagination and make believe, pretending something is here that really isn't. And sometimes at night our imagination makes believe by itself. And if you don't like what your imagination is pretending, you just have to say to your Imagination, "Stop It now, I've had enough.'"

- At bedtime: "What would you like to dream about?"

- Use the worry backpack technique, and say: "You can put all your worries in it or against it and leave them for the night."

- Suggest changing the ending of a dream: "And what if, instead of that, you . . ."

- Don't deny the feeling: The nightmare was real to the child as it was happening: "Oh, that sounds scary."

Verbal First Aid Shortcuts for Bedwetting

- Keep drinks to a minimum, empty the bladder, engage a role model to help during the night, and don't put pressure on the child to perform. Suggest an imaginary friend/role model to remind her to awaken when it's time to go to the bathroom.

- Use a role model: "What would Dora the Explorer do?"

6 Verbal First Aid for Doctor Visits and Surgery

Parental expectations expressed in words and body language affect outcome for all children in therapeutic environments.

—DAVID SPRINGER, MD, ASSOCIATE PROFESSOR OF
PEDIATRICS, UNIVERSITY OF WASHINGTON

Hey, Mom and Dad, let's go to the doctor! Time for a checkup. It's time for a round of vaccines. How does that little outing sound to you? Ask yourself: Do I enjoy getting injections, having blood taken, being examined even with kind hands, and being poked and prodded where it already hurts? We bet we can guess your answer.

Though we sound like we're joking, this is not a lighthearted question because, as you now know, what you think translates to how you feel. Furthermore, your attitude and perspective often translates from you to your little one, sometimes even from before birth. Your feelings (positive or negative) will be unconsciously internalized by your child. Even if you don't express them yourself—even if you're not consciously aware of them—your feelings will communicate directly to your child and have an effect. So, the issue is not *whether* we have an effect on how our child responds to the doctor but *what kind* of an effect we want to have.

In a conversation, early development specialist Marcy Axness, PhD, provided a number of examples that demonstrate just how much *your* inner clarity affects your child's behavior. She talked about an assertive three-year-old who wouldn't put on a pair of socks she thought was ugly but wanted the other ones until you tried putting *them* on.

You might have daily arguments about every little thing as she asserts her independence, but you likely don't have many significant arguments about seat belts, Axness suggests, because in your own mind that is nonnegotiable. You won't budge. You know you won't drive the car without the child's being buckled up; therefore, the child unconsciously reads that and knows it's simply not a fruitful issue about which to make a scene. Your consciousness, your own subliminal sense of a situation, and your thought patterns are communicated at a level way beyond words.

PARENTS' ATTITUDES ARE CONTAGIOUS

The first thing that parents of young children should realize about doctor visits is that the doctor is meeting with at least two patients per visit: you and your child. This is because, as we've said, your mood, your expectations, your fears, and your energy have a significant impact on how your child responds to the doctor and nurses around him in addition to the feelings and fears that come naturally to the child.

The first step as a parent, then, is to explore and be honest with yourself about your own attitude toward doctor visits. While no one rationally equates a doctor visit with a day at the circus, when a parent approaches a doctor visit with equanimity the child can see the visit as nonthreatening. So, ask yourself:

- How do I feel as I step foot into the doctor's office?

- How do I feel about my child's being there?

- How are those feelings manifesting or communicating themselves to my child?

Pausing to ask yourself these questions doesn't mean that you shouldn't be concerned if your child is visiting the doctor for health issues. But it's important to watch yourself and be sensible when communicating your concern, as you don't want to alarm your child or feed her any negative thoughts. How you communicate your concern and love is the variable and can make the difference between an easy office visit and one that leaves everyone stressed and exhausted.

This is the centering part of using Verbal First Aid for doctor visits. It's likely that you have had a difficult doctor's visit of your own that you can still remember to this day. Maybe a frightening diagnosis or maybe the grim and lasting discomfort of a series of tetanus shots. Run that through your brain and see if that's true for you.

Now think back to a time when a doctor or nurse comforted you when you needed it the most, put his hand on your shoulder and said, "You're fine. It's nothing to worry about." Allow yourself to remember how your doctor provided some relief or at least the relief of understanding what the problem was and had useful ideas about what to do about it.

Just as children come to us for answers, so we go to doctors for answers. And how we choose to view doctors is important for two reasons. First, a positive view of a visit to the doctor helps us better move in the direction of our own inner healing through the Placebo Effect. Next, when we hold the picture in our minds of a doctor who has the answers we need, we offer our children a similar hope. We teach our kids that things turn out better when we are confident and positive than they would have if we had been fearful and expected the worst.

To lead your child to wellness, your mind has to know the way. To that end, your exercise is to picture the best doctor visit you ever had. Or if none comes to mind, picture one from a TV show featuring your favorite fictional practitioner. Imagine the best rapport, the sincerest support, the kindness, the sense of safety. In your imagination make it a place of comfort and solutions.

This is not because we believe that modern medicine is perfect; not at all. But because, again, science has shown that healing has a great deal to do with what one is thinking. And when you eliminate fears (some that may go back to your own childhood) you are supporting your child in having an experience that allows her to come up with her own way of dealing with medical issues, an opportunity to feel brave, and a chance to explore what she needs to do to solve a problem. If she anticipates that going to the doctor is a frightening thing that turns her over to pain and powerlessness, then that is how she experiences it. If she thinks going to the doctor will lead to her feeling better, her whole being can participate in that.

The second step of this exercise requires you to consider how you would feel if someone said to you at the very last minute, "Oh, I'm taking you to see the doctor today." It would be thoroughly natural for you to want to know *why* you're being taken and what the doctor might do to you when you get there. A child with far less experience of the world will likely have even more questions and anxieties. So take the time to prepare your child and answer her questions because it will have a significant effect on how the visit goes.

Dr. Chuck Dumont, associate professor of pediatrics at Loyola University Medical Center, has observed that parental negativity passes down to children the way electricity shoots along ground wires. He often relates a story when teaching hypnosis and mindful speaking techniques to doctors and healthcare workers. It is the story of a young patient who is in the hospital for intestinal issues and has been having problems with vomiting. After treating the child, the doctor becomes certain that the child is improving. Realizing that as a doctor he has authority and that his belief in the child could increase the likelihood of a good result, he encourages the child, saying, "I wouldn't be surprised that you are ready to eat a little something and feel just fine."

Unfortunately, at just that point the mother rushes to bring a basin closer to the patient, "just in case." And, Dumont says, "her lack of belief in the child's recovery torpedoes the effect." She is an even more powerful authority figure, and in this case she wins and everyone loses.

In an e-mail, Dr. Francesca de Picciotto told us the story of two children who had diabetes. In one case, while she explained her findings to the family, she mentioned the word diabetes. "At that point the child's mother fainted. The young girl, who had been calm up until then, began to shake and cry. She was inconsolable. Her mother, through the very powerful action of fainting, had essentially given her the message that this was terrible news, news that was too overwhelming to handle.

"Several months later, another mother, upon hearing the same diagnosis of her ten-year-old daughter, assumed a *take charge, we can definitely handle this* attitude. She remained calm and rational. Her daughter stayed noticeably relaxed throughout the discussion and left calm, feeling secure that mom would be able to take care of her. And that allayed the child's fears."

Dr. Ruby Roy, chronic disease pediatrician at the University of Chicago, says that parents need to understand that *their* fears and concerns about the doctor visit or surgery are often not the same as their *child's* fears. While the child may fear an injection, the parent may fear a dreadful diagnosis. The goal is to tune in to what the child is feeling and to support the child. This is also another reason why it is so important to stay aware of our own feelings as adults/authorities. What we fear may have little relevance to what the child fears.

She added in an e-mail, "Sometimes other children or adults communicate a fear of doctors that can be quite contagious. Many pediatricians report a 'sinking feeling' when they enter a room and have a parent chastise their child for 'misbehavior' (which is usually really only an active child having difficulty waiting patiently in a small room) and tell their child 'you'd better behave in front of the doctor or you will get a shot!' A vaccination or a medical procedure is presented as a punishment rather than as a procedure to keep the child healthy. How different it might be, instead, to talk about what vaccinations are for, when the parent or their pet last got a 'shot' and to remind the child that *all* people get vaccinations to stay healthy." So once you've got a more relaxed and healthy attitude, you're ready to help your child through all sorts of medical circumstances, ordinary and extraordinary.

Dr. Ruby Roy's Tips for Parents Who Are Bringing Their Child in for a Checkup or Visit with the Doctor

- Do not be embarrassed by your child's reactions (his fear is not a reflection of your competence as a parent).

- Do not expect your child to perform.

- It is scary enough to be prodded and tested, especially when you do not really understand what is happening. Parents must understand that their children count on them for emotional support.

Be honest about your own fears. The more awareness you have, the less you will displace any negative feelings onto your child. If you think your fears may be getting in your way or your child's way it might be a good idea to talk with a professional at some length about it.

APPLYING VERBAL FIRST AID TECHNIQUES BEFORE DOCTOR/HOSPITAL VISITS

At this point, you've become more adept at using the Verbal First Aid techniques, but we'll examine them here in the perspective of dental/doctor/hospital visits so that you can see how naturally they may flow from your lips and even your heart.

Preparing a Child for a First Dental Visit

Here are a few tips for making it easier for your child to see the dentist for the first time. The first thing to do is to eliminate unnecessary surprises. If you can schedule a visit to look at the office and meet the nurse or hygienist and dentist before the visit, your child will feel much more comfortable when you come in for the appointment. Also find out what is involved in the initial exam so that you can prepare the child. Here's a brief script for general use.

Let's count your fingers. One, two . . . Let's wash your fingers. That's good. Let's count your teeth. One, two . . . Let's brush your teeth. Good. Let's look at my teeth. Can you count them? (Adult opens mouth, uses flashlight. It's fun.) Let's look at yours. When we visit the dentist, tomorrow, she will look at your teeth and count them, just like we did.

Preparing Your Child for a Routine Checkup

By the time a child is three years old, you can start helping him through the process by teaching him about cause and effect. Leading a child through cause and effect is a series of *If you/then you* concepts. So, we might say, "If you're sick, then you go to the doctor. Why? To help you be healthy." "If you're healthy you go to the doctor for a checkup, to stay healthy and keep you feeling good." In describing cause and effect at this age, we always want to make sure that we lead children in terms of positive scenarios: Why do we go to the dentist? We go to the dentist to keep our teeth clean and healthy so we can chew and eat the foods we love. You can describe other scenarios that involve cause and effect.

When we don't know what to expect, we tend to expect the worst. So, it's a good idea to call the doctor's office and ask a receptionist or nurse exactly what the next checkup will entail. Will there be a dreaded vaccination? A scary blood test? A look at the ears and eyes, a tap on the knee?

When you have a good understanding of what's coming, you can better prepare your child to find it all natural and acceptable.

Be careful about discussing embarrassing things in front of the child, such as bedwetting or things kids are teased about. If you can let the doctor know about the problem before the visit, her suggestions can seem spontaneous and be couched in words that support the child rather than shame him.

When getting your child ready for the appointment, you may want to use what is called the *truism* technique, which we will explain later in greater detail. As we've said, there's something about facts that seem inevitable, especially to children. To say "it's the rule" is to explain why something has to be done a certain way. And if it's on the calendar, well, there it is on the calendar. Just as birthdays and the first day of school and Grandma's visits are written down and approached, day by day until it's *that* day, so a doctor's visit can be noted, and—even if you prefer not to give it a long running start—pointed to at the appropriate time. "Today's the day we have a visit to the doctor. See?"

And you'll have an easier time of it, especially if he's had a bad experience in the past, by using some of the following techniques.

We've embellished Dr. Roy's list of how to make for an easy doctor visit with Verbal First Aid techniques:

- Translate what the doctor or technician says for your child (your child is under stress and may not fully process verbal commands from a stranger—repeat in words your child is familiar with).

- Model and practice breathing and appropriate body position (if your child is told "hold your left arm out straight" demonstrate for him).

- Prepare for the procedure, ask questions of the healthcare provider, and then help your child understand what to expect.

- Model on a stuffed animal or doll.

- Have the child pick out a toy or distraction.

- Focus on the parts the child can control—emotions, reactions, and thoughts.

Mental Rehearsal for Medical Procedures

Storytelling is as old as pictures on the cave wall, and that practice has lasted so long because it is so effective. You can get as elaborate as creating a book together with your child to discuss and imagine what will happen. Or as simple as pretending it all happens to Teddy the bear.

> "And then the doctor takes his temperature ..."
> "What does Teddy feel?" you ask your child.

And the story grows at a safe distance and yet builds familiarity with the procedures and offers reassurance that it all works out well. The more the child knows what to expect, the more he feels competent to deal with it, as is true for all of us, after all.

Most children around the age of four or so can remember and discuss with you the last doctor visit. While you practice the visit in advance, you can remind the child what she liked about another, perhaps innocuous visit: that nice nurse, the toys in the waiting room. The more you relive the good parts, the more *that* becomes the memory. And the sense of mastery, rather than victimhood, can be embedded as well—that you got through it and it all worked out so you could be proud of yourself. Not that we want to encourage the lollypop part, but sometimes even that can color the remembrance with a cherry-flavored glow.

Remember the age-appropriate modalities (Chapter 2), from rocking to gentle distraction to using their favorite characters and their imaginations. Remember, too, to talk to even the youngest ones: They understand more than you might expect.

On one hospital nursery visit, we listened to Dr. Bernardine Celoni, former chief of pediatrics at Methodist Hospital in Arcadia, California, talking to a newborn as she examined him. She said, "Oh, you're so smart, you picked a wonderful mother. Your sister's a little pistol, but you'll get along all right. But you did so great in picking such a good mother."

Even though she had been poking and prodding him, when she said that, the infant lay back comfortably, almost smugly, and sucked on his sleeve.

For very little children, Dr. Todd Davis, professor of pediatrics at Children's Memorial Hospital in Chicago, has the mother hold twelve- to twenty-three-month-olds during the exam. He starts by first listening with the stethoscope to the mother's knee, then moves to her hands, then listens to the baby's knee, hands, and belly, working his way slowly to the child's chest. That way the child can see and become accustomed to what is going on before it is thrust upon him.

Remember, too, the value of a role model, and that you, as the grown-up in your children's lives, are their hero. When you tell them a story about a similar incident in your childhood concerning your visit to the doctor, it makes a big difference to them. They want to be like you, even up through preteen years. "When Grandma used to take me to the doctor's office, the doctor would sometimes let me listen to my heart through the stethoscope, and it was so loud, I had to laugh. You can't just listen to your own heart all by yourself, you know. Your ear doesn't reach there."

Preparing for Vaccinations and Blood Tests

A pregnant mother we know took her six-year-old son, Logan, and her three-year-old daughter, Ashley, to one of her prenatal physician appointments. She explained to them what was happening and allowed them to watch as she underwent an ultrasound scan. The children thought they were able to make out the shape of their new sister or brother, and they loved the experience. Then their mother had her blood taken. She pointed out to them that it was very cool how the blood built up in the purple vein and then how it came through the straw to the bottle. She was very calm and easy about everything, and the kids were interested.

Then it happened that sometime in the next few weeks during a routine doctor's visit Ashley had to have *her* blood drawn for the first time, even before the mother had time to prepare her verbally for what could have been a traumatic incident. But the mother reminded Ashley how cool and interesting this procedure was. The child remembered and, involved in the details, watched the vein fill up and saw that they used a smaller needle than the one for her mother. While it was unpleasant, Ashley found it to be something of a curiosity. We asked the child what she thought about it afterward and she reported, "The nurse put it in and it hurt my elbow. I didn't like it very much." She told us that she watched until the blood came out, and they caught it in a bottle.

Later that afternoon, after Logan arrived home from school, the mother told him that Ashley had had her blood drawn that day. She asked Logan how well he thought Ashley had done with this event. He said that he thought she probably didn't like it, but their mother smiled and said, "She didn't make a peep." Logan was surprised.

Then, when it was time for his next doctor's appointment Logan's mother said to him, "If you have to have your blood drawn, do you think you might not make a peep, like Ashley?" Logan thought about it and said, "Well, maybe a peep." But when he went to his doctor visit, he was calm and easy about it. That night he told his dad with ultimate pride that not only had he not made a peep but "in fact, I smiled!" Months later, he still tells that story with pride. It was an opportunity to be brave, and he wore his badge of courage proudly.

The blood test that was used for Ashley and Logan was no different from the procedure used with everyone else. The secret is the way it was received and interpreted. Pain *is* perception and perception is at least partly attitude. And while fear increases pain, motivation has a wonderful way of decreasing it. Because Ashley and Logan's mother knew this, she was able to make an otherwise unpleasant and potentially frightful experience into an interesting opportunity for learning and growth.

Pain Relief for Vaccinations and Injections
Sometimes just hearing the word *needle* is enough to make people quiver, adults included. And sometimes the anticipation is enough to create discomfort long before they're even in the same building as the

doctor. A wonderfully potent antidote is a good story. In focusing the child's attention and absorbing her in a good yarn, stories have the power to do two things simultaneously: (1) They take children away from their own fears and move the situation far enough away that it doesn't have to be overwhelming and (2) if the story is similar to the present situation, it provides children with relevant and immediately workable solutions.

Here again, you'll want to coordinate this scenario with the doctor or begin it at home or in the car on the way. For instance, you might say:

Did you see the time that [and you can put in any character they love, such as Dora the Explorer or SpongeBob] went to the doctor? (It doesn't matter whether the child says yes or no.) Well, the doctor made a magic spot on her arm so she didn't feel anything there. Did you see that? It was so funny. Right here. (And you touch a spot on the child's arm with a little pressure.)

And then it started to sparkle. Can you feel it? Sparkling and tingling and then she couldn't feel anything there at all. Like this.

Can you imagine being Dora the Explorer going to see the doctor? And you have a magic spot. You tell me when you can't feel anything there at all. Just like Dora the Explorer. (Wait for response.) That's good.

Then you can imagine that you are Dora the Explorer at the doctor! What would she be saying while the doctor fixes her up?

If the doctor agrees, perhaps he can give the injection in the magic spot while the child talks or sings.

Dr. Roy adds other distraction techniques that she has learned from other pediatricians. She uses them regularly and encourages parents to use them (or variations of them) with their children:

1. Have the child slap firmly and repetitively on their upper arm where the injection will take place right when the nurse comes in the room. This stuns the nerves and helps numb the area. "I've had teenagers tell me they hardly felt the needle," she says.

2. Have the child practice blowing out a hundred birthday candles, and tell him to do this while he is getting the injection. This technique works well with children above the age of four but should be discussed and practiced before the nurse or doctor brings the needle into the room.

If a story doesn't come immediately to mind, you can pull out your own version by using magic:

Step 1: "What the doctor is using is a magic potion [Xylocaine] that makes it so that you can hardly feel anything in that spot."

Step 2: Then, with a washable pen, draw a circle or square or heart around the spot.

Step 3: "See? You can hardly feel anything. What you'll feel is a tiny thing like this." [Pinch but don't say the words *pinch*, *pain*, or *hurt*.]

Step 4: "The other thing you have to do is to look in my eyes [or up at a clock or some pleasant picture] and sing a song for it to work." [Make sure the child is looking away from the needle and injection site.] "Good. You'll feel a little something but that's it."

Afterward children often feel surprised or proud of themselves and say, "Oh, yeah I did feel a little, but it didn't hurt."

Or you can build a story by having a stuffed toy or doll on hand.

"Look at who's here with the doctor! This is Fluffy. He wanted to meet you. He's very fluffy, that's how he got his name. Want to shake hands? He's magic. When he touches you on your arm, you get a magic spot. Like this . . . [Move the toy's hand to touch the child's arm.] Do you feel that spot?" [Touch it yourself with a little pressure and release.]

"Now it will start to feel like it's disappearing, like it's not even there. Can you imagine that? It's disappearing, so you can't feel anything there at all. Tell me when you're sure you can't feel anything in your magic spot, like there's nothing there." [Wait for a response.]

"Good. Now would you hold Fluffy and tell him your spot is feeling very magical while the doctor gives you the medicine that will make you better?" [The doctor gives the child the injection.]

"Very nice. Tell Fluffy how it worked."

If for some reason it doesn't work as well as you might have hoped, allow both yourself and the child the opportunity to learn from the experience. Have the child discuss it with the doll and suggest how you all might do it differently next time. You should feel free to ask the child (if she is verbal enough) or the doctor, "What helps? What works?" It may surprise you to hear how willing people of all ages are to share what they know about themselves and what it takes to help them feel better.

Preparing for a Painful Procedure

Ah, the dreaded question, the dreaded answer. It is almost inevitable that when a child is presented with a new procedure he will ask, "Is it going to hurt?"

Pain, as we've said, is an interpretation of a neurologic impulse. When we are having a good time, we forget the headache, the stomachache, the *owie* from yesterday or just a minute ago. But when we're bored, restless, impatient, or upset, every little twinge seems large and insulting. And because *hurt* is not a word we like to use (because the brain starts fishing around to match up images and memories with that concept), we want to avoid the more blunt answer.

And not only can't we be dishonest but we must not be. Rapport is built on trust, and that trust is based in believability. In this case, asked about whether a shot will hurt, it seems fair to us to say, "I'm guessing you will feel something curious or different." That leaves lots of leeway. In fact, you could even suggest a feeling somewhat different from pain. You might say, "It may feel like a pinch. It may feel hot. It may feel funny or weird. What would that feel like?" Proposing possibilities other than pain initiates an unconscious search by the mind for those sensations. In less time than it takes to hear the words, the mind is processing what hot, funny, and weird actually feel like. In so doing, it is not only distracted but occupied with conjuring up sensations that are *not* pain.

You might ask a child, "Who do you think will be the most interested in how you did at the doctor's?" Maybe the child will say "Daddy" or maybe the child's best friend, "Brendon." You could say, "Think about how you're going to tell Brendon how brave you were."

Preparing for an Emergency Doctor/Hospital Visit

Of course, the most difficult visits might be those that happen as a result of an emergency. When an ambulance and an emergency room might be involved, you need all the Verbal First Aid techniques you've learned so far, remembering, for example, how Donna helped Oliver through his injury as described in the earlier chapters.

If your child is injured, even as you call for help or drive her yourself in the car to the doctor's office or the emergency room, of course you begin with a breath and then with pacing. We always go back to pacing because it is so convincing a way to give the support that your child needs and allows suggestion to be received and used in the most positive, healing way possible.

Repetition is a simple pacing technique that lets the child know she's truly being heard.

> **Child**: (Crying.) I hurt my leg.
>
> **You**: Oh, your leg. Something happened to your leg.
>
> **Child**: I fell off my bike.
>
> **You**: You fell off your bike, huh? Well, sweetheart, I'm right here with you now. Let's look at it.
>
> **Child**: It's bleeding. And it hurts so much.
>
> **You**: It's bleeding. I can see that it's bleeding. Can you move it?
>
> **Child**: It hurts!
>
> **You**: Yes, we're going to get some help for that right away. You help me by putting your arms around my neck, and we'll get you to the car, and I'll get a clean towel to wash off that nice rich, red blood and we'll see how it looks then. Want to help me? You hold the towel as I drive. And you can begin to let your body begin to heal itself. The way it always does when you have a boo-boo.

When you repeat what the child said you validate it and let her know you take her concern seriously. However, you most likely should not repeat words like *hurt* and *pain*, which can reinforce that issue. But feeling heard provides the first step to setting a platform on which healing can flourish. Just to show that there's no reason to panic, you might even say, "Look at that nice, red blood there. In just a moment or two, you can stop bleeding."

Because he or she is in an altered state, often a victim's body will respond to a command to stop bleeding as if hypnotized.

It's important, though, that your repetitions not seem like mimicking. That feels cruel and dismissive to a child. So you must be subtle about it. "I hear you," is the message.

Another way to soothe your child is to use music. One mother whose newborn had to have hernia surgery asked us for a CD of the music she had played to him while he was in utero. She had been in the Bonding with the Baby Within program and noticed her son became calm whenever he heard this particular CD.

Verbal First Aid Shortcuts for the Ambulance, the Drive to the Doctor's Office, or in a Waiting Room:

- Center yourself: Take some breaths, remember that you are there for a reason, that you have everything you need to be helpful in this moment, most especially your love and presence.

- Give presence and reassurance: "I'm right here, and we're going to the hospital, and they know just what to do to help you."

- Help the child be calm and start to make the chemicals that will aid his healing.

- Tell positive stories about survivors: "I know a guy who . . ."; "This happened to me when I was your age."

- Remind her that her body knows how to heal itself, that it always has: "Remember when . . ."

- Have her picture a better time and place while waiting for procedures: "Wouldn't it be nice to be at the farm, right now, petting those little lambs. Which one was the one that used to always come over and lick your knee? Oh, yes, Snowflake!"

- Solicit her help so she feels like part of the solution and not simply the victim. "You know what would be great? If you'd hold the towel against your arm while I check with the desk to see if they're ready for us yet."

- Employ imagery: "As you hold the towel, you can begin to notice that you're feeling a little better."

Whatever you have in your arsenal that works to make the child more comfortable, bring it along:

- Remember to bring along a favorite toy, if that will help offer solace.

- Play a calming CD, if your child responds to music.

Preparing the Child for Hospital Visit and Stay

As opposed to an emergency admission that takes everyone by surprise, you generally are given advance notice of a hospital procedure, which gives you and your child time to prepare.

If a hospital visit or stay is required, you can create a doll or puppet show describing the surgery in a friendly way. If it's Teddy's story, he can certainly come along.

When children have to go to a doctor's office, go to a hospital, undergo a painful procedure, or be separated from their families, it is good for them to have a loved object with them—a toy, a blanket, whatever soothes them and reminds them of safer times. There's great comfort in the familiar. For all people, but especially for children, in times of fear it is comforting to have familiar objects and people around.

One mother tells the story of a time that she and her husband had had a quarrel. The father had left for work but the mother just sat down in great sadness in the doorway between the kitchen and her eighteen-month-old daughter's room. Suddenly she saw her child walk over to her crib and pull through the bars her favorite blanket, which she dragged across the room and handed to her mother. She knew that the blanket had magic powers of giving solace, and she was willing to share when it was needed.

That little girl later had a stuffed kitten, which she actually named Solace. One day when they had to pack to move to another city, she asked her mother if she "could take Solace in a paper bag." That made the mother laugh, and it became a joke between them as the girl grew older. We take comfort in many things, but most especially in what is familiar when we are away from home. We can take solace in anything familiar, even a paper bag.

A pediatrician we know had a little six-year-old patient who was in the hospital after an appendectomy. She was experiencing a little discomfort and refused to get up and take a walk. The physician was concerned that without exercising, the child would build up painful gas in her midsection. The physician found out which cartoon character was the child's favorite (it was the dog Blue of *Blue's Clues*) and created a little book that had a story of that character having an appendectomy and all his friends and relatives (other cartoon characters) visiting him. "He's up and walking now," the story says, "and he wonders if you're walking and how you're doing." The doctor even found a set of Blue's ears for the child to put on as she walked the halls, speeding her recovery and imagining her cartoon friend doing the same.

While this specific incident was over and above what doctors usually do, this use of a role model illustrates how Verbal First Aid techniques can motivate healing where coercion, shaming, or cajoling would probably be counterproductive. And it is something a parent can provide for a child as well.

In terms of the surgery itself, five million children undergo surgery each year in the United States alone, and 60 percent of them develop extreme anxiety before the procedure. That's more than half of the children and to make matters worse, *anxiety* makes matters worse. It has been shown in recent studies that when high anxiety is part of the surgery experience, postsurgical pain is heightened and the recovery is negatively affected.[1] So the more and the better we can prepare the child for this experience, the more we are setting him on a course for a more comfortable, less traumatic recovery.

APPLYING VERBAL FIRST AID AT A DOCTOR'S OFFICE OR HOSPITAL

Communicating with Preverbal Children at a Doctor's Office or Hospital

Words are powerful sometimes whether they're cognitively understood or not. We somehow know intuitively what someone is saying and what we need to do in response even when we're in foreign countries or someone is whispering. We understand plot even when movies are muted. Words communicate on a multitude of levels, only one of which is the literal interpretation.

Dr. Clark tells the story of a two-year-old girl who needed a spinal tap. The child squirmed and squealed and slid out of their grasp for fifteen minutes while three doctors tried to hold on to her and make it happen. Finally, Clark said almost absently, "What am I going to do with you?" and the child stopped squirming and looked up at her with an "are you talking to me?" expression. In a gasp of a moment, Clark realized that she *hadn't* been talking to her patient. She'd been talking to everyone *but* her. So, she took a breath and explained to the baby exactly what she was trying to do and why, even though the baby was ostensibly "too young to understand." Within moments, the child lay still and let the procedure happen. Clark was stunned but admitted that she learned right then to include the patient, no matter how small or supposedly preverbal, in the conversation and the process.

Medical protocol may seem magical and monumentally important to adults, but to children they are often odd and frightening.

Children are not much impressed by technical knowledge. But they are moved by love, attention, and connection.

Communicating with Verbal Children at a Doctor's Office or a Hospital

When we train first responders, we use the word *pacing* in a somewhat different way from when we are using it with a parent or guardian. With first responders, it has to do with building rapport with someone who doesn't know you and doesn't know that he can trust you or your ministrations.

Your relationship with your child is established, and, we like to think, the trust is already there. So the pacing becomes a deeper level of connecting. For children who are about to undergo a procedure, meet a new doctor, or get an injection, we want to pace their behavior, body language, attitude, and emotional state.

You look at your little girl, and she's curled up, sucking her thumb. Or your son is whining that he wants to go home. Pacing, which can often mean reflecting back the person's words and behavior, has to take a different tack in such circumstances.

What you do here is acknowledge the child's experience and feelings, accepting them as true for the child, and then begin to lead him or her to another perspective or experience.

If he says, "I'm scared," a response of "Buck up!" or "No, you're not," does not help him or the situation. Sometimes it's hard, but it's vital to refrain from judging. Often you'll hear, "Oh cut it out, it's just a bruise. Stop being a baby." And too many times, the sense of rejection sends the child into an even more immature reaction. This is the time for support. Later, when all is well again, we can digest the more complicated or sophisticated lessons or concepts.

So we offer you this Verbal First Aid way to respond:

I can see that you're scared, because this is a new experience for you. That can be scary because you don't know how it will be. It's natural to feel that way. *I'm* wondering too what it will be like, and that makes me feel a little curious myself. I'm glad we're here together.

It's more effective—both in the short and long term—to allow the feeling, understand it, and then help the child move or transform it to something safer and healthier.

Distraction Technique: Be My Partner

Having avoided saying that it will hurt and thereby having avoided unintentionally delivering a negative suggestion, you can build on the process of distraction in simple ways. One approach, which must be coordinated in advance with the doctor, might be to say, "Look at that clock over there on the wall. You're going to be in charge of the time. You're the boss on that, here. The doctor said she was going to start [this process, the injection, et cetera] when the second hand is at twelve, and when it gets to five, you say *Stop!* and she promises to stop." Of course, it's a good idea if you know that the procedure will be over by the time you reach five.

This can work for many reasons:

- As we said, pain has to do with focus. A joke we often make in our talks is, "If you want to forget about your headache, drop a hammer on your big toe." If all you can think about is your foot, you aren't thinking about your head. If you're the clock monitor, it's hard to also think about what's going on in your arm. So the child can be distracted from the pain.

- In addition, the child may feel as if he or she has some control over the situation. When they say stop, it's all over, no matter what.

- The child knows as well that the procedure will come to an end, that whatever is going to happen won't go on forever, and that's a level of pain relief in itself.

- And the child becomes your partner in the process, not just an innocent victim of this exchange, because he or she has an important role to play.

Addressing Your Child's Fear While Waiting for a Regular Checkup: These next scripts are likely to be used over and over again in childhood, especially because kids need plenty of annual checkups and vaccinations. If you have a child who gets nervous about new things, you can prepare for the visit with the following scripts:

Yes, I understand that would be scary. But you're here now, with people who can help and protect you.

When we don't know what a place is going to be like, it could feel scary. Like when you started school. Or when you went to summer camp.

Quick Scripts to Use When Waiting to See a Doctor

Injured child waiting to be seen by a doctor: "Yes, that's quite a cut [insert injury here]. I can see that you're bleeding. But luckily, I [or the doctors] know just what to do about it."

Child waiting for a strep test: "I hear that your throat is really sore. No wonder you're unhappy. When I was your age I had a really bad sore throat and we went to the doctor for it and . . ."

Child waiting to get stitches: "Yes, that can be pretty scary. When I was ten I cut my hand trying to carve a rabbit out of a wood block, and we had to run to the emergency room! Boy, that sure was scary. I had twelve stitches, which was three more than my friend Nick had, so he was a little jealous. And I had a big bandage on it for two weeks. But see if you can find it now."

Child waiting in the emergency room with a broken bone or inflammation, or waiting for pain relief: "As you hold your arm like that I'd like you to think of the time when you were really cold, really, really cold, like in the ocean or outside playing in the winter without your jacket. Do you have that feeling clear in your head? Good. Now I want you to take that feeling and put it in your arm like you're reaching into a cooler for a soda, and let that cool, comfortable feeling go all the way, all the way into the bone."

Helping Children Who've Had Bad Experiences at a Doctor's Office or Hospital

Children who have already been frightened or traumatized (even mildly) by a checkup or procedure at the hospital or doctor's office are often very wary of the possibility of losing control and are more than normally vigilant about being manipulated. For that reason and for the purposes of maintaining or building rapport, we want to remind you of the ABCs of rapport: authority, believability, and calm. The most useful techniques with children who have already had negative experiences are pacing and leading and double-binds.

Pacing lets the child know that you truly see and fully recognize his anxiety, that you are not dismissing it and putting him back into danger. Once that rapport is reestablished, you can begin to lead him away from the awful anxiety (by reframing, future pacing, and so on).

The truth of the matter is that no one wants to stay anxious. It is terribly uncomfortable regardless of your age. When we sense that someone can successfully help us out of that state (by virtue of authority, experience, or centeredness), we are usually more than ready to grab her hands and be lifted out.

Double-binds, reframing, and future pacing are particularly useful with anxious children because they offer them a semblance of control. They can choose not only how to see the event (both past and future) but what they would like to do next time to alter it. These techniques and the frame of mind they facilitate can be powerful antidotes to hypervigilance and anxiety.

The following is an example of these techniques used very subtly.

SCENARIO I

Eight-year-old Jasper is sitting in bed, passively protesting his appointment with the family doctor. His father, Jonas, comes in.

Jonas: Time to go, buddy.
Jasper: (Lies back, arms folded.) I don't wanna go. It's gonna be just like last time.

Jonas: Which part of last time?

Jasper: When they stuck that needle in my arm and didn't even tell me first.

Jonas: Yeah, that was pretty surprising, wasn't it?

Jasper: Yeah! (Pouts in anger.)

Jonas: I imagine you surprised the doctor just as well when you knocked the magazine rack off the wall when you jumped.

Jasper: Served him right!

Jonas: You made him laugh . . . once he got over the ruckus. He really laughed hard.

Jasper: (Laughs despite himself.)

Jonas: (Laughs with his son.) I'm sorry we didn't tell you about the needle. I know it shook you up pretty bad.

Jasper: (Nods.)

Jonas: But after the needle was over, it was a really wild scene, don't you think? Wow, did he jump. We'll be talking about that day when you're forty years old and I'm—

Jasper: Really, really old.

Jonas: I hope so. The doctor was more shocked than you were! But we'll do better about telling you what's going to happen next time if you want us to. We can call the doctor together in advance so we can prepare. But you might miss some rather amazing memories. It's up to you, of course. So . . . we're going to go, and you can tell me if you want to know what's going to happen or you don't. Is that okay?

Jasper: Yeah. I guess so.

Jonas: I think the look on his face was worth it. (Smiles.)

Jasper: It was pretty good, Dad.

Jonas: Let's go then.

VERBAL FIRST AID FOR DOCTOR VISITS FOR ONGOING ILLNESSES

In reference to children with chronic conditions such as diabetes and asthma, Dr. Todd Davis says, "You can think of your child as a sickly person (which will cause long-term emotional scars) or as a normal child with an illness (and you'll end up with an emotionally healthy kid)."

One mother explained, "When my son was in the [intensive care unit], the only part of his body that could be safely moved were his feet (every other part, including his neck and both his hands and thighs, had tubes in it). The nurse gave me permission to rub his feet with lotion, which was soothing for both of us.

"In fact, he specifically requested after throwing up, 'Mom, can you distract me by rubbing my feet?' He knew what the purpose was and that it worked. It added to his trust in his nurse caregivers, who were all strangers, to see me working with them. Yes, he was willing to obey them as authority figures, but he trusted them more because I did."

With ongoing illnesses, a good rapport with her doctor is really essential to the child's faith and response to all treatments. When a child feels that the doctor cares and is doing all he can to make her comfortable, she eases into unpleasant procedures with a more cooperative air.

Remember, too, what Dr. Susan Clark said in the Foreword. This isn't just about having the child feel better emotionally. "Medical staff who work with children know that a sick, fussy, crying child is going to have a high heart rate and high blood pressure. Breathing rates increase, and the child doesn't eat well; with diabetes, being upset can even raise the blood sugar level." When a child is comforted, it changes the physical symptoms, as well.

So while there are many reasons for selecting a physician, let one of them be that he or she has some natural facility in communicating with the little patient.

Listening to Your Child

As you can see in the scripts presented in this chapter, it's important to acknowledge a child's feelings. In doing so, you make him feel heard and understood, and allow him to begin to relax a little more. When children sense that you are with them in your mind as much as in your body, they can feel supported. Pacing starts with *listening*. It's a good idea to pay close attention to a child's comments because there are often clues that allow you to find a way in to help her. For example, if a child says, "My stomach hurts when Daddy yells," this could clearly be as much about her emotional reaction to her home environment as about her digestive tract.

Sometimes with little ones we have to listen with all of our senses. One little girl complained endlessly that her stomach hurt and devoted parents and doctors went through the full regimen of tests to try to help her. Finally, someone asked the child to show them exactly where in her stomach she was hurting. And she pointed to her throat!

No one had guessed that it was her vocabulary and not her belly that needed a minor adjustment.

APPLYING VERBAL FIRST AID AFTER SEEING THE DOCTOR

The indirect suggestions you've already learned—guided imagery, contingency statements, soliciting the child's help, truisms, and future pacing—apply easily and naturally to most medical situations. The following pages offer some examples of suggestions you can offer children when you help them to focus on healing through the course of their recovery, have to give them medicine, or want to relieve their pain. These suggestions help set the course for continued progress and relief every time you deliver them.

Using the Child's Natural Imagination to Help the Healing Process

Many doctors report that when they learn how to speak to their patients using the principles of Verbal First Aid and begin to use their own imagination, they are surprised to find that the children have no trouble whatsoever doing the imaginative work with them. Dr. Clark asked one little boy, "What does your diabetes want to tell me?" He paused just a minute and said, "It wants ice cream." "Well, that was an easy fix," Clark says. Ice cream is one of those foods with a good mixture of protein, fats, and carbs to keep the child in balance overnight.

Young children don't know about coloring inside the lines and the box that we call the common rules of reality yet. They are willing to imagine most anything—even if it doesn't make much sense. And they can use their imaginations to not only entertain themselves but help to heal themselves. One young cancer patient we knew imagined angels with feather dusters clearing her brain during radiation sessions. Another young boy imagined magical boots that could kick the cancer out of his brain and astounded doctors with his completely unanticipated recovery.

Parents know their own kids the best and often think of creative and individualized ways of helping their child through their medical process. "But parents need to be empowered and encouraged to do this. Parents and doctors are often surprised by how well their children do with their appropriate support and guidance," Dr. Roy says.

Here are some ideas to help you enlist the child's imagination through guided imagery into healing:

- Let the child be free to choose the images that work for her. Some children want soldiers to fight their battles. Other, gentler children, like the girl we just mentioned, want angels to brush away cancer cells with feather dusters. Some call in superheroes. It's their image—they get to say!

- Children are so creative they may come up with their own versions of what can happen to help them heal. Ten year old Tia, whose mother is a physician in Great Britain, was complaining of a pain in the side of her neck. Her mother, who had studied Verbal First Aid, taught her the *magic finger technique,* in which Tia imagined a "blob of magic elixir" at the end of her pointer finger (that was the decidedly magic one). It was metallic blue, she explained, and the fact that it was tingling made it even more magical. She applied her finger to her neck and "lo and behold, the pain went!!!" Some time later, when she encountered another issue, she crept into her mother's bed and said,

"Mummy, I think that I have a pain that is too big for the magic finger. I think I need to use the magic hand!!!"

- Allow their expression free rein without judgment or expectation. We don't know what's going to help them and we may be very surprised to see what they can do for themselves.

- Just asking what Dora the Explorer or Spider-Man might do if he had a stomachache might entice the child to role-play in his imagination that his hero battles the infection until it is helpless and no longer hurts.

Prescribing Healing: A Spoonful of Medicine

Whenever you give your children medication or bring them to the doctor (or hospital) for a procedure, use the Verbal First Aid technique of prescribing healing: Tell them what you both want to have happen. For example, you might say:

- When you take this medicine, you're going to start feeling so much better.

- Because you're so good at taking this medicine, you're going to be surprised how fast you're feeling good again.

- Lots of kids take this medicine and then they're able to go out and play again really soon.

- As soon as the doctor holds your hand like this [demonstrating a procedure], you can start to feel more comfortable.

Soliciting the Child's Help Is a Really Important Tool

As we said earlier about the Be My Partner technique, it changes a victim into his or her own rescuer, and offers not only distraction but something more. If you're helping me help you, then we're all in this together and we can all feel a sense of purpose. Studies of elderly patients who were given plants to tend (horticulture therapy) showed that just that minimal increase in responsibility improved their stress levels and reduced their pain.[2] Children's perception of pain varies, too, with the moment and the meaning.

If you're lucky enough to have a pediatrician who is thoughtful about communication issues and willing to experiment with some Verbal First Aid, here are some helpful ways to make the visit more comfortable for all.

Whether the doctor would like you to participate or whether he'd like to use these techniques himself, partnering with the child can give the child a sense of control and participation, rather than feeling that things are being done to her. For example, the doctor or you with his permission could say:

- Here, the doctor would like you to hold this nice medicine for him, can you do that? Because he is going to need it in a minute and you can hand it to him as soon as he asks for it. And then we're going to put on this powerful medicine that makes sure it stays nice and clean and heals quickly.

- The doctor [nurse] is going to wash that cut and make it nice and clean so it can heal. When it's nice and clean, it can get better, faster. We're going to take this cloth and wash it. And you can help.

As you can see, having your child act as the doctor's or your partner can be as simple as just having him or her hold the bandage while the affected area is washed. Anything you do to involve your children helps them to be less the victim and identify more with the rescuer. We all feel more empowered if we have a job to do. When we are empowered in one way—any way at all—that feeling is translated bodywide. All parts of us become empowered. We can do things we didn't know we could do before. Which means that maybe there are other things—such as healing—that we can do, too.

Offering Truisms and the Power of Everyone Knows

Kids like facts. "My mother said . . ." or "My dad told me . . ." or "The doctor said . . ." are enough to be proof that it's true.

One wise doctor explained to a frightened young boy why he had fainted in school when he was about to give a presentation. "Sometimes when we don't want to do something, our body helps us find a way out of it. It's the body's clever way of taking us out of a situation we don't want to be in. The blood goes from our head down to our feet and we fall down and faint. Then, when we're down, the blood goes back to the head and we wake up."

Other truisms include:

- "Everyone knows that a body knows how to heal itself. Your body's done it before. Remember the last time you had a cut and put a bandage on it, and when you took the bandage off, it was all gone, just like that."

- "When your arm itches under the cast, it means it's healing!"

- "All the doctors say it can be done."

- "The scientists say this procedure is done all the time." (Depending on how old and bright the child is, you could share articles or websites with him or her.)

An offshoot of truisms are the suggestions starting with "I know a guy who . . ." In that Verbal First Aid technique we provide the power of example by sharing someone else's story, one that is relevant and meaningful to the child. You can tell her about another child who survived the very same kind of injury she is experiencing so that she can picture that life goes on after recovery. "We had a little boy just your age here over the winter with a broken leg, and today he's out playing baseball with his friends. And you know what? He just made the middle school team."

Just a reminder: Truisms are powerful tools. Make sure your information is accurate and believable.

Triggers and Anchors

Sometimes using the very problem (the boo-boo, the cough, the visit to the doctor's office) or situations that naturally and regularly occur (the sunrise, getting out of bed, walking down the block) in conjunction with guided imagery can promote healing. A *trigger* is an action or a feeling that reminds the patient to use the symptoms to facilitate healing.

- Every time you cough, you can picture Spider-Man wrapping up the mucus and throwing it out.

- Every time your arm itches, you can picture little construction workers running around repairing the bone so you can get out of that cast quicker.

Taking It One Step Further: Future Pacing

You can pace in the moment with your breath, your presence, and your acknowledgment. But you can also pace out into the future. You can, it seems, breathe into tomorrow.

Retired Tucson, Arizona, orthopedic surgeon Dr. Hugh Thompson tells the story of a high school athlete who came in with a broken leg and asked the question, "Will I be able to run again and be a track star?" Thompson says, "I said, 'You will be able to run faster than ever,' a seemingly ego-related response, but I'm not sure at the time why I said it. Twenty years later that same person came to work on my pool. He remembered me and said, 'And you know I ran the fastest five-mile after I recovered from my fracture than ever before.' Which proved to me how important what we say is, particularly in these kinds of situations where the doctors have to become much more skilled in being a facilitator and helping the patient into a situation where they can do their own healing."

When you're future pacing, use words that lead your child to imagine in as clear and vivid a way as possible what it is like when he *is* better. What is he doing? What is he feeling? What does he see? Make the future seem present. The more image rich, the more effective.

Leaving the Scene and Future Pacing

We can't always escape, even in our minds, when we're doing a job we don't like, but a visit to the doctor is a good time to help children learn a practice for themselves that shifts the focus from panic to calm, changing the chemicals that flow through their bodies. When our minds are somewhere else and not focused on fear and pain, we can avoid a lot of the misery of an uncomfortable moment. That's what a daydream is, after all. And, as you know, when someone calls you back from the reverie, it's almost with sadness (and usually with surprise!) that you return to whatever it was you were expected to be doing.

So here are some ways to suggest the daydream that takes them away from an unpleasant procedure:

> Imagine a place you'd rather be. Some place that is fun, where you're happy and doing what you really like to do. As soon as you're there, put your finger and thumb together to hold on to the good feeling and, with a good, easy breath, enjoy yourself. When you come back, you can tell me where you went. I bet I'll be able to guess . . . but maybe you'll fool me.

For short-term future pacing for a child receiving treatment, try this:

> When you're done here, you can go play with your friends. What's your favorite make-believe game? Which one will you choose?

Or even more directly:

> As soon as it's over, I'm going to look you in the eye and shake your hand and then I'm going to give you the biggest hug you ever had. You can be thinking about that as it's happening and you don't even have to tell the doctor.

We've seen children's eyes glaze over simply by suggesting, "Remember the last time you played your favorite video game with your friend." They go right there, in the middle of the action, and that distraction works to everyone's advantage.

Especially *after* a doctor visit in which children have been the patient and have not liked what was done to them, it's great fun for them to be able to be the one in control. So you can let them pretend to be the doctor and inject everybody. This allows them to regain some power when they felt so vulnerable before. As they approach you with glee, pointing their toy hypodermic needle at you and saying, "It's time for your shot!" you must take it with the grace with which you hope they ultimately will. Just say, "Thank you, Doctor. I know that will be good for me." And see how both their momentary authority and your cooperation and modeling set a good course for the future.

SELECTING A PHYSICIAN WHO WOULD WELCOME VERBAL FIRST AID

The first question to ask when you are selecting a physician for your child is whether he or she seems to be able to develop and maintain rapport with children.

Body language—being at eye level, whether that's kneeling down or sitting on the bed—can make a big difference to a child for whom adults usually look like a forest of knees but who now needs full-on attention. Doctors who meet children at their own level recognize the value of personal connection and trust.

Rapport demands integrity and trustworthiness. Children respond intuitively to reliability and honesty. They sense lies and manipulation, so, although we have techniques here for gaining their cooperation, everything must come from a level of integrity and desire for the highest good of the child.

Rapport depends on listening. Children don't always know what they're feeling and/or they can't express it, so we have to listen all the harder. Young children generally don't volunteer a lot of useful information. Therefore, tuning in through presence also helps the doctor better to sense what's needed, to read what's really going on. Good doctors do this intuitively.

The second question to ask in choosing a doctor is whether he or she is willing to partner with you in helping your child. Good doctors also welcome your input and your help. You know best how your child responds and what works to gain their compliance and cooperation. If you've developed a few successful techniques of your own to calm your child or distract him during a difficult procedure, share this information with your doctor. For instance, "I brought along Teddy. She likes to hold him when she's uncomfortable."

WHEN YOU CAN'T BE THERE, YOU CAN STILL BE WITH THEM

No parent likes to think that there may come a time when their child has to undergo a procedure without them. But should it happen, it is good to know that you can build in a way for them to hold on to the good Verbal First Aid that you've taught them.

Milton Erickson, MD, the father of modern hypnotherapy, used to tell his patients at the end of a session, "And you can take my voice with you when you go."

There are ways you can have your voice, your presence, and calm go with your child wherever she goes. Some of the simplest with children are:

- The use of totems or items that remind the child of a good, soothing experience.

- Personalized rituals that you create with your child.

We've discussed bringing along something from home that reminds the child of love and comfort. It's also possible to offer a special new magical item that will keep him safe or afford a smile when needed. It can be as simple as a heart-shaped stone you found on the beach on a walk together or a surprise pillowcase with a favorite character on it. The ritual might involve a small technique to help him feel more self-assured and relaxed when he's alone. You simply have him imagine a place of calm, his very favorite place (Grandma's lap, Uncle Jeff's barn) and then put his index finger and thumb of the same hand together (as if he were picking up something very tiny) and take three deep breaths. Whenever he feels frightened, anxious, or uncomfortable he can reenact this ritual and picture his safe place.

We each have within us the capacity to participate in our own healing. When we teach our children how to do that, we give them a gift for life. Everyone knows a wound can be stitched, but only our own bodies can knit the skin together again. Only our own bodies can repair themselves. Doctors have their part to do, and we have ours. There is no better time to learn that than in childhood. With Verbal First Aid, a visit to the doctor's office not only is a way to get a bandage or an injection but becomes an education in self-healing and empowerment.

7 Talking to Children about Illness and Death

To live in hearts we leave behind
Is not to die.

—THOMAS CAMPBELL, "HALLOWED GROUND"

We come to this chapter with a deep humility and respect for the mystery that is life and death. There are no quick and easy tricks we can perform that will change the profound nature of loss or the fact that our faces have been sharply turned toward the great unknown. It is an awe that can defy description and a pain that can bend a heart that thought it was steeled and ready.

There are many good books and many websites that provide perspectives, answers, and tools for talking with children about these devastating issues, and we will list some of them at the end of this chapter. What we believe we can add to the mix are the subtle Verbal First Aid techniques that work so well in other difficult, emotional circumstances. There *are* things we can do and words we can say that can help mitigate the loss and indeed make what might feel unbearable . . . bearable.

There is perhaps nothing harder for us to talk to one another about than death. We are desperate to find the easiest ways to say the hardest thing, to make the deepest of pains somehow more tolerable, less painful.

What can we say?

In an effort to sidestep the grief and sadness before us, we often resort to platitudes: "He's in a better place," or "She's not suffering anymore." And often we hear the hollow ring of our words as they fall flat between us and the one we are trying so hard to help. The words let us down because they seem to dismiss the feelings of loss, confusion, fear, anger, hurt—feelings that are all too real, even as we're making every effort to carry on.

In trying to avoid the unavoidable, we do things we wouldn't ordinarily do: We talk too much. We don't talk at all. And worst of all, perhaps, we think that if we ignore the pain the person is in, it will just go away.

When talking with children, we may use words that confuse, that make matters even worse: "He went to sleep," we may say, trying to minimize the loss. "She went to Heaven," trying to make it sound less threatening. "He's in the ground," trying to be realistic. "She's gone, Grandma went away," "He got sick and died." Even the often heard "We put the dog down"—which can be confused with "I'm going to put the baby down"—can make a child afraid. If people disappear permanently from going to sleep or getting sick, and everyone is sad about it and no one knows what to do about it, how can your child ever feel safe?

What *can* we say?

This is precisely where Verbal First Aid can be of so much help.

WHAT TO SAY AND HOW TO SAY IT

Children interpret death differently from adults. And very young children see it differently from older, more sophisticated children. Most children, however, even the very young, have some concept of death even if it is rarely discussed. Perhaps they've learned about it through fairy tales or stories in which someone or something (a wicked witch, a dragon) dies or because of the somewhat predictable event of finding a dead bird or butterfly on the porch.

Very young children under the age of five tend to have more magical beliefs. They may believe that death is like a disappearing act. After watching cartoon characters bounce back from otherwise sure death, they may believe that dying is not irrevocable but rather a temporary halt in the action.

By the time they reach five years of age their fascination with death becomes greater because they begin to understand that it is final. It is still a limited understanding because although they recognize that everyone dies, they don't believe that it pertains to them personally.

By the time they are preteens (nine or ten), they begin to understand that their life too will come to an end. Each child is unique in the way he interprets and uses that understanding.

To help you speak to your child about death, we've broken this difficult topic into simple steps using the principles of Verbal First Aid throughout.

Step 1: Speak Honestly with Your Child

How you talk to your child about death depends on how old the child is as well as your spiritual, religious, cultural, and scientific beliefs. Whatever those beliefs are, it is important that you tell your child the truth as you see it. It is equally important that you feel free to say you don't know the answer to a question. Prevaricating is the quickest way to lose rapport when your child needs it most.

Religious and spiritual resources can be extremely helpful if they have already been part of family life. Belief in the divine affords many people comfort, and as parents find that sustenance, they can impart it, even beyond words, to their children. But in the absence of a clear religious or spiritual belief, the following is useful for children of most ages:

> I don't know where Grandpa went. But I know that even though he's not here with us physically, he's still in our hearts.

Speaking honestly with your children, even when it means admitting you don't know the answer to their question, is fundamental to building and maintaining rapport. When you speak with your children about the death of a loved one, make sure to give them time and privacy to speak with you if they need to. It's very common for people to feel like pushing the whole subject under the rug so that the child doesn't have to suffer the hurt. But it's likely that on some level, the child knows when you're suffering and hiding it. Children learn as much from what you don't say as what you do. If you are less than truthful, he won't trust you when you need that rapport for healing.

Death is such a big mystery, especially for children. When they are faced with the loss of someone they love, they look to their caretakers for a special sense of security that only an honest rapport can provide. By using Verbal First Aid in this way, you not only help them through the moment, you build on the rapport you've been developing and let them know you can be counted on no matter what.

Step 2: Explain What's Happening

When it comes to explaining death to children, the rule of thumb is keep it simple. And the Verbal First Aid tool that will help you the most is *pacing*.

Start by telling them what you know in uncomplicated terms and sticking to the facts. After you've told them what has happened or what is about to happen, let them talk. As they do, you can pace them with your body (sitting on the floor with them, sighing with them) or with your words ("I know you're sad." "Yes, it hurts.").

If they have questions, they'll ask you. If they're very little, you can ask them, "Do you have any questions?" or "Is there anything you'd like to say?" With some very young children, once they have the facts, they're done, so you might hear an answer like, "Where's my doll?"

Whatever they're feeling, let them know it's okay. If they're crying, let them cry. If they're angry, tell them, "I can see you're angry." Let them work through their feelings at their own rate.

That does not mean allowing them to behave destructively, of course. Nor does it mean forcing them to talk when they don't want to. That would be counterproductive.

When you do see your child acting out, be sure to bring her back to what she's feeling. Even though your own heart breaks, talking about her fears or confusion and crying about the loss are the best ways to move your child through the pain and out to the other side.

Sometimes children express their pain in physical terms. You can help them by explaining the mind–body connection to them as you continue pacing them. You might be surprised to find how natural it is for children to see themselves in that way and how readily they accept the idea that what they feel in their hearts is what they feel in their bodies.

The pain of death is often experienced as a physical pain. The very idea of the metaphor of a broken heart illustrates this. If it is expressed in the body, then it seems to us that one of the ways to help is to talk to the body. What we do with Verbal First Aid in this manner is very similar to what we do in pain management, in which we use language to bypass intellect and reframe the individual's experience unconsciously. One of the metaphors children understand instinctively is *waves*. They know that things move in and move out, the way trees bend in the wind then straighten back up, the ways that rivers rise and fall, the way breath is taken in and let out. Everyone intuitively, viscerally understands the rhythm of nature when it is expressed for them in simple, descriptive terms.

A while back, in the midst of a terrible loss, a woman was simply overwhelmed by the intensity of the emotions she was experiencing. She recounted that she was sitting at her kitchen table, her hands cupping a mug of coffee as she was flooded with memories of the closed casket that had been holding her mother's body. She felt her chest sink as if molten lead had been poured into her heart and the blood drained from her face. Her husband walked in from the living room and intuitively knew what she was feeling. She turned to him and said, "I don't know how I can take this the way it's feeling. It's so huge."

"It feels like forever but it's never static," he said. "It's like the ocean. It comes in waves. Sometimes big ones. Sometimes lots of little ones. When my mother died, it happened and then it subsided. Like a wave. Sometimes I was just standing there in the sand and it knocked me on my ass when I was least expecting it. Then it would, like a wave, just go back to wherever it came from. And I'd be quiet again. It gets quiet. It does."

With a child, it would be best to express it in a simpler manner:

It's like a wave, feeling like this. It comes and it goes. In the beginning there are a lot of waves and then it slows down and the waves are smaller and smaller until it's really calm and quiet.

You can help children become more aware of their own bodies with Verbal First Aid at the same time that you help them understand how important it is to talk. For instance:

You know how you didn't feel so good after the funeral? Sometimes, the best medicine is to talk about it.

Zack

One story expresses this idea beautifully:

When little, Zack used to have an issue, he'd suppress it and then act out in a way that caused chaos and boomeranged back to him. His mother taught him to express what was going on inside, and most of the time he did. But when his favorite aunt died, that seemed so beyond his comprehension or ability to absorb, that he forgot what he'd learned and began to misbehave, which was not his way.

"What's really going on?" his mother asked. "Is this about Aunt Dawn?"

Zack paused and got a grip. "I know I'm not talking about it," he said.

"What are you doing?" she said.

He frowned. "I'm taking it out on Ian," his kid brother, he said.

His mother nodded. "Let's talk about it."

Sometimes children are so upset they shut down. It is particularly hard for them because they don't have the broad use of language that adults have. They also don't know what they're feeling. It's all new to them. And it just hurts. It can help them if we connect with and express what we see them feeling. Once again, we pace them by being fully present with them.

An example:

You've been hiding in your room all day even though your favorite uncle is here. Are you feeling sad?

It can help with small children who don't have the sophistication or experience to name feeling states yet, to let them talk about body sensations. If your daughter says, "I have a tummy ache," it might be the only way she has to express the emptiness and loss she is feeling.

At that point, what might be helpful is to ask them questions about their tummy. "How does it feel?" "When did it start?" "Does it get worse when you think about Grandpa?" And then you can share your own experience. "Sometimes, when I think about Grandpa I feel the sadness in my heart. Everybody feels it in different ways." When you describe the feelings your children don't have words for, it helps them see what is going on, put it outside themselves, and handle it.

Step 3: Use the Power of Touch

One of the stories we hear over and over from medics and rescue workers is the power of touch when there is very little else to do. One firefighter told us of how he held the hand of a woman buried under massive concrete rubble. He spoke to her but he discovered later on that she couldn't hear a word he'd said. She did tell him, though, that his presence and his touch had mattered more than anything else, that she *borrowed strength* from him, and if he had not been there and she had not felt the hope his hand afforded her, she doubted she would have survived.

Touch is a nonverbal first aid of the most natural and instinctive form. It is particularly soothing to children when they are afraid or upset. The overwhelming majority of children want to be held or embraced when they are confronted by something as vast and confusing as death. Occasionally, we have known children to be averse to touch when they are angry or distressed. In those instances, use common sense. It is best not to push a child to be held or to be open to you on your terms. Our job as adults is to be there for the child on his or her terms, to first see what it is that the child needs, and then find a comforting and healing way to provide it.

We believe that Verbal First Aid works best when we let our hearts respond fully in the moment. If a child wants to be hugged, hug him. If she wants to sit in your lap and nuzzle you for comfort, wrap her up in your arms.

There are so many prohibitions against touch now that this issue can be confusing to some. That's understandable. As a society we have become so frightened and so on guard that adults have unfortunately become hypervigilant around children. If that becomes a concern, know that there are places to touch that can be both pristine and nurturing. Rubbing a child's head as they put it against your hip. Holding a child's hand. One nurse told us that when a person of any age becomes very emotional, a gentle touch on the arm between the shoulder and elbow can stop them in their tracks and soothe them. What we're saying is, don't avoid the touch just because there are prohibitions against violating children's privacy. Let the child hug *you* and just rub a back or kiss the palm of a hand.

There is nothing sadder than to see a child look and reach up to an adult, his eyes and small hands asking to be held, to be soothed in his heartache only to be told to buck up or grow up. Let your arms and hands be as comforting as your words and let the healing begin.

Step 4: Cultivate Presence and Offer Reassurance

In a recent informal clinical inquiry, patients with chronic and terminal illness who had expressed a fear of death were asked what about dying made them the most afraid. Almost all of them said without hesitation: Being cut off from everyone else, being alone.

That sense of aloneness is one of the most frightening aspects of death for a child. Children who lose a parent or grandparent or a friend or relative they love find the notion of being without that person incomprehensible. *You mean I can't see him again?*

They are not all that different from adults in that way, except adults have had more time to refine the cognitive context within which they hold death, thus more experience with wrapping their sensibilities and feelings in intellectualisms to shield them from pain. Adults can explain it to themselves better, or at least pretend to.

For children, the sense of loss is raw and undefended. Aloneness for a child is also more closely associated (at a visceral level) with death itself. A child left all alone, especially a small child, has very little chance of survival unless an adult finds her and takes on the role (temporary or permanent) of caregiver and protector. Small, vulnerable, lacking the experience and skills for sustaining oneself on this planet, a child's fear of abandonment is a primitive and deeply ingrained response that runs throughout humanity and in much of the animal kingdom.

We see this in herd animals or highly social species such as wolves or monkeys. When one of their young is lost, it often desperately searches for its family (whether that's a herd or a band). An elephant baby does not stray more than fifteen feet from its mother's side for the first eight years. When a missing elephant calf is found, there is usually a jubilant reunion filled with nuzzling, physical contact, grooming, and reassurance.

The same is true of humans. When we experience that sense of aloneness (whether it is a concrete sense of aloneness such as being lost or an emotional isolation or fear such as grief), we need our herd for reassurance. The one thing that can alleviate that feeling is the presence of another person we trust or care about.

Presence is a spiritual, sometimes an ineffable or indefinable quality, but mostly it is an amalgam of what we discussed in the section on rapport. It is the ability to be fully in the moment, to be available physically, emotionally, mentally, and spiritually. It is the antidote to aloneness.

Step 5: Listen and Soothe Their Fears

Listening is as healing as it is because actually it is a form of pacing. As much as we think we have to explain death to our children—as if we could—we have to listen closely to what children are saying about it because they have so little experience with both life and death that they may labor under mistaken ideas. They may feel guilt if a sibling has died and they believe that it was their mean thought that caused it. They may feel diminished because the dead person is somehow getting all the attention. They may be angry at those who were supposed to make it better or afraid that this one death has invited in others. We won't know what's bothering them until we hear what they have to say. Listening in this way requires a genuine curiosity and a suspension of judgment. Be open to whatever your child has to say.

"What are you feeling?" you might say, truly solicitously, to a child who has externalized feelings by acting out or internalized them by becoming sullen. You can mirror her feelings as you see them, asking leading questions to give her an opening—all as long as you're not judging your child. If the child feels she can talk to you, even if she is not ready to say much, she may come around later and answer as if you had just asked, "Are you sad about Aunt Sally?"

Listening is not only pacing. Listening in this way is also an art. In our work with patients in clinical settings, one of the things we hear most often is gratitude that someone has finally taken the time to listen *actively*, to ask questions, to make the effort to really understand what they were feeling. Even though many of our patients are in the latter halves of their lives, they often say, "No one's ever listened to me that way before."

Heart-centered attention, listening that hears what *is* said and is *not* said, is also a way of seeing the essence of someone. This is so validating to people that sometimes that alone can be healing.

One man recalled a time when shortly after the death of his wife, he broke down in front of a friend. "Everyone up until that point had just been giving me encouragement to get on with things, you know? They were trying to be supportive, but it hurt so much to be without her. This time, though, that guy, bless him, just wept with me. It was the most healing thing that happened to me during that awful time. It was the beginning of my recovery."

Children need to be heard as much as we do. Perhaps even more because they are so unsure of what is expected in the world. How we listen actually helps shape their self-perception, which in turn is fundamental to their neurologic development. Pacing them by active listening assures them that we are available, that their reactions are not only valid but valued, and that they are safe with us.

Just as listening is a form of pacing, soothing is a form of leading. When we listen we are pacing where the child is at that moment— whether it's sadness or anger or confusion. When we soothe him we are leading him from there to a place of acceptance, calm, and clarity.

When a child experiences a death, he may have many different fears or concerns. We'll cover the most common here.

A death in the family may stir fears and questions about other losses—both past and potential. Your child may suddenly realize that Mommy and Daddy are not too different from Grandma or Grandpa or Uncle Ian and his sadness due to the death of a relative may quickly mutate into a fear of losing you. The very reality of death makes it a possibility anywhere, everywhere. If he can lose Grandpa, then what's keeping you here? The fabric of certainty that a child lives with is ripped when he is introduced to death. It is reasonable to reassure so long as there are no obvious fabrications or falsehoods.

If he expresses fear of dying, himself, or of losing you, you might say:

> I'm here and you're here, and we're going to be here for a good long time. And I'll take care of you, so you can feel safe in my arms, just like this (and then you hug him close for both of your sakes).

In the case of the death of a child (whether that's a relative or friend), children need to be reassured that they are safe, loved, and—if it is true—not in any danger of dying themselves. The fact that death can happen to someone like them, even if they don't understand it, is shocking. The adult reactions, which most likely will be horror and deep grief, will add to their sense of confusion and powerlessness.

From about age six, children may fear that they can catch death, or that they somehow caused it in another by an angry thought, or that it is a form of punishment that we can't even figure out how to avoid.

"I don't want Ivan to be dead," the child might say. And you will want to be accurate and true in your emotions, as well. "Neither do I. I miss him, too. But, I've got you, right here, and you're all right. And safe. And we can miss Ivan and still feel fine ourselves, and that's okay."

Sometimes the child who has died becomes idealized, and those remaining behind feel as though they are loved less. Without leaning on your children for support for yourself, it is very helpful if you make this a time of providing extra love.

Welcome their questions, say "I don't know" when you don't, and listen, listen, listen.

Step 6: Be an Example

They say that the best way to learn something is to teach it. Teaching your child Verbal First Aid principles is also one way you can empower yourself. In a situation of loss or impending loss, one of those ways is to take the initiative in expressing your own feelings, whether those are feelings of grief, sadness, anger, confusion, or doubt. When a child sees an adult weeping at a funeral, showing sadness and affection to others or asking for support from other adults, it gives him or her permission to do the same.

Being an example, or *modeling*, requires a sense of what is appropriate as well as what is emotionally necessary for our well-being. It would do neither you nor your child any good to look to him for reassurance or constant support. Unloading your grief on your child may make you feel better temporarily, but it reverses your roles.

Jackie
Jackie's story is an example of positive modeling.

Four-year-old Jackie just lost his favorite uncle after a long illness and has been withdrawn all day. He has clung to his father but has neither cried nor complained. His father, knowing that his son must be feeling the loss despite his youth and silence, picks him up and draws him into his lap.

"I miss him, too, Jackie," his father says as he allows the tears to flow down his cheeks.

Jackie sniffles. He wipes at his father's tears.

"Don't cry, Daddy," Jackie says.

"It's okay to cry when someone you love dies, Jackie," his father explains. "I'm here for you too, because I know you loved him as much as I did."

Jackie curls into his father's arms.

Teaching isn't preaching. Teaching is showing someone the way. It is a powerful form of pacing and leading because it is both verbal and kinesthetic. The learning for your child, then, occurs on many levels simultaneously. As it surely occurs for you, too.

Step 7: Put Things into Perspective and Remember the Good Times

Every loss is painful. However, some losses can seem more natural, more in keeping with the cyclical nature of life itself. With younger children, it might be helpful to use the attitude presented in Bryan Mellonie's book *Lifetimes,* that in nature everything has its own lifetime, with a beginning and an ending. Whether it's a day or a year, or the seven-to-twelve-year lifespan of many dogs, or eighty years—which can be the span for people—most get to complete their lifetimes unless a very serious accident or illness befalls them, which is rare. Everything that lives has an end to life. Even things that we don't usually associate with life can have a lifetime, like a bubble or a piece of fruit. To everything there is a season.

"Great-grandma Bess lived a good long life. She was born before there were airplanes! When she was little, there wasn't even television! And as she grew up, she saw so many things change. And she had children—your grandma—and grandchildren—me—and great-grandchildren—"

"Me!"

"Yes, you. And she had a good long life. And we can talk about her, and look at her picture sometimes and we can remember how much we love her."

Remembering can take many forms—it can be with stories, it can be with objects (jewelry, letters, photos), a favorite song, or a particular kind of day. In the beginning, remembering or even thinking about the one who is gone can be very painful.

"Stop talking about him. I don't want to think about it!" Caleb pouted at the kitchen table as his parents reminisced about Caleb's grandfather, who died only a week earlier.

"It hurts. We miss him, too."

Caleb is quiet.

"And when we think of the funny things he used to do, like when he did the twist at Aunt Jennie's wedding and bumped into the poor waiter with the tray full of cream puffs . . ." his mother pauses and then starts to giggle a little, even as her eyes water.

"That was pretty funny." Caleb smiles just a little.

"It makes us feel better," she continues.

"You remember when he made the spaghetti disappear?" Caleb joins in.

"Yeah, and I remember who sat on it afterward." She laughs. "God, I miss him."

"I miss him, too," Caleb says. "I'm gonna go do my homework."

Pacing and leading, once again, help a child stuck in fear and pain move into a healthy, open state in which he can remember his grandfather with love and humor even while he misses him and grieves his loss. What his parents taught him in this scenario is that joy and grief are not opposites.

Putting It All Together: One Family's Story

The following story illustrates how a family dealt with the impending loss of a beloved family patriarch. Through this difficult season of a single family's life, we see, step-by-step, how the parents managed the situation using Verbal First Aid with each of their three children.

Papa Bill was the grandfather of Jordyn, her brother, Jake, and her sister, Jara. Papa Bill had to undergo serious heart surgery when Jordyn was almost eight years old and her brother was five. Jara had only recently been born. Before his medical problems, Papa Bill had been at the center of the family. At six foot one and 240 pounds, he sang loud, laughed louder, and seemed to have the energy of a school kid in the middle of recess. He was a large man and lived larger.

Because Papa Bill was so important to the children, their mother tried to anticipate ways in which Papa Bill's upcoming medical procedures would affect them. She was instantly aware that the children were sensing her own worry and concern and attempted to counterbalance it. She sat down and explained in terms they would understand:

"Papa Bill's heart is not as strong as it used to be, so the doctors are going to help Papa's body be strong so he can play with you and be silly and sing with you again."

She explained that for this to happen, he would need some time for rest. He'd have to be taking medicine. She elicited the children's help, suggesting that they make pictures for him and talk to him on the phone to make him smile. The children of course missed him anyway, but at least they had things to do.

When Papa Bill came home from the hospital their mother had prepared a whole new roster of activities they could do with him: spend time on the Internet looking at pictures of new animals, playing guitar or piano together, putting together coin and stamp collections.

Life is seldom as simple as one complication at a time. In that family there were a number of deaths that preceded Papa Bill's. One was a close friend of Jordyn's. The other was an elderly but close cousin, and a third was the loss of Jordyn's much-beloved aunt, Pauline. By the time of Aunt Pauline's death, Jordyn began closely following her mother around the house. She became more intensely clingy when it was time for bed. "Stay with me," she'd say and reach for her mother's hand. "I'm getting nervous." It became a nightly occurrence, and soon she was not only becoming nauseated but had begun vomiting. She cried, "I don't want to die. I don't want you to die!"

Not knowing precisely what to say at the moment but knowing what to *do*, her mother took Jordyn to a therapist. Through that intermediated process, they learned to talk directly with Jordyn about death and God. They listened to her concerns. They asked her questions about those concerns. They avoided the impulse to try to minimize or dismiss those concerns with platitudes and empty assurances. "We talked about the fact that everyone dies but that we were healthy and expected to live long, happy lives together. I told her that was why we ate well and exercised and took care of ourselves."

In contrast, as might be expected, Jake was more black-and-white about death since he was only four years old at the time. He didn't speak much about it except to say, "Aunt Pauline died," then smile nervously and move on to the next subject quickly.

There came the time during Papa Bill's year-long illness that he was in and out of the hospital for long periods of time. His daughter and son-in-law kept what she called an open-door policy throughout Papa Bill's illness and after his death. They both said to the children, "Ask us anything, even if you think it might upset us . . . we always love you."

Finally the children asked, "Will Papa Bill die too?"

Though their mother's first instinct was to protect them, to hide the difficulties and the pain from her children, she ultimately understood that children are not only resilient but naturally nonjudgmental and—unless they learn otherwise—they love unconditionally. So she answered, "I don't know if Papa is going to die now."

Over time, as his illness progressed, and he had to return to the hospital, perhaps for the final time, their mother realized that the children not only had to be told what was happening but had to be a part of it, for themselves and for their grandfather. She and her husband brought all three children to the hospital. Each child had a different reaction.

Although Jara was not even two years old yet, her mother reports that she knew it was a place she didn't want to visit. "As we entered the building, she would say, 'I want to go home!' And then she became tense and quiet." She didn't want to get out of her stroller for the first few visits. She barely looked at Papa. Over time, she adjusted to the hospital environment, even becoming interested in the photographs on the walls, and would name them all as she passed. As Papa Bill became stronger, they would play peekaboo. He would save saltines for the kids.

"To this day, saltine crackers still remind Jara of Papa Bill," her mother says. Even a child as young as Jara is aware. "I talked to her about Papa as if she were older because I knew she understood. I said that Papa is sick and told her how happy it makes him to see her." As the months passed, Jara became more comfortable. It wasn't a scary place anymore. "On our last visit to my dad before he passed, they shared carrots and macaroni and cheese. Sure enough, Papa had crackers for Jara. She ran around his room laughing and playing peek-a-boo. They both had a great visit. The room was lively, it was a happy visit. I think he knew that she loved him. And she did."

Before she took the older children to see Papa Bill, the children's mother took photographs of how their grandfather looked in the hospital to show the children at home before they came to see him. She knew how different he looked and how frightening that could be for them. With words she tried to paint a picture of what they could expect. She explained that grandfather was in bed in a gown and that there was a roommate with him. She described the tubes for medicine to make him feel better and asked if they had any questions.

As it turned out they participated wholeheartedly. They made drawings and wrote letters. Then, when they visited, they sat on Papa's bed. They weren't afraid. They played cards with Papa Bill, got ice chips for him and blankets from the closet.

"They felt important. They felt comfortable. . . . Before that, the mystery had been worse. I think they were more scared by not seeing him. Jordyn didn't want to leave. They almost always wanted to come with me. As their parent, I worried and anticipated the worst and was pleasantly surprised at the outcome."

Eventually Papa Bill went to rehab, where things seemed to be taking a turn for the better. He was able to move around, to dress in his own clothes, play with the children a bit. They were far more comfortable visiting with him there where they could play cards in the sun room with him or listen to music as they held hands.

No one expected that one of those days would be their last together. But of course, it was.

Telling the kids about Papa Bill's death fell to his son-in-law. He spoke simply. "Papa Bill died today." There were no questions. Together they went to their mother, and they cried and held one another. When it was time for the funeral, the parents told the children, "It's a time to remember Papa Bill's life and what he loved, the things we want to remember about him." They also asked them if they wanted to write letters to their grandfather, which they did.

It's normal for the days around a funeral to be busy and full of distraction. But as soon as the last car leaves the driveway and the family is left to itself again, there comes what some have described as a tsunami of silence. No music. No television. No laughter. Just a seat that no one was going to sit in again. The family handled it the way it handled Papa Bill's illness—head-on. Tears were shed and fell where they landed. They talked about him. His pictures were everywhere.

Their mother noticed something interesting after a while: "Our roles reversed for a time. My kids became the caretakers. They wanted to comfort me, and they did. Jordyn said, 'Don't worry, Mama. Papa Bill will always be with you.'"

Amazingly, Jordyn, who had been so hurt by the losses of the previous year, suffered no setbacks. On Father's Day, her mother found this letter that she'd written to Papa Bill, approximately forty-five days after his funeral.

FATHER'S DAY PAPA BILL POEM
Papa Bill, Papa Bill
Lives on top of Papa hill

Never showers, never will
But we still love our Papa Bill.
I miss you so very much. And I really want to see you at your house and
do stamps together. But that's impossible now. So I just want you to
know I love you sooooooooooooooooo much! And even though I won't see
you, you'll always have a very special place in my heart. And I miss you
sooooooo very much.

—Jordyn (nine years old), June 15, 2008

What this family instinctively understood and what is so important for all of us to remember when we are hurt and saddened by loss is that those feelings are not only normal, they are a function of our love. Allowing them expression is a way of honoring our relationship with those we have lost.

As the story of Papa Bill and his family demonstrates, presence is the hub of Verbal First Aid. It enables us not only to see who we are with but feel them and understand what they truly need, so that we can be as healing with our words and our actions as we possibly can be. And it enables others to feel that we are with them, that they are the focus of our attention and love and therefore are in a safe place.

One woman who lost her son recently asked, "Is this normal, to feel this pain? It's so physical."

Yes. It is.

We asked her, "Can you imagine losing a child and not feeling any pain?"

"Oh. I guess that's true. I never thought of it that way."

It changes, we reassured her, and it fades in intensity somewhat, but it's a part of a host of memories she has of her son, some joyous, some hysterical, some now painful. Losing him has become a part of her relationship with him, a relationship that started before his arrival and now continues past his death.

Verbal First Aid Techniques Used By Papa Bill's Family

As you've just seen, the Verbal First Aid techniques can help us help our children through the loss and grieving process. Here's how they were used in Papa Bill's story.

Yes Set

When someone agrees with three or more of your statements they are more likely to agree with the next one, which should be the healing suggestion.

> You love Papa Bill. [Yes.] And you miss him. [Yes.] And you liked going fishing with him. [Yes.] Would you like to draw a picture of you and Papa Bill fishing now and think about how you love and miss Papa Bill?

Be My Partner

If you can engage the child in helping, then she feels she's doing something. How much we need to be doing something, sometimes, when it seems there's nothing to be done. The children in the Papa Bill story got ice chips for him and blankets from the closet and felt useful.

If it applies, you might say:

> Some people are coming to pay their respects to Papa Bill's memory. Would you please help me put out some teaspoons while I put out

the cups? They may be feeling sad, and sharing some tea with us might help them feel better.

Breathe with Them

If they are hyperventilating or sighing, sit with them and ask what they're feeling. Let them talk, and then you might say,

> Here, breathe with me and let's see if that helps you feel a little better. (And then breathe slowly.) As if we're filling up a balloon in our belly and then letting it go. How's that?

Truisms

Sometimes the facts are important in mitigating against fears. When Jordyn feared that other people might die as Papa Bill did, her mother explained that even though everyone dies, younger, healthier people are "expected to live long, happy lives together. I told her that was why we ate well and exercised and took care of ourselves."

Mental Rehearsal

The mother showed the children pictures of Papa Bill in his current state, thinner, in a hospital gown, so that they could be prepared to find him changed from the healthy, robust man they remembered. "She described the tubes for medicine to make him feel better and asked if they had any questions." The children understood well enough to see beyond the condition to the man they loved, and his appearance did not alter the genuineness of their joy at seeing him again.

Indirect Suggestion

Rather than trying to cheer the child up, it may be wiser to invite the child's imagination to solve the problem.

I wonder what you will think about that will help you feel good that you had such a wonderful Papa.

Pacing

After the funeral, when there was nothing left but silence, "The family handled it the way it handled Papa Bill's illness— head-on. Tears were shed and fell where they landed. They talked about him. His pictures were everywhere." When we honor our own feelings and each other's, rather than expecting anyone to buck up or deny the hurt, we learn something about ourselves and about what we value, especially as some of it goes missing. And because pacing provides the ability to share feelings in the deepest valleys of grief, it is a gift beyond words.

And a Death Shared Round the World

In the early 1980s, Will Lee, the genial grandfather figure who played Mr. Hooper, the neighborhood store owner on *Sesame Street*, died suddenly of a heart attack. Instead of simply writing him out of the script, the show's best minds decided to use this loss to help children experience death from a distance and learn a little about its mysteries and ways in which wiser people they've come to trust deal with it. Calling on psychologists, religious leaders, and grief counselors to help them forge the right message, the writers and producers created the farewell to Mr. Hooper that aired on Thanksgiving Day 1983, so that parents could watch it with their children.

Representing children everywhere, Big Bird lumbers into the midst of a social gathering of his grown-up friends to show them drawings he's done of them. They joyfully appreciate his talents but are taken aback when he shows them the picture he's drawn of Mr. Hooper and says, "Where is he?" They remind him that they'd told him that Mr. Hooper had died. But when, Big Bird wants to know, is he coming back? He's not, they tell him. "Never?" This thought is too mystifying for Big Bird. He first wonders aloud who will tend the store, make his birdseed milk shakes, tell him stories. They all say *they* will take care of him, reassuring him in the face of the loss that his needs will be met.

He appreciates that, wanders around momentarily in a Big Bird–ish circle and then says, "But it won't be the same." They pace with him verbally. He's right, they agree; it won't ever be the same without Mr. Hooper.

Then they offer him the consolations, the truisms we lean into in such circumstances. We can be glad that we knew him, that he was our friend, they say. They remind him that they have their memories of Mr. Hooper. Big Bird agrees, adding that he drew this picture from memory. We can "remember and remember and remember," he says. But he just doesn't like it. "It makes me sad," he says. And they pace with him. They all feel sad, too.

He tries one last argument, that everything was fine the way it was and why does it have to be this way. The only answer they have is "Because. Just because."

It had been an ongoing joke for years that Big Bird couldn't remember Mr. Hooper's name, so they close this part of the show with Big Bird saying, "I'm going to miss you, Mr. Looper," and Maria correcting him gently. And everyone gathers around to hug and console the grieving Big Bird.

"Just because" may seem to have left the subject hanging, but later on in the show, a baby is born, and we experience the wheel of life in all its wonder. Big Bird is in awe of how life and death work:

First you're here and then you're not; and then you're not here, and then you are.

The episode won a daytime Emmy.[1]

THE SPIRITUAL ANSWER

The *Sesame Street* story showed us that life is part of a constant stream. Beyond helping a grieving child through a loss, that philosophy and others that seek meaning or a larger picture are often sought, and often healing.

Although Verbal First Aid is a protocol that applies no matter what your belief, when we want to use words to conjure up a response to death it is easier for many to look to ideas about a soul, a heaven, other lives, an afterlife, the continuation of consciousness. This can be the most important consolation of all. But it is as personal and individual as each of us, no matter what faith or belief system we belong to.

In November 2009, the family of five-year-old Noah Biorkman of Detroit was told by the family doctor that Noah, diagnosed with neuroblastoma when he was three, would probably not live through December.

Wanting him to experience one last Christmas, his mother put out a call on Reddit and Facebook for people to send him Christmas cards. She was going to celebrate the holiday early, while he was still able to enjoy it. A television crew from WDIV visited their home on November 6, 2009, and filmed the curly-topped child as he opened the thousands of cards, letters, and gifts from around the world that flooded in.[2]

Opening an ornament of a stained-glass angel particularly delighted the cherubic child. The reporter asked him what it meant to him, and he explained, his face glowing, that he was going "to heaven. I'm going to be an angel."

Since none of us knows any different for certain, a spiritual answer can be meaningful and a blessing to those for whom this is a profound belief and relief.

SOME IMPORTANT NOTES AND REMINDERS

Here is a list of some behaviors that might indicate your child is having trouble adjusting to a death and could benefit from a professional evaluation. Most traumatic events have a pronounced impact for six to eight weeks, but if difficulties persist, please consult a professional.

- A dramatic or persistent change in eating and sleeping habits.

- Lethargy or profound lack of energy.

- Hyperanxiety or persistent irritability.

- Chronic inability to concentrate or decreased ability to perform in school.

- No interest in activities he or she used to love.

- Explosive temper tantrums.

Kara has a list of good children's books on the subject of death.[3] Hospice is a really good resource for further information.[4] Always remember that you can tell your children that it's up to us to make the most of the lifetime, to fill it with beauty and love, and that's what we do, even when we remember someone whose lifetime is over.

IN SUMMARY

- **Be honest.** If a loved one is dying or has died, we are best off telling the child what is happening quickly and simply. When possible, begin by referring back to past experiences ("Noah, you remember when Uncle Joe had to go to the hospital . . ." or "Remember when Fluffy got very sick . . .").

- **Explain what's happening.** Give the facts, but don't overwhelm a young child with details unless you are asked. He may have questions later. Be prepared to respond calmly and, again, truthfully and keep your explanations age appropriate.

- **Comforting touches.** A hand on the shoulder or an embrace can speak volumes when words are insufficient. When affected deeply by a loss, children may regress temporarily to an earlier stage of development and demonstrate a need to be held more often. This is a very common response and will usually fade with time.

- **Reassure them.** If your children express fear for you or worries that you might be hurt or killed, you can reassure them with confidence that you will be fine (unless this is obviously untrue) and will be around for a long, long time to take care of them. Death makes us all feel insecure, but this is especially true for children, who do not yet have the means to care for themselves.

- **Listen carefully and often; help them with misconceptions or mistaken notions.** Listen to what your child is saying. Sometimes her pain is aggravated by mistaken ideas about death,

Continued . . .

such as death is a punishment or the result of something negative the child thought.

- **Be a power of example.** Take the initiative in expressing your grief, fear, or anger. Accept your child's feelings and help him express himself verbally or through play, even if he is angry at the deceased. Reminiscing with your child is one way to do that.

- **Remember the good times.** Many traditions hold wakes, moments of celebrating the life of someone who has departed, to process the loss. Laughing about old memories and wonderful moments is as essential as crying.

- **Spiritual answers.** When the afterlife, heaven, angels, the flow of life and death, or reincarnation are part of the culture, it can be extremely healing in the face of the mystery of death.

8 Preparing for the Unexpected

Researchers say that in an emergency, only 15 percent of people are clear-headed and action-oriented. The remaining 10 percent panic and 75 percent freeze, stunned and bewildered, to their own peril.

—DR. JOHN LEACH, LANCASTER UNIVERSITY, ENGLAND

We know what you're thinking. The news on television is bad enough. Do I have to talk to my kids about all the terrible things there are to worry about in this world: the natural disasters, terrorism, dangers known and unknown?

But bear this in mind: Just because we recognize a possible threat doesn't mean we expect it to happen. To the contrary, being prepared can actually make you feel safer and provide a mental blueprint that could be lifesaving. Consider the fire drill that your child's school holds on a regular basis. Or the smoke alarm that you installed in your kitchen. Or the insurance you bought on your car. You still get behind the wheel every day confident of getting to your destination, feeling safer that you have some bases covered.

We love our children and want them to be prepared for the unexpected. But how can we do that without frightening them or suggesting a worst-case scenario? How do we help them be aware without becoming hypervigilant? How can we prepare our children for the really tough emergencies and decisions they may face without scaring or scarring them?

Together we can do this. First, take a breath and know that by teaching children Verbal First Aid you are giving them healthy ways to deal with whatever life might place in their path. The mental strategies you offer them with Verbal First Aid not only allow them to quickly assess what is happening but are designed to empower them so that they can instantly access concrete survival skills (It smells like smoke = get low to the ground, get out, and call 911).

Let's look at the facts. It has been shown that people who survive catastrophic events are those who have either had some prior, similar experience or those who have mentally rehearsed survival strategies in specific situations. Our minds are similar to computers in that way. We make a bookmark so we don't have to waste time searching the whole category. We note what is important so that we can find what we're looking for exactly when we need it.

To many people this is big news. Isn't survival an instinct we're born with? Don't we automatically run in the face of danger? Don't we just *know* what to do and do it?

The 85 percent of us who panic or freeze in an emergency challenge that assumption. According to Gavin de Becker, author of *The Gift of Fear*, we don't just automatically know what to do. So many of us have spent so many years in either too much needless fear or too little sensible fear due to overstimulation and numbing that we need to be taught and then reminded. In his decades of advising celebrities and politicians on security matters, de Becker has found that people in dangerous situations either don't hear their own alarms going off or they minimize their significance. Or, even when they're paying attention, they don't know precisely what to do.[1]

In her 2005 *Time* magazine article, "How To Get Out Alive," Amanda Ripley suggests that the instinct to survive in an emergency is either not an instinct at all or has been drummed out of us over years of acculturation.[2] There are numerous experts on fear who say that there are two things we most need to properly deal with a crisis:

- A solid and confident sense of intuition.

- The practical skill acquired by mental rehearsal.

We can help children develop their intuition by many of the techniques we've described so far in this book. When they tune into their bodies, they can recognize that the antennae of all our cells are working for us. That gut feeling, that pause when something doesn't look, smell, or feel right, is our intuition. It's different from a fear or panic response, and as we learn how to honor our feelings and connect with and trust in ourselves, we begin to discern that difference and pay attention.

When it comes to preparing for the unexpected, what we've typically called preparing may turn out to be fairly useless. Rather than training ourselves to adapt to emergencies by building our intuitive abilities and our resources (skills such as mindfulness, accurate interpretation of events, physical deftness, and specific practiced strategies for specific situations), we heighten random and generalized fear and encourage consumer frenzies. That there have been runs on everything from toilet paper to masking tape shows how panic can overrule common sense.

According to Ripley, one of the major reasons those who survived the attack on the Twin Towers did in fact live to tell about it is because they recognized the danger they were in and *got out quickly*. Her investigation revealed that in the case of the World Trade Center at least 135 people are thought to have had access to working stairwells and the time to reach them, but they never left their offices.

We believe that one reason the people in Tower Two got out was because they accurately perceived danger when it was present. They were present in the moment. Even though momentarily shell-shocked, they were able to gather themselves up and respond to their immediate surroundings with neither denial nor panic. (Once again, they were able to say, It smells like smoke = get low to the ground, get out, call 911.)

The other reason was that many of those who managed to escape the building had, reluctantly and resentfully, rehearsed their escape. Trained in the military, Rick Rescorla was head of security for Morgan Stanley Dean Witter, and he was insistent that the bankers and brokers up there on the high floors in the clouds drop everything whenever he declared his very frequent fire drills. His vigilance was not popular, but it was heeded. He trained them how to evacuate and how to go down the stairs; he let them know that the roof door was always locked. Essentially, he created a file folder or a bookmark in each of their minds labeled in bold letters **What to Do in an Emergency at Work.** And when they found themselves shocked and going into automatic—the way we all do when we're shocked—they looked into their emergency file folder and found the precise program they needed.

HOW WE PREPARE OUR MINDS FOR EMERGENCIES

So far in this book we've been dealing with the hurts and owies both as they've happened and in their aftermath. You've seen how using words and images can help minimize fear, shock, and pain and move your child into healing. This chapter is different because it will help your children become mentally prepared for confronting disasters and cataclysms *before they happen*.

We live, unfortunately, in a harsh world that seems to be getting harsher every day, especially for children. If it isn't terrorism we have to worry about, it's the increasing frequency of natural disasters (earthquakes, tornadoes, hurricanes, wildfires), and if it isn't that, it's the risk of human and product failures (building fires, airplane crashes, vehicle collisions, structural collapse).

Even though we don't want to instill unnecessary fears into our children about those possibilities, the fact is it pays to be prepared by giving these dangers proper thought and consideration in advance. We'd prefer not to think about the likelihood of becoming trapped in a fire, but as adults we can't go through a fire drill without thinking about the real possibility that the building could burn down. Yet fire drills are necessary and do save lives.

In a crisis, it is natural for us to resort to *automatic thinking*. In a crunch of time and resources, we automatically fall back on what we have already done, what we do by habit. To understand this, again let's consider the mind as a computer. In an effort to speed things along, nonessential systems are bypassed and our brains search for shortcuts to deal with whatever is happening. We do a file and folder search. If an emergency happens and we reach for the emergency file and find there's no information in it, no picture describing how we are to deal with this catastrophe, we draw a blank. We can't find an answer. As a result, we freeze and deny our reality. We refuse to believe what is happening. Because this unexpected situation hasn't happened before, and we have no reference for it, we fall back into what is called the *normalcy bias*. If it doesn't normally happen, it can't be happening now.

And because we have no automatic protocol for the situation, we don't act. Even though our lives may be literally at stake. That is why it is reported that 75 percent of people in emergencies freeze, dazed and confused. However, *it doesn't have to be this way.* As easy as it is to program a computer, in many ways it is even easier to program the brain for a specific skill. If we can learn to catch a ball, jump, drive a car, dance, solve a math problem, deliver a speech, write a poem, or perform any infinite number of tasks solely by mental practice, it stands to reason (and to experience) that we can learn to prepare for and survive an emergency.

Dave Grossman is a retired West Point psychology professor who trains elite military and law enforcement organizations and has written an important text on combat preparedness. He believes that when people can concretely anticipate incidents of extreme stress, and when they are prepared for them, they are far less traumatized when those incidents occur. Grossman sees preparation as a kind of inoculation against fear. In the military terms he uses, those who have been prepared for extreme situations by mental conditioning are called *stress hardy*.[3]

We're not trying to compare unexpected life situations to combat. But we find this to be compelling information; we recognize the benefit of having a prepared and readily accessible mental picture of what to do in specific situations. When we have a mental picture of what to do, we can go on automatic and act in a lifesaving way, thereby avoiding physical and emotional trauma. Mental preparation reinforces our intuitive capacities (the ability to know when *this doesn't feel right to me*) and gives us a sense of mastery, which can override both denial and paralyzing fear. It builds an all-important confidence in our abilities to care for ourselves and it makes it available when we need it most.

For smaller children, talking about dangerous situations and the possibility of someone they love being hurt can frighten them in such a way that the danger is all they can hear and think about, not the solutions.

An interesting aspect about how the very young may think about future events has been studied by psychology professor Yuko Munakata at the University of Colorado at Boulder. What she and her colleagues discovered was that children are not simply little versions of us with less capacity to do what we do. Their study seems to have shown that toddlers hear us, even when they don't respond, and that when they need the information, they think back on it and remember it.

So, it's not that they're not listening, they're just processing in a different way.

The researchers suggest that when a preschooler appears not to listen, offer the information up in another way. The example they use is this: Instead of encouraging children to put on a jacket to keep themselves warm before they go out into the cold, which doesn't compute when they're not cold, "try to highlight the conflict that they are going to face. Perhaps you could say something like 'I know you don't want to take your coat now, but when you're standing in the yard shivering later, remember that you can get your coat from your bedroom.'"[4]

In a similar way, as we show in this chapter, when we talk with little ones about emergencies, we can provide them with the information and let them know that they will remember it if they need it.

MENTAL REHEARSAL

There are four main Verbal First Aid preparedness techniques under the banner of Mental Rehearsal offered in this section.

1. **911: the magic number for help** provides ways to teach 911 information to the youngest tots.

2. **Fictional distancing** helps children over the age of four learn preparedness without feeling personally threatened.

3. **Four-count breathing** is a centering technique that can be taught to any child old enough to want to learn self-control.

4. **Plan B** helps older children see the value in being prepared.

Your choice of which is best for your child will depend most on your child's age and personality, but you'll find that these techniques will help your child to be *stress hardy* and find answers within herself that can be lifesaving.

Mental rehearsal in advance of an emergency is empowering and can build self-confidence. With Verbal First Aid, you can train your children so that their minds are, in effect, programmed to perform the lifesaving actions that will maximize their chances for survival.

But how do we mentally prepare our children for the kind of extremely stressful situations they might be at risk for encountering? How do we make them feel capable instead of terrified and preoccupied with all the bad things that can happen?

The Verbal First Aid answer is a form of mental rehearsal for the bad stuff that can be accomplished while minimizing the negative fears that often go with it. This involves helping your child attain awareness and preparedness because, as with anything we practice, we can become more adept and better able to act quickly, effectively, even sometimes automatically at times when others who are less prepared might freeze.

This process requires your own willingness to be brave and feel competent so that you can train your children to deal with anticipated risks while at the same time minimizing or eliminating the danger of accompanying fears. And because studies show that the training process is enhanced when children are able to talk about the rationale for the training steps and ask questions about new information, you'll want to create an atmosphere and setting in which this can happen.

911: The Magic Number (For the Youngest Children)

Preparedness for just about any serious emergency at home starts with learning how and when to make a 911 call and what to say when the call is connected. How old must a child be? Two recent examples demonstrate that *very* young children are capable of learning the essentials that enable them to save lives.

In Oak Harbor, Washington, a two-year-old girl saw her mother collapse on the floor and picked up the phone. She dialed 911 and used the only words she knew to call for help.

"Mommy owie," she said.

The operator repeated it to make certain she'd heard it correctly. "Mommy owie?"

"Mommy owie," the child said, and an ambulance was dispatched to the address traced to the house phone number of the caller.

In another incident, this time in central Oklahoma, three-year-old Madelyn Eaves was able to guide fire paramedics to her home when her pregnant mother collapsed from a blood pressure condition, even when they didn't have the address. The three-year-old and her nine-month-old brother were alone with their mother when she collapsed, and Madelyn called 911 on the cell phone. The neighborhood mapping system allowed the operator to track down the particular block, but not the house. The 911 operator asked Madelyn to describe the color of the cars in the driveway and the color of the house. Madelyn was asked to turn on the outside light, and to open the front door. When the operator was able to hear sirens and know they had arrived, she asked Madelyn to go outside and wave to the ambulance.

Madelyn was calm and self-possessed for the eleven-minute call. Her mother explained that she had learned a "Nine-One-One-Green" (for the green *send* button on the cell phone) song only a week before it was needed.

How can we train young children to become similar potentially heroic 911 callers? Ericka Miller, the Oak Harbor, Washington, mother of the two-year-old, explained that, "I had actually shown her, a few months ago, 'This is what you do if there's a big owie,' and showed her what buttons to push." And she added, "I am so proud of her."[5]

Generally, a young child is always accompanied by an adult,

so this training comes in only when the adult is not well or is not there.

How do we explain to a child who is only two to four years old what an emergency is and when to call for help? Our heart's tendency and desire is to want to ignore or deflect attention away from the sirens and hurrying emergency vehicles that inevitably intrude on the tranquility of our everyday lives. We don't want to worry unnecessarily about somebody else's troubles. We don't want our children to have nightmares. Thank heavens everything is okay for us. The sirens will go away.

But consider this alternative approach: to become proactive and use what is happening in their environment to begin to explain this part of life, difficult as it is, to them.

Scenario 1

You see or hear a fire truck or ambulance going by. Your child might ask about it, or you can initiate the conversation.

You: You hear that? That's a fire truck or an ambulance. They're on their way to help somebody.

Owen: Who are they going to help?

You: We don't know. Maybe there's a fire somewhere. Sometimes fires start small but they spread and a whole house has a fire in it. All the people have to get out and the fire truck comes with water hoses to spray and put out the fire.

Owen: (Considers that scenario.)

You: Maybe somebody fell down and hurt himself and needed some help to get to the hospital. The ambulance can take him to the hospital, so he can feel better.

Owen: What's a hospital?

You: A place where there are lots of doctors and nurses, you know, like Dr. Lake, who can help people get well.

Owen: Dr. Lake.

You: Yes. The sirens mean there are people who are hurrying on their way to help, to the hospital where doctors are waiting for whoever needs them.

(You will no doubt have your child's attention at this point, and here is where you turn the 911 corner.)

You: I'm so glad that we don't need help right now, aren't you? Let's hope that the people who need the help are getting it right now. (In addition to setting the stage for a discussion of 911, this facilitates the development of empathy.)

You: You know *how* the firemen and the doctors know how to come and help people?

Owen: How?

You: The people who need help call them on the phone. A special, magic number. 911. Can you say it?

Owen: 911.

You: Yes.

You can also use some situation from the child's own indirect experience:

Scenario 2

You: Do you remember when Grandma fell and had to go to the hospital, and later we went to see her and took the flowers? Well, do you know how she got there? Grandpa called 911.

Owen: He did?

You: Yes, and the helpers came and took her to the hospital.

Owen: (Thinks about that.) Grandma had a box of candies and gave them to me.

You: Yes. And then she got better and came home.

Owen: Yes.

You: It's good that we don't need help now. But if *we* ever do need help, we can get the people with the sirens to come and help us, just the way they went to help the people just now. Do you know how we can do that?

Owen: How?

You: The magic number on the phone. When you need an ambulance or a fire truck or the police, you can call for it by pressing three numbers on the telephone: 911. And like magic, you can get help. Can you say them with me again?

Owen: 911.

You: Right. When you call that number there is someone on the other end who can send the helpers after you answer a couple of their questions. Probably someone just called 911 and that's why the sirens went by.

Owen: 911.

You: Yes. And if there is ever a big owie and you need a grown-up to help you, you can call 911.

Next time there's a siren wailing, don't be afraid to use a question like the following one as a way to start the conversation.

You: What do you think is making that siren? A fire truck? An ambulance?

Owen: (You may get an "I don't know," but that allows you to reinforce the message.)

You: When there's a fire in a house and people need help, they call the firefighters who know what to do. They come with their water hoses to help.

Learning and Rehearsing Fire Safety at Home

By the time children are three or four, you can start practicing home safety, depending on the area you live in, for tornados, hurricanes, earthquakes, or—the most prevalent in all areas—fire. The following is an example of what to say and how to go about conducting a home fire drill.

Scenario 1

You: Do you remember when we heard the fire trucks and we talked about how the firefighters come with hoses and put out the fire?

Maya: Yes.

You: Well, if we had a fire here, which we probably won't, but if we did, we'd want to know what to do, right?

Maya: (Nods.)

You: So let's look around and figure out what we'd do. We wouldn't take an elevator, that's not a good idea. We'd go to the steps, or the front door to get out right away, right?

Maya: (Nods.)

You: If there's smoke, which sometimes happens in a fire, we'd get down really low, and get out as fast as we could. And if the fire was by the door, what would we do?

Maya: I don't know.

You: Maybe we'd go out the back door. Or the window. What do you think?

Maya: Yes!

You: And then we'd ask someone to call 911. Why?

Maya: The fire truck.

You: Right. The firefighters would come and put out the fire. And we'd all wait at that bench down the street, until the fire was out.

Maya: Yeah.

Then, should it ever happen, you can refer to the calmer conversation and remember what you're supposed to do: Remember the magic numbers that you call when you need help? You have a folder for it.

PARENT CHECKLIST FOR 911 AND PREPARING YOUNG CHILDREN FOR HOME EMERGENCIES

1. Be proactive in setting up scenarios and talking about how we deal with emergencies. In that way, you have something to refer back to should an emergency happen. Use a real but not personally frightening incident to illustrate, such as fire engines going by or sirens in the distance.

2. Use what's happening to reinforce what you're teaching them. If your child is slightly older, upon hearing the sirens or seeing the vehicles, you can begin a discussion by wondering aloud, "Where do you think they're going? Why? How come they're going fast? What are they doing?" And enable your child to do some thinking.

3. Help them learn concretely. Discuss making 911 calls if they need a grown-up's help. If your children have number recognition, you can have them point to the numbers on the telephone. You can suggest that they write the numbers down with crayon on a piece

Continued...

of paper that you'll tape up on the wall by the phone. Or even if they don't know how to make the numbers, you can write them down and then show them how to compare the shapes with the numbers on the telephone dial.

4. Give them guidance about speaking to the operator. Depending on your child's state of development, you can explain what kind of information they have to give to the 911 operator. It can, as we've seen, even be limited to such phrases as "Mommy owie." It is equally good to remind a child of any age that 911 is only for emergencies: "But you only can call 911 when something is really wrong. You should never call just to talk because they have to always be ready for emergencies. But if we have an emergency we can call."

5. Reinforce what you teach. Later on, you can recall your discussion: "Remember the sound of the siren? Remember what it means? That someone needs some extra help."

6. Teach your child easy ways to remember 911 principles: Jingles are a very practical and effective way to help children learn. There's a little song and cartoon on YouTube about calling 911.[6] The song and words on the screen begin as follows: "If there's trouble and you're alone, call for help on your telephone. 911." It tells children to give their name and address and shows and sings about who could come to the rescue: fire truck, police, and ambulance. It says you can be a hero for yourself or someone else and is a nice resource for parents trying to explain this process and help children remember.

The Polly Klass foundation has very specific 911 practice details for children, which include dialing and then speaking up: "I need help."[7] There are scripts for children, as well. And 911 for Kids has lots of information and activities about when and how to call 911.[8]

7. Talk about and plan exits to escape a fire and meeting places outside the home if an emergency happens. Firefighters tell us that sometimes they inadvertently frighten children when they appear during a fire with their equipment and masks on. Children run from them and they cannot rescue them as easily under those conditions. So we have to make certain that children understand who the firefighters are and what they do. Maybe there are pictures of firefighters in their full gear you can show your children. Maybe you'll want to organize a trip of youngsters to your local fire department, so they can see the engines and the people and the masks firsthand.

8. Practice mental rehearsals for emergencies in the home.

Fictional Distancing (for Children Ages Four and Older)

Many children's stories work in this way: A fictional character (the hero or heroine) experiences the problem and it is solved and resolved in such a way that everyone is happy and the child/reader, while not taking it personally, gets to learn a lesson. This technique can be especially valuable when we are discussing serious problems, those that could, if brought too close to home, cause sleepless nights and more.

Generally speaking, by the time a child is around five years of age, he can participate in the let's pretend of making up stories. The fictional distancing technique involves making up a story in which a character represents your child. The character has the same name as your child and is the hero of the story. He partners with a favorite action hero or cartoon or storybook role model, and together they help another child, this one fictional, anticipate an extremely stressful event, rehearse, and survive it.

Fictional distancing enables us to transfer fear potential to a fictional situation in which your child's character can play a hero role by training and preparing the other child, who is at risk for suffering the peril. It distances the risk and empowers your child simultaneously.

Creating an imaginary alliance between your child and your child's favorite cartoon or action hero helps promote the impression that while it is all just a story it also involves your child in performing at his or her best. This way, your child is able to be proactive in dealing with the risks and in participating in decisions with you about what survival procedures should apply, but the child who is at risk is someone else. The result is that your child has mentally rehearsed—is inoculated with—all the necessary procedures and expectations and can fall back on those procedures when an anticipated risk arises. But in the meantime, the risk remains theoretical, a virtual television drama that doesn't immediately have to be feared. And the fact that there is an adult (superhero) there also helps keep the child from feeling too brave or grandiose. It's more a matter of learning what needs to be done without taking it personally than it is about learning to be a hero in an emergency.

A grandfather we know used this technique to develop a story to help his grandson Tristan's peanut allergy. The allergy is so serious that if Tristin ingests anything that contains peanut oil, he risks going into anaphylactic shock that can kill him. Wherever he goes, an adult has to be armed with an Epi pen. So the grandfather wanted to increase Tristan's awareness of the seriousness of the problem without making him neurotic about food.

The training task was simple: to make sure that Tristan always remembers never to eat a peanut or peanut butter and to always check ingredients of any food that's offered to him to make sure it hasn't been prepared with peanut oil. In this case, it's difficult to get too far away from what's really at stake, because Tristan has to know he can face a life-or-death situation if he forgets. But too much of this reality will probably get in the way of the training purpose.

Tristan's favorite storybook character is Thomas the Tank Engine, one of the trains with human personality traits from the stories of Wilbert Awdry. Tristan's grandfather sat down with Tristan and posed a scenario in which, every month, Thomas the Tank Engine had to pull a goods train to deliver candy to children up and down the railroad line. Occasionally, there would be a child who, like Tristan, could not tolerate peanuts. The challenge was how to protect the children with the allergy.

Tristan and his grandfather created a story in which a fictional character named Tristan would accompany the train deliveries to make sure that the at-risk children were properly warned and shown how to check ingredients. Together, they worked out ways that Tristan could warn the children and show them how to read package ingredients contents to look for peanut references. As the story unfolded, the character Tristan ended up as a hero by rushing to prevent a boy who was at risk from eating a peanut candy. They finished the project by creating a storybook with pictures of Thomas, the character Tristan, and the children.

In the process, the real Tristan was able to internalize all of the warnings that the fictional Tristan was using to teach the fictional children with allergies to avoid their risks. The effect was profound and ongoing. It enabled the real Tristan to become vigilant about his own perils, all in a context that deflected away from the possible personal fears that Tristan could have had about himself.

Teaching Tornado Preparedness

Here's an example of how a parent, Mitch, might help his son, Samuel, whose favorite cartoon character is Shrek learn about tornado preparedness. Mitch looks up information so he himself knows what to tell Samuel (and in the process learns a few tips that might help him survive as well). Then he begins by establishing the basic scenario:

> **Mitch:** How about if we play a special story game. I'll make something up to get it started. Okay?
>
> **Samuel:** Okay.
>
> **Mitch:** Let's imagine that there's a boy who lives in a house out in the country, and where he lives is a place where there are lots of tornados. His parents love him, but they're very busy, and they're out working a lot, and even when they're home, they are busy, and they always forget that the boy doesn't know about tornados. Oh, and the boy is pretty shy so he never thinks to ask anybody. Now, what shall we call this boy? Can you think of a name for him?
>
> **Samuel:** Benjamin.
>
> **Mitch:** Benjamin? Okay. And we'll also have a character who looks a lot like you, and we'll call that character Samuel, just like you. Samuel lives far away from Benjamin in a place where there aren't nearly as many tornados, maybe none at all. And at the beginning of the story Samuel and Benjamin have never met. Okay?
>
> **Samuel:** Okay.
>
> **Mitch:** But one day Shrek himself comes up Samuel's street and right up to his front door. He's all excited and says: "You've got to

come with me! I'm going to visit Benjamin, and I need your help. There might be a tornado coming his way next week, and I need you to help me talk to Benjamin about what he should do if that happens." Now what does Samuel say to that?

And off we go into the story to meet Benjamin. Of course, they can take a break to have Samuel draw pictures of the characters or pictures of scenes at appropriate points. Or the story can be acted out by puppets or dolls.

When they talk, Samuel, with Mitch's help, or with Shrek's help, can tell Benjamin what a tornado would be like, what he'll have to do if he sees one, where he'll have to go to be safe. Mitch and Samuel can look for authoritative tornado resources on the Internet together. And remember, it isn't just the procedures Benjamin (and the real child, Samuel) will be learning. They are concretely anticipating an event that, if it comes, will be less traumatizing because of the mental rehearsal. At the same time, they are learning to anticipate their own courage, cleverness, and ultimate survival.

Then the parent can finish off the story by embellishing the plot with some kind of exciting finish or happy ending. Maybe the character Samuel goes with Shrek to visit Benjamin again the following week, and it turns out that there *was* a tornado, and Benjamin did just as Sam had told him, and "he wasn't real scared because he knew what to expect and what to do." He took his sisters to the basement, just as Samuel had told him to do, and everybody is safe now and fixing up the house.

You can of course adapt scenarios for whatever risk you think should be rehearsed, but the structure is basically the same.

PARENT CHECKLIST FOR FICTIONAL DISTANCING

What follows is a basic checklist for applying the fictional distancing technique for mental rehearsal and another example of how we apply it.

Here are the steps parents can use to facilitate the procedure:

1. Set up the scenario that presents a fictional child in a situation that requires the child be prepared to anticipate some critical peril (earthquake, tornado, hurricane, building fire, flood). It's a good idea to give the child a name other than the names of your child's friends and associates. You can give the fictional child some of the same worry traits or inattentiveness traits that your own child has, but don't overdo it. There will of course also be a child character with the same name as your child, who will help the fictional child learn.

2. Prepare in advance a checklist of mental rehearsal items that should be covered. This might entail doing some Internet research in preparation for various emergencies. Although you will then know what needs to be done (fire, smoke, keep low to the ground, leave the house immediately without stopping to take your belongings, meet at a designated place away from the house), you will first solicit your child's thoughts and then work together to guide the child toward the right answers, making sure that to the best of your ability all the bases are covered.

3. Place all of this in the context of your child's favorite adventure heroes, cartoon characters, or storybook figures. Incorporate settings that are familiar to your child and have the child help you decide on scenes and hero figures or role models. This will anchor the notion that this is all a story, to be taken seriously but not to

be immediately internalized as a personal fear. It will also heighten your child's interest and involvement in the process.

4. Plan to make this a physical project. You can have crayons and markers, paper, and so on available so that the child can illustrate the story. Alternatively, you can gather dolls or puppets and toys so that it can be acted out.

5. Keep notes so that you can refer back from time to time to the creation of this story. This will be useful for refreshing the training process. And if you're really resourceful and energetic, you'll create a little book that you and your child develop together, so that you can actually read it again and again.

As you do all this, you'll notice also that there's a distinct side benefit for you. You too will become mentally prepared for the same risks simply by taking the time to train your child!

Four-Count Breathing (for Older Children)

We deal somewhat differently with older children on the assumption that they probably won't be receptive to the fictional distancing story-making technique. For them, we suggest that they be introduced to the four-count breathing technique (also called 4-4-4-4 breathing and box breathing) at the onset of high stress and potential panic.

This breathing technique is a practice that can benefit everyone who is first confronted with a frightening, highly stressful, or panic-inducing situation. We include it here under the older kids category because it's unusual that very young children will be able to adopt the practice readily. But, as parents, you know your children's capabilities.

You be the judge of what age is appropriate for its introduction. It's a wonderful way for everyone who's ready to discover that we have a technique for self-control in a difficult situation.

At the onset of extreme tension, when we are inclined to panic, our breathing becomes shallow. We either forget to breathe or we begin to hyperventilate. Either way, when we breathe shallowly our brain does not get enough oxygen. When this happens, the brain panics, tells us we're in trouble, and we begin to shallow breathe even more. We lose a sense of rational present time, and we enter into a shock state. Bruce Lipton explains that the hormones created by stress constrict the flow of blood to the thinking part of the brain, the prefrontal cortex, limiting consciousness and intelligence. The blood goes instead to the more primitive brain, which is designed primarily for survival, which means that in extreme conditions we become less intelligent. Although this process is largely autonomic, according to Dave Grossman, who trains special forces, we can train against it using a particular technique.

Luckily, nature has built in a means by which we can reconnect to our more rational brain. It is simply breathing. The key is first to become aware that we are frightened or upset. Maybe we feel it in our stomachs or our hearts or our throat. We have to tune into that feeling to force ourselves to become aware of our breathing. When we become aware of our breath, we are able to come back into present time and begin to think rationally again—away from the panic state.

This is a simple technique that has been demonstrated to work for people in various situations of extreme stress that could produce panic. It is used to train rescue workers and soldiers in the Special Forces to minimize the risk of panic states. We've modified it with a few extra helpful tips of our own about checking in with the place in the body where you hold fear, so you can become aware of it. It can work for you. You can also teach it to your older children.

EXAMPLE 1

You: Sometimes things happen that can make you very frightened. Have you ever felt that way?

Emma: (Nods.)

You: One time I was so scared I couldn't even move for a couple minutes. Can you remember a time when you were very scared?

Emma: When I couldn't see you when you were supposed to pick me up at school.

You: Yes, that was really scary. Where did you feel it? In your belly? In your throat?

Emma: In my throat!

You: So here's what you can always remember to do if you ever feel that feeling in your throat happening. As soon as you feel it beginning, close your eyes for a second and hear my voice, just like this, saying, "Breathe." Listen to my voice. "Breathe." Can you remember that voice in your head when you feel scared in your throat? Try it. Remember when you were scared. Go back to that feeling when you couldn't find me and feel it in your throat. Now close your eyes and hear me say, "Breathe."

Emma: (Tries it.) I think I can.

You: Good. Now take a deep breath, in through your heart. Breathe in while you count to four—one, two, three, four—letting your breath seem to fill your whole belly like a balloon. Hold your breath while you count to four again—one, two, three, four. Then slowly release it, watching your belly go down, all the while counting to four again—one, two, three, four. Then pause for another count of four—one, two, three, four. Now do the whole thing again. Take in a deep breath for a count of four again. Let's try it now just to see how it feels . . . (You count. Emma breathes.)

You: There, good. Now let's do it again. And while you do, you might like to picture something you love, or a place you love to be, like Grandma's house in the country.

Afterward you can suggest to your children that if they ever have a nightmare or they're afraid before having to take a test, whenever something really scares them, and they get that feeling in their throat or their heart or their stomach, they should remember to do the four-count breathing first and notice how it helps. They should repeat it as many as four cycles, until they feel their minds working again to be able to solve whatever predicament that confronts them.[9]

PARENT CHECKLIST FOR BREATHING/ CALMING TECHNIQUE

1. Check in with your body or let it call your attention to itself so you realize what state you are in. When you ask "Where in your body do you feel it when you get afraid?" you're accomplishing several things. First of all, it brings the child back into his body, more grounded, and into present time instead of an older fear that hijacks his mind through his memory and makes him even more afraid because of an earlier unfortunate outcome.

One parent told us about how she learned this truth, about recognizing where in our body we hold our feelings, from her child. When Ruby was three, she was visiting a museum with her mother in France and somehow wandered away. When she realized she wasn't with her mother anymore, she froze in panic, crawled up on a bench before a portrait, curled up into a ball, and waited. Her mother, Hillary, ran through the museum, afraid to shout out her daughter's name in that quiet place but terrified that the child was lost or worse. Finally she found Ruby and they both embraced in heart-throbbing relief. Years later, Ruby told her mother that "Every time I panic, I have that very same feeling in the pit of my stomach that I had that day when I was lost in the museum." Recognizing that feeling, we can use it to launch the breath that calms us.

Second, it has been shown in studies of what is called *state-dependent learning* that what we learn in one state we tend to remember best when we're in that state again. So if you have children remember the fear, feel it, and then teach them the technique, they'll be aware of how they felt, emotionally and physically, and return to your instructions when they feel that way again.

2. Close your eyes to shut out distractions and just be present with yourself right in this moment.

3. Hear the voice of someone you trust saying "Breathe." We turn for help, even as adults, in these frightening moments, and if we can hear our parent's, teacher's, or friend's voice telling us what to do, we can avoid the freeze part of fight or flight, the dazed and confused feeling 75 percent of people in panic experience.

4. Do the four-count breathing. Let the stomach fill up like a balloon.

5. Tune into your heart and breathe through your heart. Studies have shown that when the brain and heart get in sync, we can function best. The child can even put her hand over her heart, which many of us do naturally when upset.

6. Use guided imagery to picture something or some place you love while you're breathing to increase the level of relaxation. As you've

Continued . . .

seen, remembering a safe place or happy time actually changes the physiology.

There are other variations, including putting the tongue to the roof of your mouth, breathing in for four counts through your nose silently, holding it for seven, and breathing out through your mouth with a whooshing sound for seven. This is a more meditative kind of breathing and is useful for training your mind/body for calm when you do it twice a day.

Try these techniques for yourself, and see how you can come back to yourself in a renewed way and be able to think more clearly.

Consequences and Positive Future Pacing

Just a time-out here to talk about talking about consequences. That word probably makes you think about punishments for discipline ("If you don't do this or that, you'll be grounded), but that's not what we're talking about here.

What we want to have happen is for children to know that when they do *this* . . . *that* happens. So that they realize that they can actually anticipate what might happen, which means that the world is a less scary place and that, if they pay attention, they may have some control over events.

A simple: "If you don't look where you're going, you'll bump into someone or something," is a start, but in Verbal First Aid we use positive images or future pacing. We like to tell them what to do, not what not to do. So we might say, "To avoid bumping into things and people, look where you're going. Make sure your head is moving in the same direction as your feet!"

Even very young children can begin to learn consequences. If they throw their food off the high chair, it lands on the floor. (Sometimes they love that, but it's still a consequence . . . and the next consequence might be an upset parent, and no more food.)

And that leads again into preparation, whether it's imaginary or literal, as we'll see with Plan B.

Plan B (for Older Children)

The plan B approach gives older kids the opportunity to take one step away from the direct fear that might come from imminent emergency preparedness, but it still gives them the opportunity for mental rehearsal. It's based on the premise that "This probably will never happen, but just in case it does, we can be ready."

When your child goes out for a bike ride on a beautiful sunny day, for a skateboard adventure, out on in-line skates, he wears knee pads and helmets. They don't mean he's going to fall, and he doesn't have to fear that he's about to, but with them on, he doesn't have to worry about that. It's a just-in-case measure that makes him know at a deeper level that he's safer.

EXAMPLE 1

A friend was explaining boat safety to her six-year-old who couldn't wait to be an eight-year-old and grown up enough to take sailing lessons. She was telling him that he had to be big enough to overturn his boat, swim around it, and right the boat again, pulling himself up into it.

"Tip it over?"

"Yes, that's right."

"But why?"

"Because some day, there might be a big wave that capsizes your boat, turns it upside down, and you have to know how to do all those things to get back into it."

He was clearly surprised. Up until that moment to him sailing was only about enjoying a glorious day on the water and perhaps learning a few things about jibs and sheets and all those odd sailor words.

"No," she explained. "You need a plan B. Plan B is a story you imagine, just so you can be ready if it ever happens. Sailing is mostly great fun, but you have to have some good ideas about what to do if things suddenly don't go as planned, if a cloud turns into a squall, so you'll be ready and be able to do what you need to do. That's why you have life preservers, and carry cell phones, and learn how to swim and tread water. Then if something happens that you didn't exactly plan for, you have a plan, after all. Plan B. And you go right into action on that one."

You could also tell your children about surviving a scary situation, such as a fire, a tornado, or a hurricane.

Example 2

You: When we were little, sometimes there would be a hurricane and all the electricity would go out! All down the block. And there would be no lights! And no TV!

Shane: And no computer?

You: Well, mostly no TV! But no computer too. Imagine that. And we would all huddle around candles for light, and listen to the wind and eat whatever was easy to eat, because our mother couldn't cook in the dark kitchen. But we prepared for it, because we knew it could happen in the fall. We would have a special place for candles, and matches, and even a little stove to cook on with special oil that didn't need electricity. We each had a flashlight and extra batteries ...

Shane: Let's make one of those things.

You: An emergency kit?

Shane: Yeah.

You: What should we put in it?

And then you have an opportunity to talk about how you can be prepared for the unexpected.

PARENT CHECKLIST FOR PLAN B

1. Let children know that preparing for problems is not the same as expecting them. Most likely those problems won't happen, but knowing that we know what to do, being ready for them, makes us feel safer, just as we wear a helmet on the bike or a safety belt in the car, just in case.

2. Have your own plan B and let them know that you do so because, once you're prepared, you can stop thinking about those concerns and just have fun.

3. This is not an opportunity for bravado. Just because someone knows how to defend himself with karate, for example, doesn't mean he should provoke fights. Plan B is only for emergencies, which aren't likely to happen, but for which, if they do, we will be ready.

Continued ...

While younger children like superhero stories—what would Dora the Explorer do?—older children love stories about their families. They want to hear what happened to you or Uncle John when you were young.

A REMINDER ABOUT THE
POWER OF WORDS

This book is not about the emergencies so much as how we talk and think about them. We wrap up this chapter by once again pointing out the unique power of the words parents utter to their children, especially in dangerous situations. Allow us to repeat ourselves: *Always be careful of your words!* Even idle words, uttered with good intent, can have lasting effects upon children.

Consider the mother who warned her young daughter who was fiddling with a backseat car door handle in the days before safety locks: "Don't touch that door handle! If you fall out of the car, you'll break into a million pieces, and I'll just leave you there in the road!" The daughter was rebellious. She continued fiddling. The door opened, and she did fall out as the car was starting up from a stoplight. Fortunately, because of her bulky winter coat, she sort of bounced on the pavement and wasn't hurt. But as the mother was screeching to a stop, her daughter was up and running toward the car, waving her arms and crying out: "Don't leave me here. I didn't break into a million pieces. See? See?"

Two lessons from this. The idle threat didn't work. It probably only made the enticement of the door handle all the more attractive. And the words nevertheless embedded themselves in the daughter's imagination and became a form of expected reality. What stuck in her mind was the breaking-in-a-million-pieces part, not the fiddling-with-the-door-latch part. Always be careful with words. Every one of them has literal impact on the eager mind of a young child who hasn't reached sufficient levels of sophistication to filter out those words that are uttered in jest or hyperbole.

Consider also the experience of those who grew up with the duck-and-cover training for nuclear attacks. The children were filled with Cold War fears of attack by Communist enemies, and the drills provided little if any practical help and made no rational sense to the young children who were confronted with the training in school. The lasting effect on sensitive minds was little more than propaganda-bound fear and anxiety. As one therapy patient reported during a session, years later: "There was nothing about that experience of crouching under my desk that made me feel safe. Nothing."

Unfortunately, those kinds of careless warnings that are designed to communicate messages of hate and fear that go beyond purposes of true mental rehearsal are being repeated for children around the world today. Television is filled with horrifying imagery and reminders of the dangers of modern life, but little about how to mentally and psychologically prepare effectively or care for ourselves. It becomes the task of all parents to filter and interpret these messages so that their impact is minimized.

The essence of preparedness is *presence in the moment*. When we are truly present we are able to assess what is a real danger and what is an imagined or borrowed one. Having a constant, low-level fear of germs, diseases, abduction, and anonymous bombs is quite distinct from moving through life comfortably and suddenly being alerted to an imminent crisis by the smell of smoke in the next room.

What we are imparting to you so you can share it with your children is the ability to see clearly, be calm, and respond effectively. Whatever your situation. Wherever you are. In tai chi and kung fu it is called the ability to see with *soft eyes*. With eyes that are looking outward but fixated on nothing in particular, we are able to see more, judge less, and respond far more rapidly and accurately, detecting movement even when it is coming from behind us. It is a state of gentle but broad awareness, not hypervigilance.

So remember the breathing that takes you into present time. And remember that the wise and helpful mental rehearsal images and words you use to help make your child stress hardy, to help your child plan for emergencies, can become the folders in their minds that open automatically, just when they're needed most.

POWER OF WORDS AFTER A CATASTROPHE

Tragedies are a part of life. With television and the Internet, however, every tragedy everywhere on the planet can instantly become a part of all our lives. Because of the profusion and intrusion of all this communication, it's almost impossible to keep children from witnessing disasters that are broadcast and rebroadcast (ad infinitum) on televisions in their own homes or on their cell phones or on the radio.

After the September 11 terrorist attacks, the U.S. Department of Veterans Affairs subsequently issued a report that identified two factors they believed were related to increased stress, which in turn could lead to actual post-traumatic stress disorder in children.

One was how much television of the event they were exposed to. Researchers had even coined a new name for this: *CNN stress*. This is the discomfort and anxiety that is directly due to watching a tragic scenario over and over. The other was the amount of parental distress and loss of control the children witnessed. It is interesting—and fortunate—that both of these are factors we can manage.

The first and most obviously simple strategy is to limit their exposure to the constant replays. Even if they have been overexposed, you can shift the impact of those telecasts by reminding them that this is not happening as they watch it. It's over. It's important to say:

> They keep on showing that tornado, but it only happened once. It's not happening now, even though you see it. It's an old movie of it. Like the videos of you and your friends when you were at the park. You're not there now, even though you can watch it. It's over. The tornado happened, and it was scary and some people were hurt. And firefighters and doctors helped lots of people to get better. And it's over now.

The second factor—how the adults around them are reacting—is especially important. Everything else can be spinning, but when we are still—centered—and can calmly talk and listen to children at such times, we are not only helping them feel safe in the moment but are helping make the difference in their health and their trust in the world.[10]

After catastrophic events, children will often see adults crying. There is nothing more frightening to a child than seeing their authority figures lose their composure. Even as adults we feel the same way when an authority figure we've come to rely on, someone we trust, is helpless to help us or someone we love. So, even though our hearts ache and tears flow, we have to calmly reassert our authority and offer reassurance for their sake. "I'm right here, and you're in my arms," for the young ones. "You're safe."

And for the older ones, the critical tool is pacing. They will want to know that even though you're emotional, you're with them and you understand. They want to know they're not alone and that the emotional currents are not going to sweep away everyone they need and on whom they depend. "Yes, it was scary. There are crazy people in the world. Bad things happen and we know that. That's why we prepare for bad things that can happen. Like agreeing to meet up at the tree in the park if we get separated. And having our emergency kit, with the water and bandages."

HOW SOME CHILDREN HAVE COPED

We saw the amazing ways that children in China helped themselves heal from the terrible shock and loss of the 2008 Sichuan earthquake. Because it was midafternoon when the earthquake hit, children were gathered in the schools and when those buildings collapsed, whole towns lost their most precious asset. Children who survived became another matter entirely. Using guided imagery, future pacing, and their imaginations, this is how some of the children dealt with their fright, losses, and hopes.

After the earthquake, some children said they wanted to become architects and build better buildings. Some children who were going to temporary schools in tents drew pictures of houses that had wings or feet. Houses that were ready to escape should another earthquake threaten. Some who had lost friends returned to the site of their crushed school and vowed to live good lives in honor of those who couldn't.

That is, recasting the memory with a positive outcome and seeing it happen better in the future leads to being better prepared and to positive brain changes going from victim to planner and achiever.

NOW IT'S IN YOUR HANDS, YOUR HEART, YOUR WORDS

In her book *The Unthinkable: Who Survives When Disaster Strikes— And Why*, Amanda Ripley discusses the precious skill of resilience. "People who have it tend to also have three underlying advantages: a belief that they can influence life events; a tendency to find meaningful purpose in life's turmoil; and a conviction that they can learn from both positive and negative experiences."[11]

The ultimate purpose of Verbal First Aid is to enrich a child's reservoir of responses so that whatever he encounters in life he will meet with wisdom, flexibility, resourcefulness, and resilience. Now that you have this new toolkit, you have the power to transform the inner voice that generates the running commentary on our lives and judges every downturn into a voice that is courageous, empowering, resilient, and healing.

Shortcuts for Preparing for Emergencies and Metal Rehearsals

CALLS FOR HELP (911)

■ Talk to your children about fires and emergencies when you hear sirens, and about who can come to help when someone is hurt.

- Tell your child, "This is what you do if you have an owie and you're alone or need help from a grown-up. Call 911."

- Practice it. You have them practice saying, "I need help," in a pretend call.

- Teach them their address if they are old enough to learn it.

- Tell your children that the policeman or fireman or doctor will come to help. Show them pictures of firemen in their gear.

- Tell them to call 911 *only* if they are hurt or alone and need help.

FICTIONAL DISTANCING

- To practice lifesaving techniques with your young child, make up stories in which he or she is the fictional hero and works with a favorite icon (Dora the Explorer, Spider-Man) to save other children.

FOUR-COUNT BREATHING

- Practice a breathing technique: Have children tune into their bodies when frightened, say "Breathe" to your children whenever they are frightened to remind them to hear it in their own minds when they need it, have them breathe through their hearts, in and out to a count, and think of something that makes them calm.

PLAN B

- Develop a plan B, a just-in-case scenario of preparedness that can make your children feel safer, knowing that they know what to do if the need arises.

FACING A CATASTROPHE

- Limit television time and talk with your children about what they've seen: "It's over now. We're safe."

- Model calm.

- Give children other ways of coping (drawing, writing a different outcome, using their creativity).

9 Healing the World with Verbal First Aid

A human being is a part of a whole, called by us "universe," a part limited in time and space. He experiences himself, his thoughts and feelings, as something separated from the rest . . . a kind of optical delusion of his consciousness. This delusion is a kind of prison for us, restricting us to our personal desires and to affection for a few persons nearest to us. Our task must be to free ourselves from this prison by widening our circle of compassion to embrace all living creatures and the whole of nature in its beauty.

—ALBERT EINSTEIN

For thousands of years, scientists believed that there was nothing between us and the moon, between us and the sun, between us and the stars in the sky, that there was nothing between two people but space. Recently, however, scientists have begun to discover the multitudes of fields within which we all exist and are now saying that space is far from empty.[1] It's filled with waves, particles, antiparticles, and mysteries as yet unnamed and unknown.

What we know for certain is that sounds are waves and vibrate through and in the fields between us. This is how we hear someone speak. What is now being shown is that our thoughts and emotions are literally being transmitted beyond our bodies to others through these fields in ways we do not yet understand but that are clearly and scientifically measurable.

Candace Pert, PhD, who, as section chief at the National Institutes of Health was one of the discoverers of neuropeptides, explained in an interview how thoughts affect our physiology and the physiology of those around us. She refers to the great deal of data that show that "when you assume an emotional state this somehow aligns your internal chemistry and in turn your internal vibrations." And she doesn't use the term *vibrations* idly. She means that the cellular receptors of the chemicals of emotions (neuropeptides) vibrate "as they pump ions and information through the cell membrane, so we truly are a bundle of electrical vibrations. *Our states of mind really do project very far out and affect the people close to us and this is reflected in the sequence of bio-chemicals that are released*" (emphasis added).[2]

This is measurable. There are now technologies sophisticated enough to measure the energies that our hearts and minds project into the world and out to others. This equipment, which Bruce Lipton discusses in his book *Spontaneous Evolution,* can "detect a beating heart's powerful electric and magnetic fields meters away from its source. *Field-influencing electromagnetic messages broadcast from our hearts have been shown to entangle with the hearts of others in the field*" (emphasis added).

Furthermore, he adds, magnetoencephalography, which can read the brain's neural energy patterns outside the body, offers "physical proof that brain activity is broadcast into the environment."[3]

Brain activity is broadcast into the arena that Dr. Larry Dossey,[4] among others, calls a *nonlocal field.* Like fish unaware of the water in which they swim, we swim and resonate in the nonlocal field, connecting with each other in ways we always knew but never named.

We have all experienced the nonlocal field in our own lives. You think of a person you haven't seen or heard from in years. You don't know what made you think of him, but later that evening he calls. You get a feeling in the pit of your stomach that tells you to call your child's school and see how she is. You do and find out that she's taken a fall and is in the nurse's office. You're in your kitchen preparing dinner, and your spouse or partner comes home. And without turning around or hearing anything unusual, you just know it's been a bad day.

If we are beaming out and receiving information in this way on a regular basis, and we're doing it unconsciously, imagine what we could do if we became conscious of our thoughts and words so that they were as healing as possible.

WHAT'S LOVE GOT TO DO WITH IT?

There are mysterious forces in our world, some of which scientists have spent decades, even centuries, trying to explain (gravity), some of which medical practitioners use but cannot put under a microscope (energy, chi), and some of which are all pervasive if invisible (consciousness). One of these—you can't see it directly but can detect its effects—is probably the universe's bottom line, the be-all and end-all of what it's all about (love).

There are, however, a variety of loves:

Some love is conditional: I will love you if you do that, or behave this way. The remainder of the statement "I will love you if . . ." varies, but the sentiment is that one must be worthy of love on the lover's terms. Parents have been known to withdraw love if the child is *bad* or disobeys. Earlier generations felt that this was a necessary part of maintaining discipline, and the withdrawal of love (*I'm not talking to you until you change your ways*) was considered not only legitimate but a prerequisite for the moral conditioning of humankind. Conditional love exists as long as certain criteria are met.

Then there is romantic love, known as Eros, typified by the Valentine's Day kind of love most of us think of when we use that four letter word. Most people see love as something romantic, something passive. You *fall* in love. It happens to you. You see someone across a room and are helplessly swept away.

This is the same initial falling into love people experience with their own children when they are newborn. Even if you are firmly bonded to your child by that love (the chemical oxytocin floods the mother's body at the time of birth to ensure that), you fall with an automatic swoon. And it's been documented that chemical changes that can lead to bonding are true for fathers as well. This kind of love is still a passive experience of being overtaken by something larger than oneself, unconstrained by mere reason.

Unconditional love is often seen as a higher form of love. It is all-accepting: I may not approve of your behavior, but my love remains. It's the way we love infants and puppies and kittens in general, with an innocent, unconditional love that we feel is returned absolutely, purely, and with utter trust. But in many ways, this also is passive. It emerges as a current from deep within and is similarly not driven by reason or conscious thought. Some have likened it to a state of grace, as if joy were bestowed upon them from on high.

But there is yet another love. We call it *active love*. It is known by a sense of constant forward evolving motion of positive engagement.

It goes beyond unselfish charity or the personal experience of emotion. It is *lived* love. It is love itself that begets itself anew in each moment, each encounter, each word spoken. It is a stream with an infinite source that shapes the rocks it finds in its way, that carves canyons through mountains and affirms life wherever there is the potential for it. It does not wait to receive before it gives.

You might look at these different aspects of love in another way. Yes, love is all of these things, just as H_2O is water, ice, and steam.

When it is ice, it is a solid.

When it is steam, it is gaseous.

When it is water, it is a liquid.

Love of a particular person is like ice = solid, limited by shape.

Unconditional love is like steam = passive, flows everywhere without judgment.

Active love is like water = the strongest element in the universe, wearing down rocks, nourishing; it is a generating, underlying force; there is no life without it. It changes things as it goes.

What's love got to do with it? Dr. Elizabeth Kubler-Ross was asked in an interview what factors made the difference in healing the little patients she worked with who were born HIV-positive. Her answer was easy, "The only brief way I can tell you is that they were totally marinated in love. Totally." She explained that biologically the children were also born with their mothers' antibodies, in addition to the virus, "and if there is bonding, and if there is love and cuddling and all the things children need to survive, then they begin to develop their own antibodies."[5] And some of those children have become HIV-negative.

"Marinated in love," she said. To stimulate the immune systems to heal HIV. Perhaps marinating our children in love should also be a Verbal First Aid protocol. And not just *our* children, *all* children, and in fact all of us. It involves what Einstein called for in the quotation that opened this chapter: "widening our circle of compassion." Because all of the scientists we've referenced here have made the case for how we think = how we feel, and how we feel = how we heal (and how we live)—as individuals, as families, as a planet. When we change the way we think and speak, the field changes.

The time is always now. We feel that way about Verbal First Aid. No matter what has gone on before, it's never too late to begin thinking in ways that heal and inspire—with your child or even with yourself. No matter what has gone before, you are given the opportunity, *from this moment on,* to set your own course. When you become aware of what can change as a result of higher, kinder, wiser, more generous words and thoughts, you will see that it is happening right here, right now. It's never too late to get on the moving sidewalk of creative possibilities.

EMPOWERING CHILDREN TO TAKE HEALING INTO THEIR OWN HANDS

Maybe the word *empowering* sounds a little grandiose to you. Or maybe it brings up thoughts of a movement that has something to do with drums and the moon.

Perhaps if we sum up here, defining our idea of what this empowerment entails, you will lean back comfortably and allow these concepts to flow through you, gently moving yourself, your children, and the field in which we are building our future a little deeper in the direction of what psychologist Abraham Maslow called self-actualizing.

It is our belief that when children have learned how to use imagery, how to change their thoughts, and how to listen to and gain mastery over their internal state—both emotional and physical—they will have learned the skills of a lifetime. They will have become free in the truest sense of the word.

What more could loving parents desire for their children than this self-mastery, the ability to navigate through the world as they develop with grace, ease, confidence, compassion, and a real knowledge of who they are and what they are doing here?

In the old Grimm Brothers' tale of Sleeping Beauty, twelve fairies bless the new princess with twelve generally unspecified bountiful traits to afford the little royal child a perfect life. In her book *The Twelve Gifts of Birth*, Charlene Costanzo names the gifts of the wise women:

Strength
Beauty
Courage
Compassion
Hope
Joy
Talent
Imagination
Reverence
Wisdom
Love
Faith

The gifts come with a blessing for the child's use of these characteristics in his or her life.

Costanzo expresses the hope that every child, not just royal babies, knows that he or she is blessed with these gifts, and that when the child does, we will all live in a different kind of world.[6]

A child who knows his own abilities; who reflects beauty where he walks; who is not afraid to explore with excitement and belief in a good outcome; and who is resilient, dreams, respects, and envisions in a heart-centered way is a blessing to all he encounters.

Verbal First Aid reminds us that with every word and thought we can decide in every moment how to feel and who we are willing to be. Our children are the future of the world. They are in our keeping.

Can we be the wise beings who anoint all of our precious children with these gifts, which are truly their own, anyway?

APPENDIX

Magic Words

You may want to refer to the following list of magic words to quickly remind yourself that your child's heart and body are listening and that with these words you can help to turn a painful, scary, or sad moment into an opportunity for healing and wisdom.

When you do use these words, please remember the importance of presence, rapport, pacing, and love. And also remember the power of the positive—say what you *want* to have happen, not the things you don't.

PACING WORDS

Awwww
Oh, that's sad
I see
Oh, show me where
I'm right here . . . and you can relax now

You did? Oh, my

I've got you now

Mmmm, let me see

Words for Healing Suggestions

Allow: You can **allow** your arm to relax; You can **allow** your breathing to slow down.

Notice: You may **notice** how your fingers are feeling cooler and more comfortable as I put this bandage on them; Did you **notice** that you're moving your arm better today than you were yesterday?

Wonder: I **wonder** how you're feeling when you see the surprise in the doctor's faces as you make a complete recovery; I **wonder** how comfortably you'll be able to sleep now that you have your doll with you.

How: **How** easy it is to lift your leg like that; **How** smart of you to remember to take your medicine.

Imagine: **Imagine** your favorite place with me as if you're right there right now; You can **imagine** the comfort you'll be feeling as you let the medicine do its job.

Everyone knows: **Everyone knows** that everything comes in waves, the ocean, the day and the night, the seasons, even our feelings; **Everyone knows** that your body has ways to heal itself, just the way it did the last time you had a cut and by the time we took off the bandage, it was almost gone.

Let's: Oh, **let's** take a look at that cut and **let's** stop that bleeding right away.

As I . . . You can: **As I** put this cool compress on your eye, **you can** begin to feel the comfort reach all the way deep down into the boo-boo.

Natural: It's **natural** to feel the way you do, and it's **natural** for you to feel better too.

What if: What if we asked Spider-Man how he'd take care of that boo-boo; **What if** we pretended that the knot in your stomach was a chunky piece of ice and you imagine a bright sun shining on it and melting it.

Begin to: You can **begin to** move that leg a little as you **begin to** feel a little stronger.

Breath: Blow out this imaginary birthday candle and then take a nice deep **breath**.

AUTHORS' FINAL WORDS

A SUMMONING

As the mother of two, the stepmother of two, and the grandmother of four precious beings on this turbulent jewel of a planet, I have, as I imagine you do—as everyone does—a vested interest in the future.

This book may appear to be a parenting book or a book about the power and magic of words, but I see it as a summoning to our full potential to connect and interconnect in a uniquely new way.

Here's where I learned about what we truly are: During the school day at 2:28 in the afternoon on May 12, 2008, in Sichuan Province, China, an 8.0 earthquake shook local society to its foundations. While other buildings in the towns and cities of that region remained standing, it was the schools that flattened and collapsed. It is estimated that eighty thousand people died in that one event and the aftershocks that followed. Some five to ten million people were left homeless, as floods poured in. Because families in China were allowed only one child each, the loss of these children was not only tragic, but it ended families, ended lineages. For those women over childbearing age, the disaster was intolerable. And suicides ensued.

When I was invited to work with the crisis counselors in Beijing in July 2008, the whole idea of Verbal First Aid was at risk. It is based, at least partially, on words. And yet working with these counselors, I could not depend on specific words. I couldn't tell whether the translations I was receiving accurately portrayed the situation that the counselors were reenacting for me. And I couldn't tell if the words I said in response were translated as I meant them.

How could I count on my loosely translated Verbal First Aid words giving solace to people whose loss was beyond imagination?

Demonstrating Verbal First Aid on a stage before a packed auditorium, I listened and used pacing to reflect back that I heard them. One at a time, counselors came up and told their stories. And I brought everything I knew to each encounter. One counselor came up on stage and turned her back to me, saying that she worked by phone and never saw the faces of the people she helped, so I couldn't see hers. She told the story, as if she were the mother, of losing her four-year-old daughter in the disaster. She cried. I asked her to tell me what her child loved to do. She spoke of how the little girl loved to sing and dance. I explained to the counselors in the audience that good memories are healing, and allowing her to speak of the good times was a balm to her spirit.

I looked out at the faces of the assembled crisis counselors. There we all were, me so ardently longing to help; them so devoutly looking for an answer. Ultimately, the sentence that brought tears to everyone's eyes, that changed the vibration in the room, was one of faith. But it took into account that I knew nothing of the religions, beliefs, or customs of the people gathered there, who were Christian, Buddhist, Muslim, nonbelievers . . .

The sentence, however it was translated, whatever words in which it drifted across the room to shift everything, was simple and yet complete. "She lives in your heart," I said. I wanted to find a reason for the mother not to commit suicide, for her to go on, in love. "She *lives* . . . in your heart."

In that moment I saw what seemed like a light ignite in the chests of nearly every person leaning forward toward me. My heart to theirs; theirs to mine. And everything changed.

The counselor went back to her seat in the auditorium, but then turned and demanded the microphone. She spoke passionately for what seemed like a long time. People were crying. I had learned only a little Chinese in my stay there, none of which seemed to apply, but I felt the bond among all of us growing as I awaited the translation. Finally the translator turned to me and said, "She says she feels different, lighter, that her heart has never felt this way." When we finished, people rushed the stage. Something had broken open that was new and deep and real, and they were seeing their story with new eyes.

We live in a time when the ground seems virtually to be shifting under all of us. However, when we know what kind of beings we are—that we read each other's intentions and emotions in every exchange; that nothing is wasted or lost; that our minds, bodies, and spirits are experiencing each other in every encounter—then we are obliged to speak words of caring and even to think thoughts of kindness.

This is the language of the heart. It is the way we can seed the blossoming of tomorrow's humanity at its finest.

Like the people in that auditorium, let us see with new eyes.

Pretend that you can see an energy field around every child as you talk to him or her. Does it brighten at your words? Does it fade?

Can you keep a warm sense of humor at the awkward newness of children striving to get it right?

Can you marinate children in love?

Can you speak nurturance?

Can you see *every* child as your own?

Can you be a blessing to everyone you encounter?

I happen to believe that you can.

And it is *your* doing so that will birth the future we all long for.

With love,

Judith Simon Prager

Hermosa Beach, California; Prescott, Arizona

STANDING BEFORE MYSTERY

Verbal First Aid is about words. But it is also about something far bigger than words alone.

All of us at some time stand before the incomprehensible, the unutterable, the indefinable. All of us eventually face moments of such pure beauty, such abundant grace, or such utter loss that words fail us, and the only thing that helps us communicate is a connection that defies ordinary logic. This rapport, this ability to make the most intimate, sublime sensibilities understood with only a simple word or a single gesture is, to me, the essence of Verbal First Aid.

What we say and how we say it—whether that's with our mouths, our hands, or our hearts—can move mountains.

I know this because I have been working with words in two very distinct manners for nearly thirty-four years. And I have seen what intention can do.

As a young copywriter, I saw what words could do when we used them to motivate people to buy things they not only didn't need but that hurt them. And I remember when I decided that I'd had enough.

I was twenty-eight and we got an ad order we had for a company that manufactured diet pills. Their marketing was geared to young anorexic women and without warning something in me shifted and the whole thing angered me. The ad I came up with was just a picture of the pill and the headline: "Fat Chance." Needless to say, my creative director didn't appreciate it. I left for graduate school, and in the ensuing years I made my penance by learning to use words to help people heal.

As a social worker for the last twenty years, I've also seen what words do—how they can leave a lifelong scar in a child's heart and how they can help heal those wounds, no matter how deep or old they are.

Words are tremendously powerful . . . both to help and to harm.

There is a sublime mystery to who we are and how we function. I don't pretend to understand it, how a word can make such a difference in another person's life, even though I stand before these numinous events every day and I know the science that supports it.

The concept that words are powerful is familiar to anyone who reads the Bible, where they figure prominently from the third sentence: "And God said, 'Let there be light.'" He did not create with His hands or fashion His creation with tools. *He created with words.* He spoke: "By the word of the Lord were the heavens made" (Psalm 33). To speak is to will into existence, to create with God. What we say hangs somewhere between heaven and earth, hopefully, prayerfully drawing us closer and higher.

Simple things—sometimes just a hand, a nod, a tear, or three words:

I'm right here. But with genuine compassion, words can move entire lives, taking a person from hopelessness to grace, from isolation to love, from pain to freedom.

May this book move you and those you love. May it bring you closer to your heart's deepest longing. May it bring you the relief, the joy, and the healing you hope for in ways that will surprise and amaze you every day.

Judith Acosta
Placitas, New Mexico; Butte, Montana

END NOTES

CHAPTER 1

1   "Human Emotions Hold Sway over Physical Health Worldwide," *Science Daily*, March 5, 2009. Available at www.sciencedaily.com/releases/2009/03/090304091229.htm; accessed July 12, 2009.

2   Johns Hopkins Medical Institutions, "Positive Attitude Is Best Prevention against Heart Disease," *Bio-Medicine*. Available at http://news.bio-medicine .org/biology-news-2/Positive-attitude-is-best-prevention-against-heart-disease-8844-1, and http://www.hopkinsmedicine org/press/2001/November/011112.htm; accessed January 11, 2010.

3   Ran D. Anbar and Susan C. Geisler, "Identification of Children Who May Benefit from Self-Hypnosis at a Pediatric Pulmonary Center, I," BMC *BMC Pediatrics* 5 (2005): 6. Available at www.pubmedcentral.nih.gov/articlerender .fcgi?artid=1112600; accessed January 11, 2010.

4   A. J. Barnes and D. P. Kohen, "Clinical Hypnosis as an Effective Adjunct in the Care of Pediatric Inpatients," *Journal of Pediatrics* 149 (2006): 563–565; http://www.ncbi.nlm.nih.gov/pubmed/17011334.

5   Quoted in Robert Moss, "Thoughts Can Heal Your Body," *Parade* magazine. Available at http://health.msn.com/health-topics/alternative-medicine/articlepage.aspx?cp-documentid=100197848; accessed January 11, 2010.

6   Quoted in *The Observer Effect*, "What Are You On?" Available at http://theob servereffect.wordpress.com/2008/01/10/what-are-you-on/; accessed January 11, 2010.

7   Margaret Talbot, "The Placebo Prescription," *New York Times Magazine*, January 9, 2000. A version of this article appeared in print on January 9, 2000,

on page 634 of the New York edition; http://www.nytimes.com/2000/01/09/ magazine/the-placebo-prescription.html?pagewanted=1

8 University of Michigan Molecular and Behavioral Neurosciences Institute (MBNI), *The Journal of Neuroscience*, 25(34); (August 24, 2005); http://www .med.umich.edu/opm/newspage/2005/placebo.htm.

9 L. K. Mannix, R. S. Chandurkar, D. L. Tusek et al., "Effect of Integrative Medicine i.e., Guided Imagery on Quality of Life for Patients with Chronic Tension-Type Headache, *Headache* 39 (1999): 326–334. The use of Diane Tusek's guided imagery CDs has been shown to be an effective adjunct to the treatment of headaches and migraines and are helpful for children with attention deficit disorder (ADD), depression, anger, and fears. They have a calming effect on children and help them sleep. CDs available at www .guidedimageryinc.com/g_surgery.html.

10 Thomas M. Ball, "A Pilot Study of the Use of Guided Imagery for the Treatment of Recurrent Abdominal Pain in Children," *Clinical Pediatrics* 42 (2003): 527–532; http://cpj.sagepub.com/cgi/content/abstract/42/6/527.

11 C. L. Baird and L. P. Sands. "Effect of guided imagery with relaxation on health related quality of life of older women with osteoarthritis," *Research in Nursing and Health*, 29(5) (2006): 442-51; www.pnhs.purdue.edu/directory/ publications/lsands_pubs.pdf.

12 Bruce McEwen, Rockefeller University Newswire. Available at http:// newswire.rockefeller.edu/?searchTerm=bruce; accessed January 11, 2010.

13 Benedict Carey, "Study Finds Prior Trauma Raised Children's 9/11 Risk," *New York Times*, February 5, 2008.

14 J. S. Gordon, J. K. Staples, A. Blyta, and M. Bytyqi. "Treatment of Posttraumatic Stress Disorder in Postwar Kosovo High School Students Using Mind-Body Skills Group: A Pilot Study." *Journal of Traumatic Stress* 17 (2004): 143–147.

CHAPTER 2

1 D. Spiegel, and J. R. Maldonado, "Hypnosis." *Textbook of Psychiatry*. American Psychiatric Press (1999): Washington, D.C., (1243–1273).

2 F. Ralph Berberich, "Pediatric suggestions: Using hypnosis in the routine examination of children." *The American Journal of Clinical Hypnosis*, 50 (2007): 121–129.

3   Bruce Lipton, *The Consciously Parenting Project: Fascinating*. Excerpt of Bruce Lipton's article on conscious parenting, The Consciously Parenting Project's Notes, http://www.facebook.com/note.php?note_id=103827796798.

4   Helen Thomson, "Emotional Speech Leaves 'Signature' on the Brain," *NewsScientist*, June 11, 2009.

5   Although the standard understanding up until this point has been that babies are not aware of others' minds, there is some new research that indicates that babies may be innately sociable and helpful to others: Nicholas Wade, *New York Times*, "We May Be Born With an Urge to Help," November 30, 2009; http://www.nytimes.com/2009/12/01/science/01human.html?_r=1.

6   Chris Mercogliano and Kim Debus, "Expressing Life's Wisdom: Nurturing Heart-Brain Development Starting with Infants 1999," *Journal of Family Life*, 5 (1999), http://www.appliedmeditation.org/The_Heart/articles_joseph_chilton_ pearce.shtml.

7   Alexandra Lamont, a study carried out at the University of Leicester, shown on BBC's *Child of Our Time*, July 11, 2001; www.edu-cyberpg.com/Literacy/ whatresearchwomb.asp; accessed January 11, 2010.

8   S. Hesketh, A. Christophe, and G. Dehaene-Lambertz, "Non-Nutritive Sucking and Sentence Processing," *Infant Behavior and Development* 20 (1997): 263–269; and Irène Deliège and John A. Sloboda, *Musical Beginnings: Origins and Development of Musical Competence* (Oxford University Press, 1996).

9   David Chamberlain, ed., "Life before Birth: Prenatal Memory and Learning," 1995. Available at www.birthpsychology.com/lifebefore/earlymem.html; accessed January 11, 2010; and A. J. DeCasper and W. P. Fifer, "Of Human Bonding: Newborns Prefer Their Mothers' Voices," *Science* 208 (1980): 1174– 1176.

10 F. Wirth, *Prenatal Parenting* (New York: ReganBooks, 2001), 36–37.

11 Ibid., p. 6.

12 Available at http://children.webmd.com/news/20080424/cuddling-cuts-preemie-pain; accessed January 11, 2010.

13 Benedict Carey, "Study Finds Prior Trauma Raised Children's 9/11 Risk," February 5, 2008; http://www.nytimes.com/2008/02/05/health/research/ 05trau.html.

CHAPTER 3

1   Norman Cousins, *Anatomy of an Illness*; 1980, 68-69; http://www.marquette
    .edu/library/news/2008/Sheikh.shtml.

2   Quoted in Leiden University, "Learning from Mistakes Only Works after
    Age 12, Study Suggests," *ScienceDaily*, September 27, 2008. Available at www
    .sciencedaily.com/releases/2008/09/080925104309.htm; accessed on January
    11, 2010.

CHAPTER 4

1   Donald Trent Jacobs, *Hypnosis for Medical Emergencies* [video].Westwood
    Publishing Company, Glendale, CA 1992.

2   Oscar N. Lucas, "The Use of Hypnosis in Hemophilia Dental Care," *Annals
    of the New York Academy of Sciences* 240 (1975): 240.

3   W. LaBaw, *Psychiatric Medicine*, 1992; 10(4):89-98. Available at http://www
    .ncbi.nlm.nih.gov/pubmed/1289965.

4   Robert Rosenthal and Lenore Jacobson, *Pygmalion in the Classroom* (New
    York: Irvington, 1992).

CHAPTER 5

1   Child Anxiety Network, "Fears, Phobias and Anxiety." Available at http://
    childanxiety.net/Fears_Phobias_Anxiety.htm for more information; accessed
    January 12, 2010.

2   Robert Coles, *The Spiritual Life of Children* (Boston: Houghton Mifflin, 1990),
    p. 138.

3   American Academy of Child and Adolescent Psychiatry, "Bedwetting," up-
    dated November 2002. Available at www.aacap.org/cs/root/facts_for_fami-
    lies/bedwetting; accessed January 12, 2010.

CHAPTER 6

1   University of California Irvine Feature, Tom Vasich, University Communica-
    tions, "Making Surgery Less Scary For Kids." Available at www.uci.edu/uci/
    features/feature_kain_web_090706.php.

2   Canadian Garden Centre & Nursery, "Horticulture Therapy," www.canadian
    gardencentre.ca/content/view/1193/38.

CHAPTER 7

1 The farewell to Mr. Hooper is available online at www.youtube.com/
   watch?v=YZTvDZHRFrU, and discussion of the birth at the end is at http://
   www.emmytvlegends.org/interviews/shows/sesame-street-farewell-mr-
   hooper.

2 The news story is available online at www.clickondetroit.com/video/21525126/
   index.html.

3 "Kara Reviews of Books for Children & Teens." Available at www.kara-grief
   .org/Children%20Books.htm; accessed January 11, 2010.

4 Hospice, "Talking to Children about Death." Available at www.hospicenet
   .org/html/talking.html; accessed January 11, 2010.

CHAPTER 8

1 Gavin de Becker, *The Gift of Fear* (New York: Dell Publishing Company, 1998).

2 Amanda Ripley, "How to Get out Alive," *Time*, April 25, 2005. Available
   at www.time.com/time/magazine/article/0,9171,1053663,00.html; accessed
   January 11, 2010. See also Ripley, *The Unthinkable: Who Survives When Disaster Strikes—and Why* (New York: Crown Publishing Group, 2008).

3 Dave Grossman and Loren Christensen, *On Combat: The Psychology and
   Physiology of Deadly Conflict in War and in Peace*, PPCT Research, Millstadt,
   Illinois, 2004.

4 University of Colorado at Boulder, "New View of the Way Young Children
   Think," *Science Daily*, March 25, 2009. Available at http://www.sciencedaily
   .com/releases/2009/03/090324131554.htm; accessed February 2, 2010.

5 *Good Morning America*, ABC-TV News, "Toddler 911 Call: 'Mommie Owie,'"
   September 19, 2007. Available at http://abcnews.go.com/GMA/story?id=
   3623131; accessed January 11, 2010.

6 Monique Healy, "911 Video For Young Children," www.youtube.com/
   watch?v=cVObBXma7bM; accessed January 11. 2010.

7 The Polly Klass Foundation: 9-1-1 Practice for Children, Available at www
   .pollyklaas.org/safe/9-1-1-practice-for-children.html; accessed January 11.
   2010.

8 9-1-1 Safety for Kids, Comission on State Emergency Communication, Texas.
   Available at www.911.state.tx.us/kidshome.html; accessed January 11. 2010.

9   Our version of four-count breathing is based on Dave Grossman, and healer Pat Aoki. The breathing through the heart and research on brain/heart sync is from a similar protocol from the Institute of HeartMath® called The Quick Coherence Technique,® http://www.heartmath.org.

10 Jessica Hamblen, "Terrorist Attacks and Children," United States Department of Veterans Affairs, National Center for PTSD. Available at http://www.ptsd .va.gov/public/pages/terrorist-attacks-children.asp, www.ncptsd.va.gov/ncmain/ ncdocs/fact_shts/fs_children_disaster.html; accessed January 11, 2010.

11 Ripley, *The Unthinkable*, p. 91.

CHAPTER 9

1   "Empty space, we have discovered, is actually not empty at all. Quantum effects constantly produce particles and antiparticles 'out of nothing,' only to have them disappear few moments later." Fermilab, "Inquiring Minds: The science of Matter Space, and Time," available at www.fnal.gov/pub/inquiring/matter/index.html; accessed January 12, 2010.

2   Quoted in Robert Millett, "Healing Emotions," Julia Johnson, 2009. Available at www.juliajohnson.co.uk/pages/articles/interview-with-candace-pert. php; accessed January 12, 2010.

3   Bruce Lipton and Steve Bhaerman, *Spontaneous Evolution: Our Positive Future (And a Way to Get Here from There)* (Carlsbad, CA: Hay House, 2009), p. 273.

4   Larry Dossey, *Reinventing Medicine* (San Francisco: Harper 1999).

5   HealthyNet, Interviews With People Who Make A Difference, "On Death and Dying;" interview with Elizabeth Kubler-Ross by Daniel Redwood, 1995. Available at www.healthy.net/scr/interview.asp?Id=205; accessed January 12, 2010.

6   Charlene Costanzo, *The Twelve Gifts of Birth* (New York: HarperCollins, 2001).

INDEX

state-dependent learning, 253

State University of New York University Hospital, 12

steps to the goal, xxvii, 57–78
  See also Centering Yourself (Step One); Ground Rules (Step Three); Oliver and Donna's story; pacing (mirroring); presence in the moment; Rapport (Step Two); Verbal First Aid Manual

stitches, 119–23, 180

stomachache/headache example, 85–86

storytelling
  doctor visits and surgery, 163, 167, 168–69, 173
  mind of a child, 41–42, 49

strep tests, 180

stress hardiness, 232–33, 234

stress (mother's) impact on prenatal babies, 42–43

success of Verbal First Aid, xiii–xiv, xvii–xxii

Sufi story, 61–62

suggestibility of children, 29–31, 51

suggestions. *See* healing suggestions

summoning to our full potential to connect and interconnect, 279–82

superheroes. *See* character or superhero, using

support vs. criticism, 75–76, 78

surgery. *See* doctor visits and surgery

survival-maintaining hindbrain (reptilian brain), 40

survival skills, 228–29, 230

Sweden, 28

sympathetic nervous system, 70

Talbot, Margaret, 13

talking about illness and death, 198–204, 225

teachable moments from traumatic, 3–4

temporal lobes, emotional imprints in, 35

theory of mind (unique), 39–51

THETA brain wave lengths, 30

thinking=feeling=healing, xiv–xv, xxi, xxiii–xxvii, 7–12, 14, 271
  See also Verbal First Aid

Thomas the Tank Engine, 245

Thompson, Hugh, 191

thoughts, affecting physiology, 267–68

three steps to the goal. *See* steps to the goal

Time magazine, 229

toddlers (one to four years of age), 39, 46–48, 130, 198, 233

tornado preparedness, 246–47

totems, 195

touch, power of, 44–45, 204–5, 225

toys (familiar), 163, 167–68, 173, 174

translating doctor's words for child, 162

triggers, 190

true learning, 40

truisms, 162, 189–90, 220

Trujillo, Timothy, 19, 39–40

trust, honoring, 32–33, 170

"try," avoiding, 76–77

Tusek, Diane, 17, 49

Twelve Gifts of Birth, The (Costanzo), 272

Twin Towers, September 11 terrorism, 4–5, 22, 230

unconditional love, 269, 270

unexpected, preparing for, 227–65
  adult distress, 42–43, 261–62, 265
  automatic thinking, 228, 231–32
  careless warnings caution, 258–59
  CNN stress, 260–61
  computer, mind as, 228, 231–32
  consumer frenzies, 229–30
  duck-and-cover training for nuclear attacks, 259
  empowerment from, 228, 234, 263, 271–73
  facing a catastrophe, 260–61, 265
  fear and, 228–29
  idle threats caution, 258–59
  intuitive skills, 229, 230, 233
  mental rehearsals, 228, 229, 230
  minds, preparing for emergencies, 231–34
  normalcy bias, 232
  post-traumatic stress disorder, 260–61
  presence in the moment, 259
  replaying of tragic events, 260–61, 265
  resilience, 263
  responses to emergencies, 227, 228–29, 230, 232
  September 11 terrorism, xxiv, 4–5, 22, 230, 260–61
  Sichuan (China) 2008 earthquake, 262–63, 279–81
  soft eyes awareness, 260
  stress hardiness, 232–33, 234
  survival skills, 228–29, 230
  young children checklist, 241–43
  See also mental rehearsals; Verbal First Aid Manual

unique theory of mind, 39–51

"universe," 266

University Medical Center of Geneva, Switzerland, 35

University of Chicago, 159

University of Colorado at Boulder, 84, 233

University of Kansas, 9

University of Leicester's School of Psychology in England, 41

University of Michigan, 14

University of North Carolina, 41

Photo by H. Youtt, 2009

Judith Simon Prager, PhD, is a teacher, writer, and practitioner, with a PhD in psychology, specializing in trauma release. She has trained doctors, nurses, firefighters, and other first responders across the United States, in England, and in China in using Verbal First Aid™ for adults and children.

Photo by author

Judith Acosta, LISW, CHT, is a licensed psychotherapist, classical homeopath, hypnotherapist, and crisis counselor in private practice. She specializes in working with law enforcement and first response personnel, school-age children, and adolescents and their families.